D1595530

The Spectacle
of Accumulation

PETER LANG
New York • Washington, D.C./Baltimore • Bern
Frankfurt am Main • Berlin • Brussels • Vienna • Oxford

Sut Jhally

The Spectacle
of Accumulation

Essays in Culture,
Media, & Politics

PETER LANG
New York • Washington, D.C./Baltimore • Bern
Frankfurt am Main • Berlin • Brussels • Vienna • Oxford

Library of Congress Cataloging-in-Publication Data

Jhally, Sut.
The spectacle of accumulation: essays in culture,
media, and politics / Sut Jhally.
p. cm.
Includes bibliographical references.
1. Culture—Economic aspects. 2. Mass media and culture.
3. Advertising—Social aspects. I. Title.
HM621.J44   306—dc22   2006017727
ISBN 0-8204-7904-7

Bibliographic information published by **Die Deutsche Bibliothek**.
Die Deutsche Bibliothek lists this publication in the "Deutsche
Nationalbibliografie"; detailed bibliographic data is available
on the Internet at http://dnb.ddb.de/.

Cover design by Joni Holst

The paper in this book meets the guidelines for permanence and durability
of the Committee on Production Guidelines for Book Longevity
of the Council of Library Resources.

Printed in the United States of America

Contents

Acknowledgments

A book of this sort, which collects writings and interviews over a twenty-year span, has gathered too many intellectual debts to list accurately. I hope my coauthors and editors over this time span will recognize their immense contributions to the work drawn together here under my name.

In terms of this book directly, I would like to thank Damon Zucca, my editor at Peter Lang, for his faith that there is value in bringing these essays and interviews together in this form; Lynn Comella, who painstakingly copyedited the manuscript for stylistic consistency and accuracy; and Jeremy Earp, who was instrumental in the final stages of editing. I am also immensely grateful to Henry Giroux for writing such a gracious and generous Foreword.

Foreword

Henry A. Giroux
McMaster University

Given the current state of American politics in which the very nature of democracy appears at risk, if not under siege, it has never been more important for intellectuals to take a concerted public role in addressing the major issues of our time. Of course, I am not talking about the public-relations intellectuals who appear regularly on FOX, CNN, and other dominant media that increasingly and willing serve as adjuncts of the American Heritage Foundation or the American Chamber of Commerce. On the contrary, I am referring to public intellectuals who are concerned with finding ways to develop a more democratic and humane future, intellectuals who refuse to consolidate authority by questioning it and holding it accountable for its consequences, intellectuals whose projects are rooted in the need to alleviate human suffering and create public spaces that promote critical discourses, collective action, and the return of resources back to communities.

When I think of all of the many notable public intellectuals in this country, Sut Jhally stands out as one who engages in diverse forms of publicness while taking seriously the obligation to provide what Pierre Bourdieu has called a permanent critique of the abuses of authority, especially by those who are in positions of power. He not only teaches, gives public talks, and publishes scholarly books and articles, but he also runs a progressive foundation—the Media Education Foundation. In addition, he directs, writes, and produces films, and orchestrates a Web site that is a theoretical and strategic gold mine for accessing alternative, critical views on a variety of subjects, including American foreign policy, globalization, and a host of other issues. In many ways, Sut Jhally provides a model for what it means to connect learning to politics, pedagogy to a wide variety of forms and public sites, and cultural politics to social change. His diverse body of work addresses the important insight that the power of the dominant order is not just economic but also intellectual—residing in the realm of ideas, knowledge, values, and beliefs. For Jhally, a politics for the twenty-first century has to engage not only matters of political economy but also the educational force of culture as it makes its way across the globe, shaping all aspects of life and everyday experience. His ongoing concern with social justice attempts to break down the illusion of unanimity that seems so prevalent in the dominant media, all levels of government, and the commanding heights of corporate power. Equally important are his sustained attempts to foster modes of critical public pedagogy whose purpose is to reach a diverse number of publics and audiences—all of which have the potential to come to grips with their own power as individual and social agents. And that is precisely why he supports a cultural politics based on the presupposition that the worldly space of criticism is the democratic underpinning of social agency and a cultural politics that combines a public pedagogy with a politics aimed at restoring a sense of utopian possibility, collective resistance, and social transformation. For Sut Jhally, making the pedagogical more political suggests creating robust theoretical discourses and practices that offer people a critical vocabulary, a space for dissenting, and a set of experiences for considering the possibility of connecting critique to political action. As one of the most important theoreticians of cultural studies, public pedagogy, and visual culture in North America, Sut Jhally's work has always embodied the assumption that the greatest danger facing the twenty-first century is not the risk of illusory hopes but those undemocratic forces that deny social, economic, and political justice.

Just before his death, Edward Said, the great social and cultural critic, suggested that intellectuals in the United States and throughout the world have a greater responsibility than ever before because democracy is being threatened unlike no other time in our history. In many ways, *The Spectacle of Accumulation* embodies, deepens, and extends Said's sense of what it means to be an engaged intellectual. This is a book that is concerned with the ongoing threat to democratic culture; the corporate control of mass media; the intersection of race, class, and power; the war on youth; and the power and reach of the spectacle of accumulation and commodification. Rather than separate knowledge from commitment, political economy from cultural politics, and theory from practice, this book connects all of these issues within a broad political and cultural landscape that makes visible how the spectacle of appearance, commodification, and accumulation functions to reproduce ongoing attacks on minorities of class and color, the hijacking of the political state by the corporate state, the commercialization of public space, and the increasing reduction of young people to consumers. As this book indicates in brilliant fashion, Sut Jhally offers a much needed critique of those intellectuals who have either become largely silent in the face of a growing authoritarianism or are simply reduced to clerks of empire, appearing daily on FOX News or speaking ever so softly on National Public Radio. An underlying concern of the book is a critique of those cultural workers and intellectuals who have turned away from the idea of engaged criticism, which increasingly collapses into a form of banal and accommodating politics. Intellectuals in this sense do more than keep a particular discourse going or simply map out and adjudicate positions, they take a stand and do so with the greatest possible sense of justice. Critique in this instance becomes a form of public pedagogy, an oppositional discourse that reminds us that there is no genuine democracy without genuine opposing critical power. But there is more here than an implicit critique of disinterested and accommodating intellectuals; there is a demonstration of what it means to be a publicly engaged intellectual who takes seriously the educational force of the larger culture and the politics it reproduces.

Underlying Sut Jhally's political project is both a language of critique and one of possibility. Critique in this case works to show not only how culture deploys power in the service of domination, but also how many intellectuals have simply turned their backs on the great narratives of the search of freedom and emancipation. In the place of such silence, *The Spectacle of Accumulation* is grounded in a project that frames its essays in a call for intellectuals and cultural workers in a variety of sites to exhibit a critical and engaged interaction with the world, an engagement mediated by a responsibility for challenging structures of domination and for alleviating human suffering. *The Spectacle of Accumulation* is more than a series of brilliant essays on media and culture, it is the embodiment of an ethical and political stance that embraces a political worldliness and sensibility that is afraid of neither raising controversy, making visible connections within the culture that are otherwise hidden, deflating the claims of imperial jingoism within the spectacles produced by the dominant media, nor bridging intellectual work and the operation of politics. Refusing the now popular sport of academic bashing, and refusing to embrace a crude call for action at the expense of rigorous intellectual and theoretical work, *The Spectacle of Accumulation* combines rigor and clarity, on the one hand, and civic courage and political commitment, on the other, all as part of a larger attempt to understand the cultural politics of power and to transform it in the interest of developing a more just and democratic society. In this book, Sut Jhally demonstrates what it means to live in a world that demands a certain kind of worldliness, a wakefulness, if you will, a recognition of interdependence, and a willingness to speak not simply as an engaged intellectual but as an intellectual for the public, an intellectual who represents a varied range of important issues and understands that an inclusive democracy matters, that it must be struggled over first and foremost within the realm of culture, and that such a struggle needs to be done with a fierce sense of commitment, solidarity, and hope. As a public intellectual, Sut Jhally embodies in both his work and action the ideal and the practice of what it means to give meaning to the notion of a militant and educated hope, one that registers politics as a matter of desire, intervention, and struggle.

As Fred Jameson has pointed out, we live at a time when it is easier to imagine the end of the world than it is to imagine the end of a market economy creating vast inequalities throughout the globe. Corporate ideology increasingly drives the meaning of citizenship and social life. One consequence is that the principles of self-preservation and self-interest increasingly appear to undermine, if not sabotage, political agency, if not public life itself. Moreover, as democracy succumbs to the instrumental politics of the market economy and the relentless hype of the commercially driven spectacle, it becomes increasingly difficult to preserve those public forums where private troubles can be translated into public concerns, or to maintain under the onslaught of privatization those public spheres that do the crucial pedagogical work of democracy by offering resources and possibilities for resisting the dissolution of sociality, reciprocity, and social citizenship itself. *The Spectacle of Accumulation* is a crucial book that takes seriously the task of addressing the intersection of culture and politics, texts, and power. Its original contribution lies not only in its ability to combine the study of symbolic forms and meaning as a form of public pedagogy with concrete social formations and relations of power, but also in its provocative ability to unmask the workings of the spectacle in media culture, to make power visible, to foster public debate, to lift the discourse of private problems to the level of public considerations, and to make cultural politics central to the struggle for an inclusive democracy at home and in the larger, global public sphere.

January 8, 2005

Preface

The essays, talks, and interviews published in this volume are drawn from my academic and political work over the past two decades. My hope is that they demonstrate the necessity of a coherent vision of rigorous intellectual work within a highly politicized context, where the popular dissemination of knowledge has never mattered so much for the project of democratic renewal. While the majority of these pieces have been previously published in other venues, I believe there is some value in collecting them together in this form.

I hope also that the collection can be seen as an attempt to grapple with the central issues that constitute the field of critical media studies. Like many other areas of analysis, the field is defined not only by what holds it together (issues of power and politics), but also by divisions that threaten its coherence and unity. On one side of this contested boundary line sits *cultural studies*, with its central concerns of identity, subjectivity, and consciousness. On the other side is *political economy*, with its focus on ideology, ownership, commercialization, and control. The papers collected in this volume are an attempt to work on both sides of this divide simultaneously, not so much by synthesizing these concerns into a new framework, but by pursuing work located precisely at this boundary, where fields of analysis overlap and intertwine, where purity fuses into an unpredictable hybridity defined by contradiction and complexity.

The cultural studies/political economy debate has taken place around a number of familiar axes, the most prominent being the relationship between the symbolic and the material (and, in that sense, has reproduced age-old issues around idealism vs. materialism and base vs. superstructure). These essays and interviews, then, are located on intellectual terrain that has been contested for centuries, and it would be arrogant (and very foolish) to suggest that they offer any kind of resolution to those enduring issues. Nonetheless, I hope that, in their totality, they suggest the immense possibilities that emerge from straddling the lines, working away from the center, and working in the spaces between established intellectual fields.

Occupying this terrain, I have been powerfully influenced by the work of Stuart Hall, especially by his insistence that the central philosophical and scientific question of *determination* is much more fruitfully posed as thinking about it not in the (in)famous "last instance," but in the "first instance." This shift in emphasis is to draw attention always to context, and is designed to flesh out Marx's famous dictum that "men make their own history, but not in conditions of their own choosing." This tension between form and content, figure and ground, is the thematic that runs through this collection. If critical media studies at its heart is concerned with questions of identity, subjectivity, and consciousness, then in the contemporary context the integration of these dimensions into the material organization of the global economy ensures that any approach that falsely decontextualizes these issues is doomed to reproduce incomplete understandings.

I have also been profoundly influenced by Stuart Hall's insistence that, while progressive intellectuals must remain at the forefront of intellectual theoretical work, they also carry "the responsibility of transmitting those ideas, that knowledge, through the intellectual function, to those who do not belong, professionally, in the intellectual class." This is a project of translation, both of language (from the realms of philosophy to everyday commonsense) and also increasingly of mediums. In my case this has meant producing and distributing video programs that address the central questions of the contemporary world. While these cannot be represented in a print volume of this kind, the political impetus behind such a project also runs through this collection.

Sut Jhally
Northampton, MA
January, 2005

Advertising, Cultural Criticism, and Pedagogy: An Interview with Sut Jhally

Conducted by William O'Barr

William M. O'Barr, Professor of Anthropology at Duke University, interviewed Sut Jhally in the spring of 2002 for the online journal Advertising & Society Review.

O'BARR: What do you hope to accomplish through your role as a cultural critic?

JHALLY: I really don't see myself as a cultural critic. I define myself much more as a teacher. Everything I do, everything I've done with the Media Education Foundation (MEF), and with my publishing, I see as an extension of my teaching role.

O'BARR: Then let me ask what you are trying to accomplish through your role as a teacher?

JHALLY: I believe that the role of teachers is to give students the tools they need to be able to negotiate a complex world and to give them the tools that they need to be in charge of that world—to be active participants rather than passive recipients of other people's actions. So what I always want to stress in teaching is that the world that we live in is a created world, that it's been constructed by someone, and that there is no such thing as a "natural" version of the world. The world we live in did not fall fully formed from heaven. It is always created by someone, and therefore the issue of *power* is what is central to how we analyze the world.

O'BARR: So how do you explain the construction of the world, that is, how it came to be how it is today, to your students?

JHALLY: History is absolutely essential to understanding this. It helps us to see that the world in which we live—the world that seems normal to us—wasn't always like that. It was created by specific institutions for specific ends. It was created with the motivations of specific individuals who had very specific things in mind.

O'BARR: Where does that history begin for you?

JHALLY: When I first started teaching, I used to go all the way back to the Stone Age in terms of looking at communication. If communication is always about power, if communication is always about constructing the world, and if communication is always about symbolic communication, then we have to look at the social and material conditions that are the determining aspect of that.

O'BARR: What is it that students need to know about communication in the Stone Age?

JHALLY: They need to know how language first started: Why do we have language? Language wasn't always a part of the communication "vocabulary" of what we consider to be the ancestors of the human species. If language is *the* key element of the development of the human species from our primate ancestors (and I think it is), and if the content of language is always arbitrary (that is, the result of social process and not given by nature), then the issue of power and communication is there right from our origins. And it's locating communication in very concrete, everyday circumstances. Let's not forget that our ancestors developed language as a survival mechanism when we were driven out of the thinning forests of Africa and onto the flat savannas.

O'BARR: How do you get from there to now? What do you need to look at?

JHALLY: You do it by understanding that communication is always a response to something. Communication is a creative act but is always a response to something. Every new development in communication—initially it was language and face-to-face, then it was mediated communication, such as drawing on cave walls. You have to ask, "Why are people drawing on cave walls?" It's because people started to think about broader issues, such as where do I come from, how was the world created, what else is going on around me?

O'BARR: So the way that advertising comes into this history is that advertising *is* communication?

JHALLY: Absolutely. The way I always frame why I study communication is that communication is a fundamental social process. I think we are human beings because we communicate. Our ability to tell a story—and to tell *our* story—is essential to us as human beings. That is central to our construction of our identity and therefore part of what it means to be human. Communication is a part of what is natural to being a human.

The question then is: What are the *conditions* of communication? What are the contexts within which communication takes place? That's why you can never divorce communication from power. Even when language first develops, you start to have monopolies of knowledge around that ability very quickly.

O'BARR: Can you make this specific? What concrete example comes to mind?

JHALLY: Well, in terms of who gets to tell the stories within a traditional culture. Not everyone tells stories. The storytelling function quickly becomes specialized.

O'BARR: You are talking about sitting around the campfire?

JHALLY: Yes, sitting around the campfire not everyone tells stories. Some people tell stories—and they get to tell certain stories—and some people only listen to stories.

O'BARR: Later this becomes the church, for example?

JHALLY: Yes, the first form of monopolization of knowledge is around religious ideas. It gets codified around the church.

O'BARR: And this kind of situation is then true in all kinds of religious traditions, not just Christianity?

JHALLY: Absolutely.

O'BARR: So this is the historical road that you take your students along?

JHALLY: Yes, what I want to do is show my students how advertising is not just about selling products. I want them to understand that advertising is a part of the whole process of communication. Communication is fundamental, and advertising is one of the major forms of communication in the modern world. So we have to think of how it's always linked up with power.

The other reason we need to look at advertising is that it's dealing with a fundamental human relationship—*our relationship with things.* One of the other ways you can define the human species is as the maker and user of things. We create the material world. We don't just take the world as is. In fact, we change the world, and change it in very specific ways. That's the basis of what anthropologists and historians do—they look at the *material world* that people created, and they read from it the social world that surrounded it. The reason they can do this is the assumption that in objects are the social relations of their production as well as the social relations that surround production. That's what archaeology is about, that's what anthropology is about, and that's what history is about—an understanding that the relationship between people and things is central and fundamental to a culture. From that understanding it's relatively easy to get to advertising because it is the modern form of talking about that relationship between people and things. It's talking about a very fundamental part of human existence and of the way we operate as human beings.

O'BARR: When you consider advertising within this broad frame of interpretation, where do you see its beginnings?

JHALLY: Well, you can go back a long way in terms of traders giving information about their goods and services, but I normally start in the middle of the nineteenth century (around the 1850s or so). It was brought about by the development of a market society and national markets in the United States and in Europe. It goes hand-in-hand with that. You can always talk about whether one creates the other, but the point is that those two things are fundamentally connected.

This is when it's especially crucial to look at history. You ask: Before the national market, what's going on? What kind of information about objects is there? If you go to a small town in America in the 1850s, what is people's relationship to objects? A lot of the goods they used, they made themselves through farm labor. How do they interact with goods in terms of the market? They buy things that are unbranded. They buy things from local retailers mostly, like lumber and textiles, which they then fashion into things for themselves. Flour is another example. They take the raw materials and fashion those themselves into whatever they need at that time. Their interaction with the market is relatively limited.

But there's always been a market to some degree where people have to interact with others around objects and services, say with the occasional traveling trader who brings in things from outside. Even in this context, when people do deal with things coming in from outside—there are some things that you do need from outside that can't be produced locally—the major players in providing market information are retailers, not producers. The major advertising in the nineteenth century is the advertising of retailers, where shopkeepers are announcing that this product is available. If you look at a newspaper, for example, in the mid-1850s, it's nothing but the advertising of local retailers saying that new objects from outside have arrived. There's no advertising for local products. There's no advertising for, say, a local lumber mill or the flour of a local gristmill. The advertising is the advertising of retailers about things coming in from the outside.

It's very interesting that if you look at those newspapers in the 1850s, you also see the future right next to the retailers' ads—and that's the ads of patent medicine manufacturers who are trying in fact to sell their very particular products. What they are doing is not announcing that this is available; they are trying to *brand* their product. The middle of the nineteenth century is a very interesting period in which you can see the early development of a market society, which is largely the information of retailers. And right next to it, you've got what is going to be the future of advertising—which is branding and the voice of manufacturers. We know, in fact, that many of the early advertisers came from patent medicines. They used the knowledge they had from branding patent medicines to then brand other products. The idea of branding comes from the fact that manufacturers have to distinguish their objects from other manufacturers'.

O'BARR: Well, it's gone pretty far since then. Even fruit is branded nowadays.

JHALLY: It's very useful to look historically at that because the branding comes about because manufacturers had no market power. The market power lay actually with retailers. So the retailers would say to wholesalers, "Look, I need so many barrels of crackers" if it wasn't available locally. And what wholesalers would do is go to producers of crackers and they would be able to play them against each other based on price—because at this point there's no other distinction. And so the profit margins of manufacturers were tiny because they could always be played off against each other on price. And so market power in that sense lay with wholesalers. National advertising starts to develop partly because manufacturers say, "Well, hold on, what I need to do is create a demand for *my* product, not just for crackers, but for *my* brand of crackers." How do you do that? You do that by advertising directly to consumers so that consumers will go in and ask for a particular brand. When that starts, wholesalers cannot continue to play the manufacturers off against one another in terms of price. That's the way market power shifts. So advertising's absolutely fundamental in shifting market power away from wholesalers to manufacturers.

O'BARR: What have been the critical steps in terms of advertising moving from that beginning to the present state of things?

JHALLY: We get from there to here based upon the further isolation of the mass of the people from the means of production so that now those people are totally dependent upon the market for survival in all aspects of their lives.

O'BARR: By isolation from the means of production you mean that hardly any one is producing what they use anymore.

JHALLY: Yes, very few people are producing things that they can just make themselves and use. As people are driven off the land, they then have to go to the marketplace for food. One of the major ways you can think about this is to look to see how bread has moved from being produced at home to being produced commercially. Over the course of fifty years from the middle of the nineteenth century to the beginning of the twentieth century, there's a huge shift in the way bread is produced. By the beginning of the twentieth century, something like 60 percent of bread is commercially baked bread, and that's an indication of a general movement whereby the market becomes much more important in terms of how people live their lives. When that happens, there's more competition for the dollars of those people buying things in the marketplace. Advertising expands exponentially along with this shift.

Throughout the course of the twentieth century, different communication technologies are integrated into advertising. In the beginning, what was available were newspapers and billboards. Newspapers changed form from political news-papers to newspapers that we would recognize as based on commercial funds. At the end of the nineteenth century, the yellow press is brought about because advertisers needed to reach new audiences. Magazines also develop as advertis-ing delivery vehicles around this time. Then comes the development of radio, which again starts off not being part of this commercial mix, but very soon becomes a fundamental part of the commercial system. And then you get tele-vision. Actually, once radio was determined to be commercial, the course was set. The last time we had a real public debate about how important advertising was going to be in the culture had to do with whether you were going to have a radio system funded essentially by advertisers or a system that could be sup-ported in other ways.

O'BARR: The cases of Canada and Britain make interesting comparisons with what happened in the United States.

JHALLY: Canada and Britain operate in very different ways from the United States. They decided to operate their broadcasting systems as a state monopoly. The commercialization of communication is much, much less not just in Britain, but in Europe in general.

O'BARR: Are things really any different in those countries where communica-tion is more controlled by the state?

JHALLY: Up until about twenty years ago, you could find some fundamental differences in the level of commercialization that was present on an everyday basis—how many messages people are exposed to, how powerful advertisers are in terms of the presence they have in the discourse of everyday life. I certainly think that you could measure that empirically.

O'BARR: In this age of globalization, do those distinctions still hold up?

JHALLY: That is the key. In the last twenty years or so, as media became more and more global, as giant corporations have put pressure on the national state broadcasting systems, those kinds of distinctions have started to break down. And so now we have broadcasting systems all over the world that are increas-ingly being penetrated by a commercial logic. And so I think the global differ-ences are much, much less than they ever used to be.

In one sense that's what globalization is. Globalization is the commercial logic moving to center stage in more and more places. And even if it is not the dominant logic all over the world, it is the logic that's present everywhere, and every other logic has to at least deal with that.

If you go to India right now, you'll see that the commercial logic is there because of Star TV, because of satellite TV, and because of their targeting of a middle class that is largely Western educated. Religious organizations in India now have to deal with that commercial penetration. It's not as though it has taken over everything, but it is now a constant presence all over the world, and that's where its power comes from. It will operate differently depending upon local conditions and upon local discourses, but it is there and present all the time. If you had asked me, what kind of power do you want if you want to influence something, I would say: Give me the power of presence, the power to be there all the time, so that someone always has to deal with me.

O'BARR: Up to this point, we've been talking about the historical steps. I'd like to ask about your sense of what is good and bad about this process that you've described.

JHALLY: To go back to teaching, which is where I started, what I want to say to people is: Look, this is the world that's been constructed. We know why. It doesn't require rocket science to figure out why advertising occupies the place in the world that it does today. The next question is: What is important about this? Why is it worth studying this? Why should we bother to look at this?

The typical way we've dealt with advertising in the past has been, I believe, the wrong way. In the past, we've typically said we need to study advertising because it fundamentally affects product demand. Our whole analysis of advertising until very recently has been about whether it's effective in increasing product demand. I think that is an interesting question if you are a manufacturer or if you are interested in using advertising to increase your profits. But from the viewpoint of society, this is the wrong question.

One of the things teachers have to do is to pose the right questions. My question about this world—in which advertisers and corporations have this enormous amount of power—is what is that power being used for? What values are being stressed through it? What is the morality that's being communicated? What are the ethics that are being discussed? It's important to ask this because the ideology communicated through advertising has an enormous influence. Even if people don't buy the products advertised, they are influenced by advertising anyway.

O'BARR: What are some examples of the values communicated through advertising?

JHALLY: Well, first of all, let me say that I don't think advertising is some kind of trick. If it were a trick, it wouldn't work so well. I don't think advertisers simply manipulate people. Human beings are much too complex to be manipulated in some easy way just by controlling communication. You can do it, but it's a very difficult process.

O'BARR: You are talking now about things like subliminal advertising?

JHALLY: Yes. I think a lot of our discussion about advertising has asked the wrong question. Whenever people think critically about advertising, they think, "Oh, there's sex and death in those ice cubes!" Or they will look at a Ritz cracker to see what things are baked into it. What I want to look at is not what's hidden in advertising but what you can see up front, what's there on the surface, because that's what's impacting us.

I think that the fundamental thing that advertising does as a discursive form is that it tells a story about human happiness. That's how it sells. That's how it does its job. It sells products by convincing people that their happiness is connected to buying products. And particularly by buying *this* product. It is a story that says human happiness is connected to the provisions of the marketplace, is connected to *objects*. That's the fundamental story told in every ad. If you're successful in telling that story, it is not just a story for individuals but the story by which you organize the whole society. If the story is true, then what we need to do is to make more products, and we need to make more products in a better way, because that's the way toward human happiness. This story has been fundamental in highlighting the strategy of economic growth. What politicians then have to do is to get the economy to grow and grow. It has put economic questions at the center. Not the questions of whether economics is connected to justice and who has a role to play in how we think about economic policy. Instead, it's done it in a very simple way by saying that economic policy is always about *growing the economy,* to use President Clinton's famous words, and the promise that human happiness will come from that growth.

It's an interesting story, but what if it's not true? What if, in fact, human happiness doesn't come from things? What happens if we don't get happier if we get richer? That's the heretical question that never gets asked.

O'BARR: How do you answer it? How do you assess the degree to which people are happy or not?

JHALLY: Well, first of all, I think asking it is the most important thing you can do. The assumption is that the story we get told about objects and happiness is true. In asking it, you are questioning the assumption.

The way you answer it is empirically. I am a social scientist. As a teacher I don't want to impose my views or my ideology on people. The classroom is not the place for that. Now, I don't think the classroom is some kind of objective place where there is no power. There's always power. But what I try to do in a classroom is to tell people, "Look, there's always power operating in communication. If someone tells you there's no politics in a class, they are lying to you. Choosing the very subject matter is a form of power. It's a form of politics. So I tell you up front that this class is a place where power is operating. And my power is, in fact, pretty strong here. I can define what questions are going to be asked. It's up to you to figure out if those questions are the right questions. Then we use the best tools to study the issues, whatever they may be. But the real power lies in defining what is going to be asked in the first place."

So, once you've defined happiness in the way this story does, that becomes an empirical question—how to measure happiness, how to determine if the equation between wealth and happiness is true. Luckily, people have studied this. It's a difficult question because you are talking about how to measure *subjective* happiness.

O'BARR: Happiness is always subjective, isn't it?

JHALLY: Yes. The issue is how you reach some objective conclusions about something that is ultimately subjective. Luckily, I don't have to come up with ways to do this because there are researchers who study this, who have tried to measure the level of human satisfaction across time and across space.

O'BARR: What does the body of that research show?

JHALLY: It shows that the link between happiness and wealth does not hold over time. In the United States right now, we are, in absolute terms, a richer society than we were fifty years ago. We have access to a higher standard of living. We have better cars. We have better houses. We have better washing machines. However, that does not seem to be linked with higher levels of satisfaction for the society as a whole. The same proportion of people seem to be happy, and the same proportion of people seem to be dissatisfied within the society. If happiness is supposed to be connected to things, and if we have access to more things, why aren't more of us getting happier?

O'BARR: Why not?

JHALLY: We have to understand how happiness and satisfaction function. Human beings are very complicated social animals. What the research shows is that our level of happiness is not defined in some isolated way. Our level of happiness is always a relative issue. Whether we are happy with the material objects we have is connected to what other people have. There is a level of what Thorsten Veblen called *conspicuous consumption* in which people who have access to a higher standard of living within a society seem to be happier than people who don't have access to that. Happiness is always relational. You are always comparing yourself to something. The question is what you are comparing it to. If you were comparing it historically and said, "You know, actually, I have much more than my parents did, I have access to more things, my cars are better," and if the correlation worked, then you would be happier. But that's not the comparison we make. We don't make the comparison to our parents' generation, and we don't make the comparison to people in poorer countries. We don't say, "Look at me in comparison to people in Africa, in India, in Eastern Europe." If we did that, then Western societies would be far happier overall. What we seem to do is to make our judgments relative to the people closest to us and to other people in our society in our particular time. So, as the overall level of material well-being rises for everyone, the average rises for everyone as well. The same proportion of people are above and below the average. And the same proportion of people are happy and unhappy.

O'BARR: Have psychologists explained this principle of the relativity of happiness and how it works?

JHALLY: It is a good question. Why are we always comparing ourselves to others near us right at this moment? That may have something to do with the immediacy of human experience. In one sense, we are always a local species rather than a global or historical species, although, interestingly, television is changing that, so that the Joneses we are now trying to keep up with don't live on our street or on the next street over—they live on television in unbelievably upscale environments. So our comparison is with Rachel and Ross on *Friends*. That's why we are in such financial debt as individuals. We are chasing a lifestyle that exists in the symbolic dream life of the culture (advertising-based television) as though it's real.

There's a very interesting book, one of the best books I've read on happiness, by an economist, Tibor Scitovsky, called *The Joyless Economy*. The joyless economy was *our* economy. He looked at all the psychological literature and looked to see what the psychologists have concluded makes us happy. He found that what seems to make us happy subjectively is stimulation—a change in a level of stimulation. We like novelty. We like it when new things happen. That is what seems to be connected to happiness. Think about the basic things that give people pleasure, like food. You get hungry, and, before you get to discomfort, you eat food. There are different ways of eating food. It's not just putting nutrition into your body. People have a high degree of pleasure or displeasure depending on the kind of food that goes into their bodies and the level of taste that it has. No wonder that so many of our social activities are based around food. Food changes our level of stimulation. We go from possibly being hungry to then having intense pleasure because of the taste that we get from food. That's what makes us happy. The same with sex. Why so much focus on sex? Sex is about going from one state to another state. There's a change in the level of stimulation. That's why drugs work and why they have such an initial hold on people. In the same way, art gives us stimulation. When you see something that moves you, that change in the level of stimulation is what seems to be at the base of happiness.

Given all this, and that we know that what makes people happy is new experience, the question then becomes what are our social institutions doing? Do they stress novelty? Do they stress pleasure? Do they stress the things that make people happy? Or, in fact, is our bad luck that what the society provides for us as a source of happiness (goods) can't deliver what really makes us happy? That's the situation we are in.

Look at the research. Look at the quality-of-life studies that have been done. If you ask people what they want out of life, very few people respond with "a BMW" or "a big house." If they do, and you ask, "What's the BMW going to give you? What's the big house going to give you?" Once you start probing those, you find that the things that make people happy are relatively simple. What people want out of life is a life in which they have control. They want a life in which they have some autonomy through which they can express themselves. They want to have good friendships. They want a social life. They want a family life that is meaningful and rewarding for them. They want intimate, romantic lives. They want leisure time that is really free and that really allows them to relax. People want independence. All of these things have to do with social relationships, and they have nothing to do with products.

O'BARR: Are these findings true cross-culturally, or are these findings specific to America?

JHALLY: No, these things are pretty much cross-culturally true. Although I try to stay away from essentialism, the more I teach, the more I come to think that there are some things that are pretty essential about human beings. We are a social species. We like being in contact with other people. We are a species that is connected to our bodies in a very fundamental way. We like pleasure; we like novelty.

O'BARR: This is very interesting. What you are doing is something that I have seldom heard—linking up advertising to the human condition. You are interpreting it in terms that take into account the kinds of creatures to whom it is addressed.

JHALLY: Yes. The reason I talk about all of this is that I want to get back to advertising. As somebody who studies advertising and wants people to think about the world they live in and question that world, what I'm trying to do through my teaching is to give people the kinds of tools they need to become active participants in the world in which they live. That means they have to question the world in which they live. And if they question it, and if they come to an understanding that the world is not providing us what we need, both individually and societally, that is an impetus to change. That requires them to ask how can we have a world that reflects what human beings really want, to ask how can we have a world that reflects genuine human needs?

O'BARR: What kind of personal answer do you give as to how to have that kind of world?

JHALLY: Do you mean what would a different world look like?

O'BARR: Yes, and how would we get there?

JHALLY: That becomes the political question.

O'BARR: If this is just a rhetorical question for the classroom . . .

JHALLY: Oh, no, no, no. The reason I think advertising is such a great teaching tool is that it points to fundamental questions about the world in which we live. It's an entry into those broader questions because advertising is fundamentally connected to the ways in which our society is organized and to the ways in which we think about ourselves. The reason I'm teaching advertising is that I want to get to those broader questions. Advertising works as a rhetorical tool because everyone thinks they're experts in it. In one sense, everyone loves it. They are surrounded by it. And the most creative stuff is in advertising.

O'BARR: Where else is everyone an expert?

JHALLY: That's actually one of the major things I have to fight at the start of a course.

O'BARR: Believe me, I know.

JHALLY: The fundamentally heretical question is to ask what happens if we take advertising seriously. Everything we've talked about here, advertisers know. They know people get no pleasure from goods. They know that people's major forms of pleasure and satisfaction come from social relationships. If you know that and yet you are stuck with the problem of selling objects, because that's your job, then what you've got to do is connect what fundamentally moves people to the things that you have to sell. You have to convince people, at least for a brief moment, that somehow buying the object that you have to sell for your client is connected to the things that will make them happy, even though we know it will not.

One of the only ways in which goods are connected to happiness is through the concept of novelty bringing pleasure. So, when people say that when they get depressed, they go shopping, there's a real basis for the alleviation of unhappiness. When you first buy something, it does bring you happiness. The moment you leave the store, the moment you get home, the happiness changes. That should tell us why our relationship to objects is always shifting. There's nothing in objects themselves that make us happy. What makes us happy is the act of buying and the novelty that initially comes with that. If we were always happy because of the objects we've bought, then our dustbins would be much less full, and we wouldn't do as much shopping. But that's the thing. It's the novelty that keeps people coming back.

What advertisers have to do is to link up what keeps people happy with the things that they have to sell, which are objects. That's the falsity of it. What's real about advertising are the dreams that it recognizes in the population. And that's why advertising is full of adventure. It's full of independence, it's full of sex, it's full of family, and it's full of social relationships. It's full of meaningful work. What advertising has to do is to take those images of what makes people happy and connect them to objects. There's something that's true about advertising, and there's something that's false about it. What's true and what's real about advertising is that it reflects the desires and dreams that people have. But it takes these things that are very real—and that's why advertising works so effectively—and it links them up to a place that, by its very definition, cannot provide it: the marketplace and the world of things.

We know that objects won't really bring us happiness, and yet we are constantly seduced by this idea. People know their real-life experiences. They buy stuff, and they get it home, and it doesn't work the way it is supposed to work. It doesn't give them the same kind of pleasure that it's supposed to give. Advertising is like a drug dealer in that way. It's the pusher on the street. We know products are not particularly good for us, but every time we try to break this, advertising is there offering us another hit: "This will make you really happy. Look at what this product will deliver." It has a way of keeping us from asking whether the equation between happiness and goods is actually true, or if there is a different way of organizing our lives and our society.

There are a number of different images that I call on to describe advertising. I think the ways we describe advertising are much too benign right now. One of the things I want to do is to change the metaphors we use. I think the drug dealer is a good metaphor for advertising. It hooks us on the world of things.

I also think it's a child abuser, as well, in the way in which it targets children as part of the market. Nowadays, advertising targets kids while they are still in their cribs. If you think about the whole concept of children's advertising, by its very nature what it is doing is child abuse—given that kids don't have their own money to spend. Mostly, the reason that kids are being targeted is that kids are being trained to become lobbyists for products against their parents. They are being targeted so that they will become lobbyists for particular kinds of products, so that the parents will be pestered to buy them. And they are also being targeted so that by the time they really have money, they will already be branded in some way. What advertisers are doing in that sense is targeting children, not for children's own needs and desires, but for the advertisers' needs and desires. The only defense of advertising you see is always based around the argument that people are rational; people are always independent; they can always evaluate the information they get, and they can reject it; and there are always other people who can provide alternative information. Well, when it comes to kids, kids are not rational. We know that rationality is something that develops over time. So you take the most vulnerable segments of the society, and you target them, so that they will give you their money when they start having some. And you also want to turn them against their parents, so that they are constantly nagging their parents for the right product. I'm amazed that families have allowed an alien presence into the corner of their living rooms when that alien presence is designed to break down family life and to cause nothing but tension within it. So that's why I think that the whole idea of children's marketing is, from a moral point of view, abhorrent. If I had my way, I would ban all advertising to children under eight years old. Even eight is, I think, a problem.

O'BARR: Do you think the Canadian efforts to restrict advertising directed at children have been successful?

JHALLY: The question is about national policy in a globalized environment. Does Canada's doing that in the media that it controls have any real influence when in fact you can turn on a satellite station and pick up all these other channels?

O'BARR: Plus, the vast majority of Canadians live very close to the U.S. border.

JHALLY: The Scandinavian countries also tried this as well. They wanted no advertising whatsoever directed to children. Children are going to be reached in a general way by marketing campaigns directed at the general population, but what I'm talking about are those specific campaigns that are directed toward kids and that adults are not supposed to see. Although it's difficult within a global society to isolate those effects, I think that any society that doesn't even think about those questions, any society that simply gives advertisers carte blanche to do whatever they want with the kids, is essentially opening up kids' bedrooms to child molesters.

O'BARR: That's a pretty powerful metaphor. I think it's useful in teaching sometimes to have that shock value because it really makes people think about what you are saying. I guess that's part of what you are doing, right?

JHALLY: It is shocking, but I also fundamentally believe what I'm saying. The other reason to use the metaphor is that it also refers to the media, as well as advertisers. And that's got to do with how commercial television is organized, because when you are watching commercial television, you are engaged in labor the same way you would be in a factory. What the networks are trying to do is gather you together the way the factory owner would gather laborers together. They are drawing value out of your watching, out of your labor. So the image I'm creating here is not that you are being given messages but that value is being drawn out of your labor. If people didn't watch television, networks would have nothing to sell. If NBC turned out the evening news tonight and no one watched, they couldn't give that advertising time away. It's fundamentally dependent upon people watching. And, therefore, you are trying to organize an audience, and you are trying to extract value out of them the same way you would be in a factory. And when you start doing this to two-year-olds and three-year-olds, it is like child labor, like a global factory. And we have opened up our doors and allowed people to come into our homes to manipulate our children and to draw value out of them. That's why I think the metaphor of child molestation is so powerful. It makes people examine these issues I've just described.

O'BARR: Well, it certainly is an eye-opener. When you explain how you think about the issues of advertising to children, it explains why you need such a powerful metaphor to describe something so powerful.

When you say all of these things to your students, what do they think about all this? What kind of attitude do they have toward the possibility of going into advertising after hearing ideas like this laid out over the course of a semester?

JHALLY: I don't think that one course is going to change people's lives. But I do think it encourages a questioning attitude toward the career path they've laid out for themselves. What I say to people is, "Look, I'm not here to tell you what you should or should not do. What I've laid out for you is an analysis, a perspective that says that the world you are going into—if you are going into advertising—is a fundamentally powerful world. It has a huge amount of cultural impact. If you go into that world, you have responsibility that comes along with that power. You have to think as moral beings. You have to think as ethical beings. What kind of world do you want to participate in? I'm not here to tell you whether you should go into advertising or not. I'm here to say to you that if you choose to go into advertising, it is not like going into, say, making shoes or something peripheral. You are cultural workers who are implicated in the major ways in which the society is thinking about itself. That gives you responsibility. That gives you moral responsibility. I want you to think about that. I want you to think about that in terms of what your own values are and whether what you do reflects what your own values are." That's the only thing teachers can do. You can't give people answers. Often, people will say, "You've said everything that's bad about it, but you haven't told us what to do." My answer to that is, "Look, I have already too much power in your lives. My role is not to tell you what to do. My role is to give you the tools to be able to understand the world in a new way and to point out that there is no such thing as innocence in this world. No one is innocent. Everyone should go into whatever they go into with their eyes fully open. And if my analysis makes sense, you've got to take that on as part of how you understand your role in the world."

O'BARR: Do you have some students who've gone into advertising?

JHALLY: Absolutely.

O'BARR: What do they tell you about dealing with these issues when they are in the business?

JHALLY: I don't have too much feedback on that. Oftentimes I do get people saying back, "Yeah, everything you said was correct. It's a dead world. And I got out of it quickly. It was all about making money, and it was deadening as a world." Other people say, "Actually I love doing the creative stuff. I really love it. And everything you say is true, but you have to make a living. I think I can work better on these issues from the inside. I think I can have an influence by changing some of the images, changing some of the content from the inside." That's fine with me.

If you gave me a choice and said, "Here are two groups of people in front of you. Here's one group of people who are not going to go into advertising, and here's another group who are going to go into advertising, which one do you want to speak to?" there's no question. I want to speak to the group that's going into advertising. I want them to recognize the immense amount of power that they have and the immense amount of responsibility that they carry and to really think about it in a serious way.

I want them to care as much as I do about these issues. What people often say about me in my teaching is that I care about what I teach. Oftentimes, people disagree with what I have to say, but they are so unused to teachers standing before them and believing passionately in what they are teaching about and believing passionately in the intellectual vocation. That it is not just job training but is central to how citizens are supposed to operate. I guess I got that from watching Stuart Hall lecture when I was at university. To see that you can have great ideas and be at the intellectual cutting edge and, at the same time, you can be speaking to a group of undergraduate students and make absolute sense to them and give a sense of not only why intellectual work is important, but also why it's fun. Hall was able to communicate that to me. Not everything is based on this, but I did get a notion that intellectual life is not only about doing intellectual work, but it is also about communicating that intellectual work.

O'BARR: Do you have any optimism for change? There is a certain pessimism that comes from this analysis.

JHALLY: Yes, there is. The response to my analysis, from my teaching perspective and from some of the tapes we've done at the Media Educational Foundation—MEF is the way I've tried to put my teaching into a form that gets beyond my classroom into other classrooms and community groups and have this kind of discussion—can be one of two things. Some people say they are just paralyzed by it. "Wow, everything you say is true. When you do the analysis, I see it is true. But what it's done is to paralyze me, because what you have talked about is power, the unbelievable power that corporations have in this world. And it seems there is no way anyone can fight against it." So, on the one hand, it leaves students feeling impotent. When people tell me that, I am horrified. I don't want this analysis to paralyze people. I want my analysis to drive people toward activism. It's a fine line to draw, because you have to do the analysis. Intellectually, you have to do the analysis.

O'BARR: What would activism look like? What would be, in your opinion, a constructive approach to these kinds of questions? Given that we live in this kind of society, it's hard to imagine the value of a Walden-like approach to things. That wouldn't solve any problems. We went through that kind of thing in the sixties. What prospects are there for people to live in the kind of world that we live in and yet really change things in ways that are more productive and gives them things that they are really after?

JHALLY: I'm actually quite optimistic. Let me tell you why. In one sense, you have to be. The optimism is about a vision for the future. If you don't have a different vision for the future, then you are condemned to live the present and the past over and over and over again. I have a vision for the future. I can imagine a different world that is based much more on justice, on equality, on actually giving people the lives they want to live. I have that vision, and I think it is my moral responsibility to try to take actions toward actualizing that vision.

There's another reason that I'm optimistic—and it's sort of perversely related to the pessimism—and it is this: Why do corporations, why do advertisers, why do media have to spend billions of dollars every day to convince us of these things? If the game were over, if there were no possibility of change, then why would they keep doing this day after day after day? And why would they go out of their way to make sure that no other idea gets into the minds of the population? They have to do that because they know that if they don't, then the world will change. In fact, if people are left to their own devices, and if other voices come into it, and if people are given real choices, then the decisions that they make will be based on real alternative choices.

O'BARR: When you say "real choices," what do you mean? You've said this before in the things you write, but what does it mean to say "if people were given real choices?" Is it like people saying in another situation, "We don't really have a choice about the political system because we only have two candidates to pick between?"

JHALLY: Well, I don't think we do have real choices in politics either. The question is whether we can have a choice that breaks with the limited choices that are given to us. There is a reason why a progressive, such as Ralph Nader, has to be marginalized and to be kept out of things like presidential debates. Not that he was going to win, but what he would have brought into it was, in fact, a different vision based on a sort of populist understanding of democracy. And so what you have to do is to make sure that Ralph Nader, as representative of that vision, was not allowed entry into the discourse. And that the discourse had to be about whatever difference there was between the Democrats and the Republicans. If Nader was that marginal, that much of a lunatic, that much of a no-hoper, why wouldn't they let him in? Why wouldn't they let people see how idiotic he was? They didn't let him in because they knew that if they let him in, his vision, in fact, would resonate with the vision of large parts of the population. And so you have to keep it out. You have to keep out this notion of a radical economic democracy in which workers would have some say over how their workdays are based.

O'BARR: Do you think that people would actually respond to someone with that kind of vision?

JHALLY: I think people would respond to that vision because it more closely reflects what people actually already believe. It's really a myth that most people are conservative. If we had a world that reflects public opinion as is, we would have a military budget that is a fraction of the size that it is, we would have much more money spent on education, and protecting the environment would be high up on the list. When you look at actual public opinion, it's much more to the left than our political elites are. And so what our political elites have to do is somehow convince us that the only choice is what they offer and to isolate individuals in their own beliefs. So individual people think, "That's not really what I believe, but no one else believes what I believe." There's this notion that you have to go along with it, because everyone else believes in these polices and these values. That's why you have to keep people separated. Once people can see another public vision that reflects what they think, there'll be tremendous support for that. I think our present political leaders know that, and that's why they have to keep that vision out. The present commercial leaders know that if there is alternative product information that comes across, people will start to question and challenge their consumption. That's the basis of boycotts. The whole movement around the global practices of the sneaker industry has been an incredibly successful way in which people have used Nike advertising, for example, to raise issues of global justice.

O'BARR: But we still have Nike. We still have advertising.

JHALLY: Social change doesn't happen overnight. But now you have, in fact, a generation of people who have on their radar the issue of third-world labor. Phil Knight, CEO of Nike, said, "I'm fed up now that whenever people think about Nike, they think of exploitive practices in the third world." Nike can do a lot to change all that by the power of their own advertising, by the billions of dollars they spend on advertising. They have to do that, because they know there is this grassroots stuff coming up. You've now got a generation of kids in college who think about Nike in a different way. Whether that will make a difference in whether they buy Nike or not, that's another open question, because this, again, is limited to what choices there really are in the marketplace. If I want to buy, say, underwear, where do I buy underwear that's not produced in the third world? The fact of the matter is it's very, very difficult to buy sneakers, underwear, and other clothing that are not a part of the system. So you can't change the world through shopping. Shopping will never change the world. It's like pollution. If you live in a polluted environment, you can't do anything by yourself to change it. What you've got to do is change the causes of that pollution. So what I want to do when I talk about Nike, about globalization and where products come from, is to have people understand this new world in which we live, in which products are made for pennies by third-world labor, and then huge amounts are spent by Nike on advertising to build up the Nike brand, to link up Nike with sports, and then that idea is put on these worthless products so that they can charge $90 for them. I want people to understand that system, and I think that if you understand that system, it won't change consumption immediately, but I think that Nike is worried enough that it will change consumption that they've had to adjust their practices. They've had to give voice at least to this notion that somehow they are not going to use poorly paid labor or that their subcontractors are going to have a different code of behavior. I don't think it will change consumption, but you now have a generation of kids at the college level who now have this on their radar and for whom now this is how they are going to operate. That's how social change works.

O'BARR: Tell me what you think the world will be like in another decade or two? Where are we headed?

JHALLY: It depends on what we do. It depends on what kind of opposition there is to our present mode of operating. As I said, I'm actually fairly optimistic that there will be at least the movement toward change.

O'BARR: Coming from where?

JHALLY: Coming from young people, from the generation that is going through college right now. People talk about them as Generation X, a generation, and therefore a demographic, that's cynical and jaded. Well, they are. But you are only cynical and jaded if you don't know where to go, and I think part of the job of political activists is to give a really positive vision of social change. I think that has been part of the problem of the Left. We've said, I mean, everything has been about the problems of capitalism, and you have to be an activist almost out of duty. I think the Left has been very bad at this. Activism needs to be talked about much more positively. It's going to be fun to change the world in a positive way, much more fun than buying Nike sneakers, much more fun than buying the latest car that's going to give you pleasure for about two minutes and then it's going to be a drain on your pocketbook. Changing the world is fun; it's about pleasure. The Left has not talked about pleasure. Advertisers talk about pleasure, and that's why everyone is buying the products of our system. Because they think that somehow pleasure will come from that. I think that we have to talk about pleasure in a different way and ask where does pleasure really come from?

For instance, what would happen if we take advertising seriously as a vision of the future? We would have a world in which everyone's work would be valued. How do you create that? The present world is not a world in which people's work is valued. We'd have a world of economic democracy. We would have a world that stressed family life. We'd have a world that was about relaxation and linking friends up in some way. None of our institutions do that at the present time. The institutions of the marketplace, in fact, work against all of those things. If you wanted a world that looked like advertising, we would, in fact, have to create a very different set of institutions. Again, this is what makes me optimistic. What we have in advertising, I think, is a vision of what a different world will look like. I've always been struck by the fact that capitalism has had to go to a different vision of society to sell itself, to a world that looks much more like a vision of socialism. In one sense, the images of the future are already there. What we have to do is uncouple them. At the moment, those images are coupled with the marketplace and with capitalism. The reason these images are there is that they are very powerful, they reach deep into the popular psyche. I want to take them and uncouple them from the present system and couple them with a different kind of society in the future.

O'BARR: The so-called socialist economies didn't fare very well in the twentieth century. How do you explain all of what happened?

JHALLY: Well, they were not really socialisms. We haven't had a society that manifests this vision yet, a vision of *democratic* socialism. That is not going to be a socialism like we had, which was a state-dominated socialism in which one form of power, capital, was replaced by another form of power, the state, with the same kinds of impacts upon ordinary people. Also, communism never gave up on the idea that somehow more things would make more people happy. They eventually went broke trying to compete with the West on that basis (as well as at the same time squandering so many resources on the military).

O'BARR: What you've described is a socialist situation that had a vision of capitalist wealth in it and a capitalist situation that has a vision of socialist theory in it.

JHALLY: Those socialist societies were never able to free themselves from the global influence of the capitalist market. You are always connected to that in the present world. My views are less about policy than they are about vision. If we can get people to think about the world in a different way . . . for example, how do we have a world in which people have more fun? I'd be quite happy to have that as the basis of political discussions. If you can't answer that question, then you are not on the train of politics. The Left's visions of fun have to be more powerful than those other visions of fun. At the moment, the Left has not talked about fun and about pleasure. I want to talk much, much more about that. I think that, in fact, the Left is much more committed to pleasure, much more committed to fun, much more committed to satisfaction, much more committed to individual freedom, and much more committed to democracy than capitalism. I want to use the images that are in capitalism. That's what makes me optimistic.

O'BARR: What will happen to goods if your vision is realized?

JHALLY: There will be less of them. We will, of course, never do without them. We need goods. But I think that there will be less of them and that we will, in fact, have a deeper relationship to goods and a deeper relationship to the material world because it really will be linked up to the kinds of things that make us happy. At the moment, we are not happy. Objects are linked up to the interests of corporations. I want to have a world in which objects are linked up to the interests of ordinary people. We will have goods, of course. This is not an argument for poverty. We need to have a certain level of material existence so that we can live every day in comfort. But going beyond that, the material world doesn't give people the kind of satisfaction that advertising insists is there. I think that if we recognize this and ask, "What other kinds of things would give us that satisfaction?" it will get us to think in very different ways about the future and about politics.

O'BARR: Thank you very much. You've managed to start at the beginnings of what you understand about the origins of modern advertising, to put it in a really interesting historical context, and to find, in all your analyses, some optimism for the future about how things might work themselves out.

You did something very interesting when we started this interview. I suggested that you are an important cultural critic—which I still consider you to be despite your disowning the term. What's the problem with being a cultural critic?

JHALLY: There's not a problem. I think we need cultural critics. I guess I am just used to a different way of describing my approach. I want to focus on connecting to the audience, not just being a critic or just commentating, but on how to communicate with the audience.

O'BARR: Emphasizing the dialogic nature?

JHALLY: Yes, absolutely. Again, I think the Left has not been very good about this. There's been incredible thinking on the Left around these issues, incredible critiques, but a lot of those critiques have remained at a very intellectual level. I don't object to this notion of a cultural critic, but I want to stress the idea of being a teacher, of linking up with the audience. Unless cultural criticism is put in a form that links up in a way in which ordinary people understand the world, I think it will remain impotent and marginal to the real lives of people. We have to figure out a way to connect intellectual work with nonintellectual lives and nonintellectual work. We have not been very good at that. The Media Educational Foundation is, I hope, an attempt to try and do some of that.

O'BARR: Well, thank you very much. I think this is a good place to stop.

Political Economy

Watching as Working: The Valorization of Audience Consciousness[*]

with Bill Livant

Does the audience *work* at watching television? Is the notion a real economic process, or does it serve as a metaphor? Our short answer is that it is both. It is a metaphor *because* it is a real economic process, specific to the commercial media that produces value. How this process occurs is the argument of our article.

The metaphorical power of *watching as working* arises from the particular relationship of the media and the economy as a whole. In the media, the whole economy exists as an image, an object of watching—more precisely, an object of the *activity* of watching. At the same time, the media exist as a reflection of the whole economy of which they are a part. The media, therefore, are at once a real part of the economy and a real reflection of it. This is why we say that *watching as working* is both a real economic process, a value-creating process, and a metaphor, a reflection of value creation in the economy as a whole.

Metaphor and Reality: The Production of Watching Extra

Let us begin with the advertising-supported commercial media as part of the whole economy. How do they make a profit? A short answer would be that the

* This essay first appeared in the *Journal of Communication* 36, no. 3 (1986): 124–143. Reprinted by permission.

media speed up the selling of commodities, their circulation from production to consumption. Hence, they speed the realization of value (the conversion of value into a money form) embodied in commodities produced everywhere in the economy. Through advertising, the rapid consumption of commodities cuts down on circulation and storage costs for industrial capital. Media capital (e.g., broadcasters) receives a portion of surplus value (profits) of industrial capital as a kind of rent paid for access to audiences. The differences between this rent and its costs of production (e.g., wages paid to media industry workers) constitute its profit.

But what is it precisely that industrial capital rents? Media capital sells something, sells the use of something, to capital as a whole. If media capital could not sell this something, if this something, when used by the buyer—capital as a whole—did not speed the realization of value embodied in commodities in general, the media would receive no payment (rent). Thus, the production of this something is the central problem for commercial media.

This something has been fuzzily described in the communications literature. Is it attention? Is it access, and, if it is, access to what? To markets? To audiences? And what are these audiences? Are they materials, tools, conditions? What is fuzzy about these answers is that they describe the something from the point of view of the interest of the *buyer*: in terms of how capital as a whole proposes to *use* it. But they do not describe the something from the point of view of the *seller*: in terms of how it is *produced*. In short, such answers do not describe the something as a problem for the media, which is the clue to the development of their specific practices.

For the media, above all, this something is *time*. But whose time? What kind of time? What happens in it that takes time? It is clear that this time would be empty and unsellable if people didn't watch. It is therefore something about watching-time that is sold by the media to advertisers.

This watching is, first, a human capacity for activity. It is not a thing, not simply a product in which value is, in Marx's word, "congealed." It is a capacity for doing something. We use *doing* generically to include seeing and listening—in general, capacities of perception. Watching is human activity through which human beings relate to the external physical world and to each other.

Watching is guided by our attention, so we often see or hear less than there is to be seen or heard. But we also see or hear more than there is. Elementary psychology books are filled with examples in which watching completes a figure, makes a connection, fills in the blanks. Gibson (1979) has found that we actually see behind obstructing or occluding objects: We see hidden surfaces. Indeed, this seeing *more* is the basis of Williamson's (1978) analysis of decoding advertisements. All watching contains an element of what we call *watching extra*.

Precisely because watching is an unspecialized, general-purpose capacity, it is capable of being modified by its objects, by what we watch, how we watch, and under what conditions we watch. Watching has a historical character; this is especially true of *watching extra*. What is so striking about the modern commercial media is that for the first time this *extra* has a specific social form: it is a commodity. Recall that this something that media capital sells is a human capacity for a certain kind of activity, which can be put to use by the buyer. The trade literature offers many testaments to the problem of getting people to watch. As ex-sportscaster Howard Cosell noted, "You've got to deliver 40 million people. Do you know the strain of that? You've got to deliver them. . . . If you don't, you're gone. The business chews you up" (*Sport*, February 1979). But when the activity of watching becomes subject to commodity production, the central problem for the media is not simply to get people to watch but to get them to watch *extra*. The problem for the commercial media is to maximize the production of this commodity and to attempt to minimize the costs of doing so.

What is the form in which these costs appear? We can answer this if we ask the following question: when we, the audience, watch TV, for whom do we watch? It is not hard to get people to tell you that some things they want to watch and some things they don't particularly want to watch but they do anyway. Indeed, as Jerry Mander's son Kai remarked, "I don't want to watch but I can't help it. It makes me watch it" (Mander, 1978 p. 158). Although formally free to watch or not to watch, we are often practically compelled. The literature is full of the phenomenology of felt compulsion (see Mander, 1978; Winn, 1977). This phenomenology in itself does not directly describe the commodity form of watching, but it does point to the fact that somehow this extra watching is being extracted in our interaction with the media. But extra watching does exist as a commodity. Some of what appears on television is a cost of production to media capital; some of what appears is not a cost but revenue that media capital receives from those who will use it. The costs are incurred to produce what we will call *necessary watching-time*—necessary to reproduce our activity of watching. The revenues are received for the *surplus watching-time* that is extracted. The problem for commercial media is to extract the maximum surplus watching-time on the basis of the minimum necessary. The logic of the media is governed by the expanded reproduction of surplus watching-time.

We argue that necessary and surplus watching exist as real economic magnitudes, identifiable and measurable. They are conceptually defined on the basic generalized human capacity for watching, the fundamental activity that constitutes a population as an audience. Watching-time is the mode of expression of value. What we are exploring is the struggle over the valorization of the activity of watching.

We believe that this argument offers an understanding of important features in the modern history of the commercial media: the changes in its technology; its composition and segmentation of audiences; the development of the blended forms of messages, such as the *advertorial* and the *infomercial*; and, above all, the acceleration of time that pervades the media. The test of our conception, of course, will be the understanding that it offers of this history.

We have found the real meaning of *watching as working* by looking *into* the media, by "putting the audience into the tube" so that we can watch its watching. But having done so, we can now look *out from* the media into the whole economy; we can treat the media as a metaphor for the economy.

We know that virtually anything can appear on television and that, today, virtually everyone watches. In short, the media are potentially a reflection of everything. But the vast literature of what TV teaches has overlooked the possibility that it might show us, right there on the screen, the production and realization of surplus value; that all its devices might reflect the organization of human labor in the economy as a whole; that, through the relation of the watching populations to media capital, it might reflect the relation of the working population to capital as a whole.

In our view, the media are a great fishbowl. Every economic process, every movement of value, every step in the circuit of capital appears as a reflection, not simply through or in the media but *as* the media-audience process itself. The media economy is a fishbowl that reflects the whole thing of which it is a part. In particular, the struggles over the valorization of human activity in the media reflect these processes in the whole economy. The media are indeed a metaphor.

Watching as working? Really? Metaphorically? Again our answer is "both." It is metaphorical because it is real; it is real because it is a part of something real, which it reflects and for which it therefore can stand as a metaphor. We will look into the commercial media in order to see how the whole economy, embodied in it, is reflected there.

From Use-Value to Exchange-Value: Breaking with Message-Based Analysis

Most studies of the media (both in the mainstream and critical traditions) have focused on messages as their central unit of analysis. Despite the many differences within the field, there is a broad unstated agreement that the discipline of media communication is about the production, distribution, reception, interpretation, and effects of messages. From two-step theory, to uses and gratifications, to cultivation analysis, to agenda setting, to the study of ideology and texts, to the controversy over the New World Information Order, and even to the debate concerning the effects of the new information technologies, the focus has been on messages. More specifically, the concentration has been on how these messages are used, on what meanings are generated in the interaction between messages and people. The history of communication, then, has been a study of the use-values of messages, their meaning.

That this should be the focus of the study of the commercial broadcast media, in particular, is somewhat surprising when we view the industry in historical perspective, for messages have *never* been the central commodity that has been produced and traded. In the early years of broadcasting, as Williams reminds us, there was little attention given to the content of the new media: "Unlike all previous communications technologies, radio and television were systems primarily designed for transmission and reception as abstract processes, with little or no definition of preceding content . . . the means of communication preceded their content" (1974, p. 25). In the United States, the first role of the electronic media was to stimulate the sale of radio sets (Barnouw, 1978). Later, as the commercial networks developed, the sale of audiences took precedence as the industry's major activity. Messages were integrated within this wider industrial production.

There has been increasing recognition in recent years, particularly among critical scholars, of a failure to penetrate to the core understanding of the role of media in advanced capitalism. The traditional concepts of base/superstructure, relative autonomy, ideology, and hegemony are not sufficient to explain the dynamic changes taking place in mass media. As Garnham wrote,

> So long as Marxist analysis concentrates on the ideological content of mass media it will be difficult to develop coherent political strategies for resisting the underlying dynamic of development in the cultural sphere in general which rests firmly and increasingly upon the logic of generalized commodity production. In order to understand the structure of our culture, its production, consumption and reproduction and of the role of the mass media in that process, we need to confront some of the central questions of political economy in general. (1979, p. 145)

Smythe (1977, 1981) also expressed explicit dissatisfaction with the existing state of critical media analysis. For Smythe, Marxism has had a blind spot about communications, concentrating on the concept of ideology instead of addressing the issue of the economic role of mass media in advanced capitalism. Smythe gave two original formulations to this problem. First, he argued that mass media produce audiences as commodities for sale to advertisers. The program content of mass media is merely the so-called free lunch that invites people to watch. It is the sale of their audience-power to advertisers, however, that is the key to the whole system of capitalist communications. Second, he claimed that advertisers put this audience-power to work by getting audiences to market commodities to themselves. Audiences thus labor for advertisers to ensure the distribution and consumption of commodities in general. While one cannot overestimate Smythe's contribution to a proper understanding of the political economy of communications, the stress on audience labor for the manufacturers of branded commodities has tended to deflect the specificity of the analysis away from communications to the ensuing consumption behavior of the audience. Ultimately, Smythe was concerned with drawing attention to the place of communications in the wider system of social reproduction and the reproduction of capital. We believe that the exploration of the blind spot needs to be located more firmly *within* the media industries rather than focusing on their wider role.

Broadly speaking, Garnham and Smythe were attempting to break with *symbolism* and *meaning* as the starting point of materialist analysis: They were seeking to break with message-based analysis and the study of use-values. We strongly support this attempt but wish to phrase it in slightly different terms in trying to establish a general framework for a critical materialist analysis. While all messages have a use-value, within the commercial media messages are part of not only a system of meaning but also a system of exchange. They form part of the process wherein media industries attempt to generate profit by producing and selling commodities in a market setting. Within the sphere of commercial mass media, messages have both a use-value *and* an exchange-value. More precisely, the use-values of messages are integrated within a system of exchange-value. To understand use-value, we have to adequately contextualize its relation to exchange-value. This means a switch in focus from the question of the use-value (meaning) of messages, not because the understanding of meaning is unimportant, but because we can understand it within its concrete specificity only once we fully understand the conditions created by exchange-value. The remainder of this article attempts to unravel the system of exchange-value that constitutes the system of advertising-supported media.

To properly comprehend the system of exchange-value within which the commercial media are based, we need to understand its economic logic and to answer three related questions: What is the commodity-form sold by commercial media? Who produces this media commodity and under what conditions? What is the source of value and surplus value in this process? Once we have answered these questions, we can then formulate an adequate context within which we can understand the role of messages.

What Is the Commodity-Form Sold by the Commercial Media?

At first glance, the answer to the question of what commodity-form is sold by the commercial media seems obvious and straightforward: Media sell *audiences* to advertisers. We need, however, to pin down specifically what about audiences is important for the mass media. For all his emphasis on communications, Smythe does not ask this question directly. For him, it is audience-power put to work for advertisers that is important. There is no doubt that this is what advertisers are interested in, but it does not mean that the media are interested in the same thing. What advertisers buy with their advertising dollars is audiences' watching-time, which is all the media have to sell. That advertising rates are determined by the size and demographics of the audience is ample confirmation of this. When media *sell time* to a sponsor, it is not abstract time that is being sold but the time of particular audiences. Furthermore, this is not (as Smythe contends) time spent in self-marketing and consuming advertisers' commodities, but rather time spent in watching and listening—communications-defined time. What the media sell (because they own the means of communication) is what they control—the watching-time of the audience.

Most critical analyses of advertising and media have been stalled at this point. The watching-time of the audience has been (quite correctly) characterized as the domination of so-called free time by capital to aid in realizing the value of commodities in general. For example, Ewen (1976) and Baran and Sweezy (1966) concentrate on this point, as does Smythe. No matter how much Smythe stresses the oppositional activities of audiences in constructing alternative lifestyles, however, he drifts back to the use-value of messages—meanings and their relationship to consumption. The discussion of audiences should not stop here. The audience as a market is the first form of organization of this commodity but not the last.

The recognition of watching-time as the media commodity is a vital step in the break with message-based definitions of media and audiences. It makes the problem an internal one to mass communications. The focus on watching-time is crucial to establishing an audience-centered theory of mass communications from a materialist perspective based on the analysis of exchange-value.

Who Produces This Media Commodity and under What Conditions?

Networks consider themselves the producers and sellers of audiences (see Bergreen, 1980; Reel, 1979, pp. 4–5), and critical thinkers have tended to take this at face value, accepting the notion that, because networks *exchange* audiences, they also *produce* them. It is surprising to find this confusion in the writing of Marxist critics on the topic of communication, since they do not make this error in writing on, say, the auto industry or petrochemicals or, indeed, on communications hardware itself. But, when it comes to communications, the myth of the "productivity of capital" (Marx, 1976) still befuddles us.

To avoid this trap we have to distinguish several common confusions. First, we must distinguish the production of messages from the production of audiences. The staff in a network newsroom produces news. The viewers watching it do not produce the news, but they do participate in producing the commodity of audience-time, as does the network staff. Networks could produce messages that no one might watch, in which case they would barely be able to give away that time, let alone sell it. The commodity audience-time is produced by both the networks and the audience.

Second, we therefore have to distinguish between the production of audiences and their exchange. There is a lot of talk in the industry about the media producing audiences, but they have not produced what they are selling.

The networks merely sell the time that has been produced for them by others (by the audience). It is only because they own the means of communication that they have title to the commodity, which has been produced for them by others. Like Manchester manufacturers more than a century ago (see Engels, 1891), networks suffer from the self-serving myth of the productivity of capital. Once we have sorted out these confusions we can see that the answer to this second question is that *both* audiences and the networks produce the commodity audiences' watching-time.

What Is the Source of Value and Surplus Value in This Process?

Through their own station licenses and those of their affiliates, and through their ownership of the means of communication, the networks have control of twenty-four hours a day of broadcasting time. How is this time that the networks control made valuable—how is it *valorized?*

The surface economics of commercial television seem quite simple. Network expenses can be defined as operating costs plus program costs. Their revenues are advertising dollars from advertisers who buy the time of the audiences that the programming has captured. Networks hope that revenues are more than expenses— more than an empty hope, of course, for it is almost impossible to lose money if one owns a network station. The average cost of a thirty-second network prime-time commercial in 1985 was $119,000. Based only on prime-time (8:00 p.m. to 11:00 p.m.) sales, each network collects $60 million per week from advertisers. We need, however, to dig beneath the seeming superficiality of commercial television economics and ask specifically how and by whom value and surplus value (profit) are produced. Let us trace through the process in detail. The networks buy (or license) programs from independent producers to entice the audience to watch. Networks then fill this empty time that they control by buying the watching-power of the audience. Having purchased this "raw material," they then process it and sell it to advertisers for more than they paid for it. As a concrete example, a network pays independent producers $400,000 per episode for a half-hour situation comedy. The program is in fact twenty-four minutes long; the other six minutes is advertising time. Let us presume that this six minutes is divided into twelve thirty-second spots that sell for $100,000 each. They thus yield $1,200,000 in income, which results in a surplus of $800,000 for thirty minutes of the broadcasting day.

If we keep in mind that it is the watching activity of the audience that is being bought and sold, we can see precisely where value and surplus value are produced. It is necessary for the audience to watch four of the twelve spots to produce value equal to the cost of programming. For four spots, the audience watches for itself; for the remaining eight spots, the audience is watching *surplus-time* (over and above the cost of programming). Here, the audience watches to produce surplus value for the owners of the means of communication, the networks or the local broadcasters.

Networks wish to make necessary watching-time as short as possible and surplus watching-time as long as possible. The struggle to increase surplus time and to decrease necessary time animates the mass media. One way in which this ratio can be manipulated is to make the advertising time longer. Program time is made into ad time, so that, in the previous example, two more thirty-second spots could be added by making the programming only twenty-three minutes long. In that case, the ratio between necessary and surplus time (presuming program costs remain the same) extends to 4:10 from 4:8, resulting in more surplus time. This, indeed, is what local stations do to syndicated shows. Portions of the program are cut out to make space for more ads. This strategy, based upon extending advertising in real time, can be labeled *the extraction of absolute surplus value*. In this scenario, there is a continual attempt to expand total advertising time.

However, at a certain point, there is a limit to the expansion of advertising time. Audiences will simply stop watching if there is too much advertising and not enough programming. The TV Code of the National Association of Broadcasters (NAB) limits nonprogramming time to 9.5 minutes per hour in prime time (although most stations violate this limit [see Ray & Webb, 1978]). The networks in this situation must adopt new strategies to manipulate the ratio between necessary and surplus time. If the networks cannot make people watch advertising longer in absolute terms, they can make the time of watching advertising more intense—they can make the audience watch *harder*.

From Absolute to Relative Surplus Value

Since the late 1950s, as market research has grown in sophistication, and as advertisers are able to pinpoint quite precisely their target market, the media have found it profitable to deliver these segmented audiences to sponsors. Barnouw (1978) has given a powerful account of how the obsession with producing the right demographics has come to dominate the everyday practices of broadcasters (see also Gitlin, 1983). Advertisers judge the effectiveness of various media in terms of their *cost per thousand*—how much it costs to reach one thousand people. However, the watching-time of all types of audiences is not the same; some market segments are more valuable because that is who advertisers wish to reach.

For instance, advertisers will pay more to buy time during sporting events, because the audience for sports includes a large proportion of adult men whom advertisers of high-price consumer articles (such as automobiles) are anxious to reach. As John DeLorean put it,

> The difference in paying $7 a thousand for sport and $4 a thousand for "bananas" [prime time] is well worth it. You know you're not getting Maudie Frickert.

You're reaching men, the guys who make the decision to buy a car. There's almost no other way to be sure of getting your message out to them. (Johnson, 1971, p. 224)

Now men certainly do watch prime time, but, in prime time, automobile advertisers are paying not only for the male audience, but also for the rest of the audience, many of whom are presumed to have no interest in purchasing cars. For every one thousand people whose time is bought by advertisers on prime time, then, there is much wasted watching by irrelevant viewers. Specification and fractionation of the audience leads to a form of *concentrated viewing* by the audience in which there is (from the point of view of advertisers) little wasted watching. Because that advertising time can be sold at a higher rate by the media, we can say that the audience organized in this manner watches *harder* and with more intensity and efficiency. In fact, because the value of the time goes up, necessary watching-time decreases, and surplus watching-time increases, thus leading to greater surplus value.

The other major way in which relative surplus value operates in the media is through the division of time. Whereas the concern with demographics reorganizes the watching population, the concern with time division reorganizes the watching process. This involves a redivision of the limited time available to increase the ratio between necessary and surplus time (Bergreen, 1980, p. 289). The major way to accomplish this is to move toward shorter commercials, and, indeed, over the last twenty-five years, the number of nonprogram elements has dramatically skyrocketed, although the absolute amount of advertising time has increased only by 2.5 minutes per hour. In 1965, the three major networks showed an average of 1,839 ads per week. The figure rose to 2,200 in 1970, to 3,487 in 1975, to 4,636 in 1980, and to 4,997 in 1983 (*Television/Radio Age*, June 1985). Today, the thirty-second commercial predominates, although there are a great number of fifteen-second commercials also. They comprised 6.5 percent of all network ads in 1985, and it is estimated that, in 1986, this figure will climb to 18 percent (*Fortune*, December 23, 1985).

The basic economic logic works as follows: Assume there are five thirty-second commercials in a commercial break. If each sells for $100,000, income to the network is $500,000. To increase the revenue derived from this time, the network divides it into ten fifteen-second slots offered to advertisers for $60,000 each. If there were enough demand to sell these spots, the income to the network would be $600,000 instead of the previous $500,000.

But why would advertisers agree to this price hike? After all, they are now paying more per second, although less per spot. Advertisers, however, are not concerned about the value of time but about the frequency with which the market can he reached. The shorter spots give them twice the number of ads without raising the price by a proportionate amount. And, indeed, advertisers believe that a combination of thirty-second and fifteen-second versions of the same ad works well in conveying almost the same information. If the program price remains the same, viewers will have to watch for less necessary time to cover its cost. We must emphasize that the time of audiences is the key to the process by which networks valorize the time they control. It is also the limits of human perception (that is, the limits to watching) that guide the division of time. Advertisers may be able to construct beautifully crafted ten-second commercials, but these are useless if they do not work on the audience in that short time. "If we can demonstrate that the American consuming public can absorb and act on a 15-second unity, can the 7.5-second commercial be far behind?" (*Fortune*, December 23, 1975). Human watching, listening, perceiving, and learning activities act as a constraint to the system.

Watching and Labor

Our use so far of the familiar concepts of Marxian economic theory to analyze the valorization of time by the networks has been a pointed one. Central to the whole paradigm of Marxian economics is the notion that human labor—not capital or technology—is the basis of the productivity of societies. Similarly, in the analysis of broadcasting economics, it is audience watching that is vital to the whole process. In a very real sense, we can see that there are many similarities between industrial labor and watching activity. In fact, watching is a form of labor.

Again, this relationship should be seen as both metaphorical and real. Watching is a real extension of the logic of industrial labor, even if it is not the same as industrial labor. However, as metaphor, it illuminates the obscure workings of the economy in general. As Ricoeur writes, "metaphor is the rhetorical process by which discourse unleashes the power that certain fictions have to redescribe reality" (1977, p. 7).

Watching as metaphor reflects the dynamic of the capitalist economy. In Marx's analysis of the work day, the productivity of capitalism is based upon the purchase of one key commodity—labor-power. This is the only element in the means of production that produces more value than it takes to reproduce itself. Like all commodities, it has a value, a cost—the cost of its production (or reproduction). The cost of labor-power (the capacity to labor) is the cost of the socially determined level of the means of subsistence: that is, what it costs to ensure that the laborer can live and be fit for work the next day. The amount of labor-time that it takes to produce value equivalent to this minimum cost is labeled by Marx as *socially necessary labor* (necessary to reproduce labor-power). Socially necessary labor-time produces value that is equivalent to wages. The remaining labor-time is labeled as *surplus labor-time,* through which surplus value is generated. In the nonwork part of the day, workers spend wages (on shelter, food, children, etc.) that will ensure that they will be fit and healthy enough to go to work. During nonwork time, they thus *reproduce* their labor-power.

How is this process reflected as metaphor within the broadcast media? The network owns the means of production—communication—which makes possible the production of commodities and gives the network ownership of those commodities. While workers sell labor-power to capitalists, audiences sell watching-power to media owners; as the use-value of labor-power is labor, so the use-value of watching-power is watching, the capacity to watch. In addition, as the value of labor-power is fixed at the socially determined level of the means of subsistence (thus ensuring that labor-power will be reproduced), so the value of watching-power is the cost of its reproduction—the cost of programming, which ensures that viewers will watch and be in a position to watch extra (the time of advertising). In this formulation, it is only the time of advertising that comprises the so-called work day for the audience. The programming, the value of watching-power, is the wage of the audience, the variable capital of the communications industry. It is also time for the reproduction of watching-power, the time of consumption, the time of nonwork. As the work day is split into two, so the work part of the viewing day—advertising time—is split between socially necessary watching-time and surplus watching-time.

For instance, the early history of industrial capitalism is tied up with attempts by capital to extend the time of the working day in an absolute sense, thus manipulating the ratio between necessary time and surplus time. Within the development of the commercial media system, this phase is represented by broadcasting from the late 1920s to the early 1960s. In the first years of commercial broadcasting (extending into the 1930s), broadcasters struggled to persuade advertisers to sponsor shows. The more shows were sponsored, the more audiences could be sold to advertisers. This was an extension in the amount of time that people watched and listened for capital. It also has to be remembered that, until the introduction of spot selling in the 1960s, programs were advertising agency creations, with the sponsor's name and product appearing everywhere (not only in ads) (Bergreen, 1980).

However, as Marx realized, this absolute extension of the working day cannot go on indefinitely. Unions and collective bargaining limited the length of the working day, forcing capital to increase the *intensity* of labor. The concept of relative surplus value initially meant the cheapening of consumer goods that reproduce labor-power, so that the amount of necessary time would be decreased. In the era of monopoly capitalism, two other major factors contribute to the extraction of relative surplus value—the reorganization of the workplace and the introduction of technologically efficient instruments of production As Marx writes, "The production of absolute surplus value turns exclusively upon the length of the working day: the production of relative surplus value revolutionizes out and out the technical processes of labor and the composition of society" (1976, p. 645). We have already referred to the stress on demographics (reorganization of the working population) and the redivision of time (reorganization of the work process). Watching and labor, then, display many historical similarities in the movement between absolute and relative surplus value.

From the Formal to the Real Subsumption of Watching

In a very important text published in English for the first time in 1976, Marx distinguishes between the *formal* and the *real* subsumption of labor (1976, pp. 943–1085). As capitalist relations of production expand, they come into contact with other types of relations of production—for example, feudal relations in agriculture. Capitalism does not effect a change in these other relations but merely "tacks them on" to its own operations: "capital subsumes the labor process as it finds it, that is to say, it takes over an *existing labor process*, developed by different and more archaic modes of production" (1976, p. 1021). Thus, while capital subsumes the process, it does not establish specifically capitalist relations of production in that sphere; it does not need to. The old relations are used in ways that benefit capital without being organized under its relations of production. Marx argues that the formal subsumption of labor is based upon increasing the length of the working day: that is, on absolute surplus value.

In broadcasting, the formal subsumption of watching activity is linked to the period when advertisers had direct control of programming (when they wrote and produced it). Broadcasting did not develop initially as an advertising medium; its first purpose was to aid in the selling of radio sets. Only later was time on the airwaves sold by AT&T to bring in additional revenue. Even when advertising became prominent in the late 1920s and 1930s, networks did little more than lease facilities and sell air time to advertisers who had total control of broadcasting. Thus, capital (advertisers) took over more archaic modes of watching for their own ends. Advertisers were interested primarily in the activities of the audience as it related to the consumption of their products. Watching here was tacked on to specifically capitalist relations of production without being organized in the same manner.

But the two different relations of production cannot exist side by side indefinitely. Indeed, capitalism constantly works to wither away the other mode of production and to introduce capitalist relations of production into that domain. This is labeled as the *real subsumption of labor*. At this stage (which corresponds to the extraction of relative surplus value), "the entire real form of production is altered and a *specifically capitalist form of production* comes into being (at the technological level too)" (Marx, 1976, p. 1024). The archaic forms of production are replaced with capitalist relations of production. The old realm is no longer directly subordinate to other domains but itself becomes a proper capitalist enterprise interested primarily in its own productivity rather than being peripheral (yet vital) to something else.

By the late 1950s, it was proving inefficient (for the network) to have the audience watch exclusively for one advertiser for thirty to sixty minutes. The media could generate more revenue for themselves if they could *reorganize* the time of watching by rationalizing their program schedule. The move to spot selling was an attempt to increase the ratio of necessary to surplus watching-time.

There was a limit to how much one advertiser could pay for a thirty- or sixty-minute program. If the networks could control the programming and the advertising time within it, then they could generate more revenue (by selling spots) from multiple advertisers, all of whom individually paid less. Initially, advertisers resisted this rationalization and the subsumption of their individual interests under the general interests of media capital. In the end, however, rising program costs, legal objections to advertisers' control, and scandals drove the networks to move toward full control of their schedules (Barnouw, 1978). This resulted in the double reorganization of the watching population and the watching process under specifically capitalist relations of production.

Alienated Watching

There is another dimension along which watching-labor shares characteristics with labor in the economy in general—both are viewed as unpleasant by the people who have to perform either activity. The history of working-class resistance to the process of wage labor and various sociological studies illustrate that, for many people in modern society, work is not an enjoyable activity. People, on the whole, work not because they like their jobs but because they have to work. Work has become a means to an end rather than an end in itself; labor is a form of alienated activity.

Similarly, consider the attitudes of the watching audience to the time of advertising. Despite the fact that huge amounts of money (much more than on programming) are spent on producing attractive commercials, people do all they can to avoid them. Data indicate that almost 30 percent of viewers simply leave the room or attend to alternative technologies during the commercial breaks (Fiber, 1984). They also simply switch channels in the hope that they can find another program to watch rather than more ads. (Switching between the major networks is rather unproductive on this score, as they all tend to have their commercial breaks at the same time.) Indeed, a 1984 report by the J. Walter Thompson advertising company estimated that, by 1989, only 55 to 60 percent of television audiences will remain tuned in during the commercial break. Commercial viewing levels are decreasing. The remote channel changer is a major factor in this so-called zapping of commercials, as is the spread of video cassette recorders (VCRs). When programs are recorded to be watched at a later time, one can simply skip over the commercials by fast-forwarding through them. The owners of the means of communication are faced here with a curious problem—the audience could watch programs (get paid) without doing the work (watching commercials) that produces value and surplus value.

These findings have not been lost on the advertising or television industries, who have increasingly recognized that the traditional concept of a *ratings point* may no longer be valid. Ratings measure program watching rather than commercial watching. Indeed, it seems that there is much disparity between the two, and advertisers are starting to voice their discontent at having to pay for viewers who may not be watching their ads at all. This has led the ratings companies to experiment with new measures of the audience. The most intriguing development is the *people meters,* a device on the TV with a separate button for each participating household member. Individuals punch in when they start watching and punch out when they stop, providing advertisers and broadcasters with a more precise measure of the level of commercial viewing. There could be no clearer indication of the similarities between watching and labor. Just as workers in a factory punch in and punch out, so too will viewers be evaluated along similar lines.

It is instructive to note that no one would be worried if people were zapping the programs and watching ads in greater numbers; the industry would be undisturbed. But when the new technologies of cable and VCRs threaten the viewing patterns of commercial time, then the very foundations of the broadcasting industry begin to shake in anticipation of the consequences.

Although we have pointed out many similarities between watching and labor, we do not regard them as identical activities. For instance, watching has no formal contract for the exchange of watching-power, and there can be no enforcement of the informal contract. We have sought to identify the broad dynamic through which watching activity is brought into the realm of the economic and the manner in which watching activity, under the conditions of advanced capitalist production, reflects in a spectacular way the workings of the real.

Narrowcasting and Blurring

Since the continued spread of cable in the 1970s and 1980s, there has been a very dramatic shift in viewing patterns in the United States. In 1975 and 1976, according to Nielsen figures, the three major networks commanded among them 89 percent of the watching audience during prime time (*New York Times,* October 16, 1985). By 1985, that figure was down to 73 percent. This does not mean that people are watching less television; indeed, by 1984, the average family viewed an all-time high of almost fifty hours a week. People thus are watching more TV and less of the networks. The extra viewing has been diverted largely into offerings available on cable television. Those homes with access only to regular over-the-air broadcast television watched only forty-two hours and twenty-two minutes a week in 1985, while those with cable and subscription services watched almost fifty-eight hours a week. Clearly, cable television (based upon narrowcasting to specific audiences) increases the total amount of time that people watch television. While some of this extra watching goes to pay TV services (without advertising), much of it is still bound up with commercially sponsored programs. Narrowcasting, then, also increases absolute surplus value.

Up until now, we have made a rather strict distinction between programming and advertising. In the historical development of the commercial media system, however, the boundaries between the two were very often blurred. The function of programming is much more than merely capturing the watching activity of a specific demographic group of the market. Programming also has to provide the right environment for the advertising that will be inserted within it. Advertisers seek compatible programming vehicles that stress the lifestyles of consumption. Thus, in the 1950s, the very popular and critically acclaimed anthology series were dropped by the networks, because they focused on working-class settings and complex psychological states, neither of which was conducive to the advertisers' needs for glamorous consumer-oriented lifestyles and the instant and simple fixes offered by their commodities to the problems of modern living. The anthology series were replaced by programs that were much more suited to the selling needs of advertisers. Furthermore, actors and stars moved easily between programs and commercials. At a more explicit level, advertisers sought to have their products placed *within* the program itself. In all of these ways, we can see a blurring between the message content of the commercials and the message content of the programming.

Although many writers (see Barnouw, 1978) have commented on this phenomenon, they have not noticed how this blurring is enormously intensified by the move to narrowcasting. In each portion of the fractionated audience, from the point of view of the message content the difference between the program content and the ad content constantly diminishes. Both ads and programs draw upon the specific audience to construct their message code. The drawback of the mass audience for broadcasting is usually thought to be that the program may attract a mass audience without necessarily attracting a mass market for certain commodities; hence, the importance of demographics for advertisers. But the problem has not usually been perceived within the sphere of watching itself. Broadcasting produces only a loose compatibility between programs and commercials. Broadcasting limits blurring while narrowcasting overcomes these limits.

Although there may appear to be a formal symmetry at work, within the sociomaterial conditions of the media the first aspect dominates the second. The commercial form is the dynamic element in the process. If part of the program is really an ad, then part of the program time is not really consumption-time: rather, it is labor-time, and the length of the working day has been extended. The program as the extension of the ad shows us the increase in the magnitude of labor-time of watching. It contributes to absolute surplus value. Within narrowcasting, the progressive fractionation of the audience intensifies both absolute and relative surplus value. From such a viewpoint, there appear to be two *media revolutions*. The first—broadcasting—converts nonwork leisure time into the sphere of watching-time (both consumption watching-time and labor watching-time). The second—narrowcasting—converts consumption watching-time (programming) into labor watching-time (ads). Because there is a limit to advertising time, media have to gain more surplus from the existing time. Blurring accomplishes this by converting program into ad, by converting consumption watching-time into labor watching-time. While this process is observable within broadcasting, it is greatly intensified by narrowcasting.

Televised sports are one such example of blurring. Values of masculinity and fraternity are present in both ads and programs; sports personalities flit between the two. The sponsorship of televised sporting events (e.g., the Volvo Grand Prix of Tennis, the AT&T Championships) is also an attempt to convert program into ad.

Within the field of broadcasting itself, segmented programming leads to blurring. For instance, in 1983, Action for Children's Television petitioned the Federal Communications Commission to recognize certain Saturday morning children's programs—those that featured toys successfully sold in stores as their primary characters—for what they really were: thirty-minute-long commercials.

The formation of the MTV cable network highlights this movement most dramatically. On MTV, the entire twenty-four-hour viewing day is advertising time—between the ads for commodities in general are placed ads for record albums (rock videos—the so-called programming). Objectively, all time on MTV is commercial time. Subjectively, also, it is very difficult to distinguish between ad and program. The same directors, actors, dancers, artists, etc., move between videos and ads until the lines between the two blur and disappear (Jhally, 1987).

The best example of the blurring under consideration is that of the *commercial on the commercial. The Commercial Show*, a cable program in Manhattan, "consists of old commercials; advertisers can buy time to put new commercials between the old ones" (*Wall Street Journal*, February 4, 1982). The blurring here is so complete that it shows dramatically the difference between consumption-time and labor-time. There is no better example of the fact that the same kind of message has two fundamentally different functions. One could hardly find a better reason to abandon a message-based definition of the messages themselves.

Conclusion

We believe that this theory explains in a unified way a number of recent developments: the move to shorter commercials, the stress on demographics, the evolution of narrowcasting, the creation of new ratings measures. Looking farther afield, this framework also lends an explanation to the movements in Western Europe toward commercial broadcasting in which the watching activities of the audience can be more fully integrated within a productive sphere.

Moreover, this framework allows us to understand the basic division in the message system between programs and ads. Many writers have commented that ads are much better constructed than the bulk of network programming. Barnouw

(1978) believes that ads are a new American art form; it does indeed seem that the artistic talent of our society is concentrated there. On the average, ads cost eight times as much to produce as programs. Why should this be the case? Our theoretical framework provides an answer: The reason ads are technically so good and programs are generally so poor is that they have a different status within the communications commodity system. Programs are messages that have to be sold to consumers—they are, in fact, *consumer goods*. Like most consumer items in the modern marketplace, they are products of a mass production system based upon uniformity and are generally of a poor quality. Program messages, like consumer goods in general, are designed for instant, superficial gratification and long-term disappointment that ensures a return trip to the marketplace. They are produced as cheaply as possible for a mass audience.

In contrast, we can label commercials *capital* goods—they are used by the owners of the means of production to try to stimulate demand for particular branded commodities. Like machines in a factory (and unlike consumer goods), they are not meant to break down after a certain period of time. Although the objects of their attempted persuasion are consumers, commercials are not sold to consumers, and consumers do not buy them (as far as we know, people do not tune in to television to watch commercials as a first priority).

As with other objects used by capital, no expense is spared in producing the best possible good. Also like capital goods, commercials are tax deductible. During programming time (consumption watching-time), audiences create meaning for themselves. During commercial time (labor watching-time), audiences create meaning for capital. It is little wonder that commercials whose function is to communicate (and not just get attention) should be the "best things on television" and the only part of television to have realized the potentials of the medium.

The main contention of this article has been that the activity of watching through the commercial media system is subject to the same process of valorization as labor-time in the economy in general. This is not to suggest that they can be identified as exactly the same type of activity for, clearly, they produce different types of commodities. Factory labor produces a material object, whereas watching activity does not. However, the modern evolution of the mass media under capitalism is governed by the appropriation of surplus human activity. The development of this appropriation is a higher stage in the development of the value form of capital. Its logic reproduces the logic described by Marx for the earlier form, but its concrete form is, in fact, a new stage: the value form of human activity itself. The empirical reflection of this is that the process of consciousness becomes valorized. There is thus a partial truth in the label attached by Enzenberger and others to the modern mass media as *consciousness industry*—except that they have so far conceptualized it upside-down. Mass media are not characterized primarily by what they put *into* the audience (messages) but by what they take *out* (value).

References

Baran, P., & Sweezy, P. (1966). *Monopoly capitalism*. London: Pelican.

Barnouw, E. (1978). *The sponsor: Notes on a modern potentate*. New York: Oxford University Press.

Bergreen, L. (1980). *Look now, pay later: The rise of network broadcasting*. Garden City, NY: Doubleday.

Engels, F. (1891). Preface. In K. Marx, *Wage labor and capital: Value, price and profit*. New York: International Publishers.

Ewen, S. (1976). *Captains of consciousness: Advertising and the social roots of the consumer culture*. New York: McGraw-Hill.

Fiber, B. (1984, October 31). Tuning out ads a growing trend. *Globe and Mail*.

Garnham, N. (1979). Contribution to a political economy of communication. *Media, Culture & Society, 1*. pp. 123–140.

Gibson, J. (1979). *The ecological approach to visual perception*. Boston: Houghton Mifflin.

Gitlin, T. (1983). *Inside prime time* (1st ed.). New York: Pantheon Books.

Jhally, S. (1987). *The codes of advertising: Fetishism and the political economy of meaning in the consumer society*. New York: St. Martin's Press.

Johnson, W. (1971). *Super spectator and the electric Lilliputians*. Toronto: Little, Brown.

Mander, J. (1978). *Four arguments for the elimination of television*. New York: Morrow.

Marx, K. (1976). *Capital: A critique of political economy* (B. Fowkes, Trans., Vol. 1). London: Penguin.

Ray, M., & Webb, P. (1978). *Advertising effectiveness in a crowded television environment*. Cambridge, MA: Marketing Science Institute.

Reel, F. (1979). *Networks: How they stole the show*. New York: Scribner.

Ricœur, P. (1977). *The rule of metaphor: Multi-disciplinary studies of the creation of meaning in language*. Toronto: University of Toronto Press.

Smythe, D. W. (1977). Communications: Blindspots of western Marxism. *Canadian Journal of Political and Social Thought, 1*(3). pp. 1–27.

Smythe, D. W. (1981). *Dependency road: Communications, capitalism, consciousness, and Canada*. Norwood, NJ: Ablex.

Williams, R. (1974). *Television, technology and cultural form*. London: Fontana.

Williamson, J. (1978). *Decoding advertisements: Ideology and meaning in advertising*. London: Boyars.

Winn, M. (1977). *The plug-in drug*. New York: Viking.

The Political Economy of Culture[*]

Introduction

Democracies, by definition, are fragile and unstable social formations. To remain democratic, there must be at all times a vigorous and diverse debate under way concerning social policy over a whole range of subject areas. Without open debate, it is all too easy to lapse into a homogenizing authoritarianism. The diversity and richness of the cultural realm are not merely "ornaments of a democracy but essential elements for its survival" (Bagdikian, 1985, p. 97). It is for this reason that the First Amendment of the Constitution guarantees freedom of belief, expression, and assembly. For many different reasons, the framers of the Constitution recognized that such freedom was a prerequisite for political freedom and a bulwark against centralized control of the social and cultural realm.

However, although freedom can be discussed as an abstract concept, it is always played out in specific historical and material circumstances. The freedom of expression (and the press) that the Constitution guarantees is freedom defined in a particular way—it is freedom from control by *government*. In the American mind, freedom is integrally linked with the role of the government (hence, the

[*] This essay first appeared in *Cultural Politics in Contemporary America*, ed. S. Jhally & I. Angus (New York: Routledge, 1989) pp. 65–81. Reprinted by permission.

perceived loss of freedom under a centralized authority—Communism). However, this one-dimensional definition of freedom ignores the possibility that freedom can be diminished not simply by government restrictions, but also by other factors that prevent freedom of belief, expression, and assembly. In freeing culture from government, the Constitution entrusts it to the *marketplace of ideas* which, presumably, ensures freedom. But, we shall be asking ourselves here, is this necessarily the case? Is the *marketplace* a truly democratic site?

The metaphor of *the marketplace of ideas* works in two ways: ideologically and materially. Ideologically, it conveys the notion that ideas battle for people's minds in a realm in which competition of belief is encouraged and that, from this free and equal struggle, so-called truth will emerge as the victor. It is diversity and choice and freedom of speech that are stressed in the ideological reading of the metaphor. The way to ensure this—it is argued by democracies—is to block government interference in the political and cultural realms. There are thus no constitutional laws restricting freedom of expression in the United States.

The material interpretation of *the marketplace of ideas* takes the notion of marketplace literally—as a place where ideas are bought and sold. It refers to the concrete framework within which the right of free expression exists. As Supreme Court Justice Walter Brennan says,

> Freedom of speech does not exist in the abstract. On the contrary, the right to speak can flourish only if it is allowed to operate in an effective forum—whether it be a public park, a schoolroom, a town meeting hall, a soapbox, or a radio and television frequency. For in the absence of an effective means of communications, the right to speak would ring hollow indeed. And, in recognition of these principles, we have consistently held that the First Amendment embodies, not only the abstract right to be free from censorship, but also the right of an individual to utilize an appropriate and effective medium for the expression of his views. (as quoted in Owen, 1975, p. 1)

However, the courts have never been able to agree whether the First Amendment merely prevents Congress from restricting free expression or whether it implies that Congress should take legislative action to widen and protect free expression.

The question that is left to be answered here is what is the relationship between these two interpretations of the marketplace of ideas? Is there a contradiction between expecting the marketplace to provide genuine diversity while, at the same time, treating ideas as economic goods to be bought and sold? What are the implications of expecting the marketplace to work in the *public* interest and, at the same time, leaving the control of the institutions expected to accomplish this in *private* hands?

This paper examines the economic context of our mass-mediated culture. In the modern era, questions of freedom of expression and culture are intimately and inextricably tied to systems of mass communication. While culture cannot be reduced to mere economic factors, it cannot be understood, either, without understanding the economic context that surrounds and shapes it. Culture is not an abstract phenomenon. The process of consciousness and representation is a real material process that requires material resources for its existence and survival. Within the United States, questions about the provision of material resources for the cultural realm have been given largely industrial answers. What we specifically need to focus on then are the workings of the cultural industries; we need to ask the heretical question of whether the First Amendment (as presently interpreted) leads to domination rather than freedom.

Consciousness Industry

All societies seek to reproduce their constitutive social relations over time. If they cannot accomplish this, then a new set of social relations will develop, and a new type of society will emerge. All societies are characterized by this constant tension between stability and change. There are no historical laws governing these processes, but, in general, groups that benefit from the existing distribution of power and rewards work for stability, whereas groups denied access to power and resources work for change. Capitalism is characterized by power and rewards being increasingly concentrated in the hands of those who own the means of production at the expense of the much larger group of people who own only their own labor power, which they sell in exchange for wages.

For societies, such as capitalism, that are characterized by a wide disparity in the distribution of wealth and power, the vital questions of reproduction concern how a minority but dominant social class (capitalists) can maintain power over the vast majority of the population. There are two ways in which this reproduction can be accomplished. First, by sheer force (the use of the police and military). The ruling elites of nations such as South Africa and Chile rule through this method. Second, reproduction can be accomplished through the consent of the dominated, by convincing the majority to identify with and to support the present system of rewards and power rather than opposing it, in fact to live their own domination as freedom. In this situation, the media are vital institutions that, far from providing a free marketplace of ideas, work to legitimate the existing distribution of power by controlling the context within which people think and define social problems and their possible solutions.

In one very important variant of critical communications theory, the function of the media and the cultural realm in general is to produce the appropriate *consciousness* in the majority of people to ensure the reproduction of what is essentially an exploitative system of social relations. Hans Enzensberger coined the phrase "consciousness industry" to describe the media (1974). The media here are literally an industry that attempts to produce a form of consciousness in the audience that benefits the class that controls the media and industry in general.

But why would the media act in this way rather than for the public good? The answer, of course, is that media are not public institutions but private ones. They are owned and controlled by the corporations who have concentrated wealth and power in their hands. They thus reflect the needs of their owners. Ben Bagdikian writes of this situation: "Today there is hardly an American industry that does not own a major media outlet, or a major media outlet grown so large that it does not own a firm in a major industry. These media report the news of industries in which they either are owners or share directors and policies" (1983, p. 4).

Ownership and control are not merely structural phenomena—they affect the everyday operations of media organizations. This control is achieved concretely by means of interlocking directorships, by persons who serve on the board of directors of multiple corporations and thus can coordinate the various interests that they represent. For example, in 1983, the Gannett Company (which owns eighty-eight daily newspapers with a daily circulation of 3,750,000) shared directors with Merrill Lynch, Standard Oil, Twentieth Century Fox, Kerr-McGee (oil, gas, nuclear power, aerospace), McDonnell Douglas Aircraft, McGraw-Hill, Eastern Airlines, Phillips Petroleum, Kellogg Company, and New York Telephone Company, among others. The authors of a study that examined interlocking directorships among the twenty-five largest U.S. newspaper companies reached the following conclusion:

> The directors of these companies, whose dailies account for more than half the circulation of all American newspapers, sit on the boards of regional, national and multinational business corporations. . . . Overall the directors are linked with powerful business organizations, not with public interest groups; with management, not labor; with well established think tanks and charities, not their grass-roots counterparts. (Drier & Weinberg, 1979, p. 51)

These directors are responsible for hiring and firing people in important media posts. That is where their power rests, not in interference with reporters and editors at an everyday level. People, in whatever occupation, normally will not engage in actions that will displease superiors, and journalists are no exception to this.

For the cultural realm, the implications of such connections between the media and the economy are immense. Take the following three issues, for example: (a) The debate concerning *the arms race*. Any of the companies who benefit from huge defense contracts are intimately connected with media. How is the debate going to be affected by that relationship? For example, General Electric (GE) is a major defense contractor for the government. GE (through its ownership of RCA) owns and operates NBC. Within this context, how will the Strategic Defense Initiative (SDI or "Star Wars") debate be framed and structured on NBC? If SDI proceeds, GE will reap rewards in the billions of dollars! It is little wonder that serious and informed debate about the arms race is almost totally absent from network television. (b) The *energy crisis*. The energy crisis will be one of the most contentious issues facing American society from now to the end of the century. The information presented about oil companies by media is going to be vital in forming public opinion about these issues. What happens if the oil industry has a deep influence on news media? This is not simply an academic question—oil representatives sit on the boards of all the powerful news media. (c) The reporting of *foreign affairs*. Major media companies themselves have investments around the world and they are interlocked with other companies who have investments around the world. How is the reporting of news affected when media companies, own interests (or the interests of their partners) are involved? For example, the major networks have investments in South Africa—how does this effect the way in which they report struggles against apartheid?

There is a second variation in critical theory of the notion that the media are a consciousness industry. This is represented in the work of Dallas Smythe, who claims that too much attention has been paid to the way in which media produce ideology. Instead, we should focus on what their role is in the economy directly. Viewed from an economic perspective, Smythe claims that the principal product of media is not ideology but *audiences*.

Industrial corporations do not only need to produce commodities; they also have to ensure that they are sold. In response to this need, in the nineteenth century, newspapers and magazines underwent a process of modernization whereby they would deliver the appropriate audiences to advertisers. In the twentieth century, the commercialization of radio and television ensured that advertising considerations would become *the* predominant factor shaping the structure of the American media system. Smythe writes the following:

> The secret of the growth of Consciousness Industry in the past century will be found in (1) the relation of advertising to the news, entertainment and information material in the mass media; (2) the relations of both that material and advertising to real consumer goods and services, political candidates, and public issues; (3) the relations of advertising and consumer goods and services to the people who consume them; (4) the effective control of people's lives which the monopoly capitalist corporations dominating the foregoing three sets of relationships try to establish and maintain. . . . The commercial mass media *are* advertising in their entirety. . . . both advertising and the "program material" reflect, mystify, and are essential to the sale of goods and services. (1981, p. 8)

The mass media then sell audiences that perform three key functions for the survival of the system: audiences market goods to themselves, they learn to vote for candidates in the political sphere, and they reaffirm belief in the legitimacy of the politico-economic system.

Smythe's version of consciousness industry differs from Enzensberger's in that he stresses the absolutely fundamental necessity of the consumption of commodities for the survival of the system. The consciousness industry produces a particular kind of human nature or consciousness, focusing its energies on the consumption of commodities . . . for about a century the kind of human nature produced in the core area has, to a large degree, been the product of Consciousness Industry. People with this nature exist primarily to serve the system; the system is not under their control, serving them. (Smythe, 1981, p. 8)

Both versions of consciousness industry referred to previously do have a common characteristic—they are functionalist in their treatment of the cultural realm. The first looks at the role of media in the reproduction of society in general. The second emphasizes the role of media in the reproduction of the economy in general. In both accounts, the attention is not so much on the cultural and media sphere itself, but on what function it plays within the *system as a whole*. While this is not an incorrect way to approach the study of culture, it is an incomplete and partial approach. Focusing on the wider role of the media deflects attention away from what could be learned if one focuses closely on the media themselves.

The Industrialization of Culture

Focusing on the specificity of the cultural realm forces us, in an important sense, to treat it in its own terms, rather than focusing on its relationship to another realm (such as the economic). The first issue to be addressed from such a perspective concerns the nature of the cultural realm under capitalism (see Jhally, 1989). There is a wide agreement across the political spectrum that the culture of modern capitalism is a very distinct phenomenon from what preceded it. In the early part of this century, as society was moving from an agricultural to an industrial basis, both right-wing and left-wing writers decried the triumph of *mass culture* over local or high culture (Swingewood, 1977).

The move to urban industrialization weakens considerably the traditional cultural influence of the extended family, the community, and religion in the everyday lives of people. As a direct result, a cultural void opens up. The marketplace moves in to replace older forms of cultural activity. Culture itself is made into a commodity and is bought and sold in the marketplace. The first body of scholars to write about cultural commodification was the Frankfurt School. Two of its representatives, Theodor Adorno and Max Horkheimer, argued that, under capitalism, the profit motive is transferred to cultural forms in that more and more artistic products were being turned into a commodity, "marketable and interchangeable like an industrial product" (Adorno & Horkheimer, 1977, p. 377). This implied a change in the traditional conception of the artist and of art itself. While in earlier epochs, artists also sold their works, monetary exchanges did not prevent them from engaging in "the pursuit of the inherent logic of each work." Under modern capitalism, however, art is first and foremost a commodity, and it is this commodification of art that dominates the logic of cultural forms. Commenting on the work of Adorno and Horkheimer, David Held writes the following:

> Advertising and banking lay down new aesthetic standards. Even where the culture industry does not directly produce for profit its products are determined by this new aesthetic. The economic necessity for a quick and high rate of return on investment demands the production of attractive packages designed either to sell directly or to create an atmosphere of selling—a feeling of insecurity, or want and need. The culture industry either has to sell particular objects or it turns into public relations, the manufacturing of "good will" per se. (1980, p. 90)

In choosing the term *culture industry*, Adorno and Horkheimer wanted to stress that this was not *mass culture* or something that arose from *the masses* themselves but was instead imposed by the dictates of the marketplace. Culture then is not the product of genuine demands—its driving force is the need to sell itself as a commodity. The products of cultural industries are divorced from art and become pure entertainment. Their purpose is to divert, to distract, and to amuse people away from the alienation and drudgery imposed by capitalist work relations. The culture industry offers an escape through pure illusion.

For Adorno and Horkheimer, there is no variety in mass culture. It is all essentially the same and interchangeable. There is a "ruthless unity," and what differences there do appear to be in terms of types of films or magazines

> depend not so much on subject matter as on classifying, organizing and labeling consumers. Something is provided for all so that none may escape; the distinctions are emphasized and extended. The public is catered for with a hierarchical range of mass-produced products of varying quality, thus advancing the rule of complete quantification. Everybody must behave (as if spontaneously) in accordance with his previously determined and indexed level, and choose the category of mass product turned out for his type. Consumers appear as statistics on research organization charts, and are divided by income groups into red, green and blue areas; the technique is that used for any type of propaganda. (Adorno & Horkheimer, 1977, p. 351)

An important part of the Frankfurt School critique is that the products of the culture industries do not challenge people to think and to reflect on the world—instead, as standardized products, the response to them is built into their own structure. In this way, cultural meaning is imposed upon the audience rather than being created by the audience.

While there is a sense of overkill in their writings, and there is no place for audience resistance and subjectivity to intervene in this process that produces what Herbert Marcuse called *one-dimensional* people, their warnings need to be taken seriously. However, in the critical tradition of cultural studies, their work has been (mistakenly) seen as part of the *consciousness industry* approach outlined previously. Although there is little doubt that Adorno and Horkheimer see the cultural industries as producers of capitalist ideology, they believe that the dynamic process that is producing this mass production of ideology has not been properly understood. The cultural industries produce ideology not primarily because they are controlled by corporations, but because that is necessarily the result when culture is treated as a *commodity*. It is not conspiracy that is the cause but the logic of industrial production applied to cultural products.

In this, what we are witnessing is the movement from the formal subsumption of culture to its real subsumption within the capitalist mode of production. The *formal subsumption* refers to a situation in which an area of society becomes vital for the functioning of the economic system without taking on the structures of the economic system. The *consciousness industry* approach analyzes media as only formally subsumed. The media are seen as vital for the functioning of the capitalist economy, but they are not viewed as principally economic institutions. Investment by capitalists in media is not primarily to make money but is to ensure that the media (by producing the appropriate consciousness) provide the context within which the whole economic system can survive and expand.

Real subsumption refers to a situation in which the media become not ideological institutions but primarily economic ones. That is, investment in media is not for the purpose of ideological control but is for the purpose of reaping the biggest return. Culture is produced first and foremost as a commodity rather than as ideology. Of course, these are not exclusive of each other (see Marx, 1976; Jhally, 1987).

In attempting to formulate the correct relationship between the economy and cultural institutions, we are on the terrain of debate referred to as *the base/ superstructure* metaphor within critical cultural studies. The British communications theorist Nicholas Garnham is the most sophisticated of recent scholars to explore the implications that stem from recent movements in the cultural sphere (i.e., treating culture as primarily a commodity to be bought and sold in the marketplace) for the conceptualization of this metaphor. He argues that there are two principal ways in which cultural institutions can be supported. First, they can be supported from revenues that derive from other spheres of the economy. If this is the case, then the *superstructures* (such as the media) remain subordinated to the *base*—they are dependent upon surpluses created elsewhere in material production.

> Material production in this direct sense is determinate in that it is only the surplus produced by this labor that enables other forms of human activity to be pursued. Thus the superstructure remains dependent upon and determined by the base of material production in the very fundamental sense. (Garnham, 1979, p. 126)

Thus, either through patronage or public expenditure, cultural activities can be supported. This is at the level of formal subsumption.

Second, the cultural realm can support itself by producing and selling cultural commodities, resulting in surplus being generated internally. Culture here becomes a part of material production, a part of the base itself, and is subject to the same laws of economic production as other industrial spheres. This leads to what is called *the industrialization of culture*, a process whereby the superstructures become commodified. Thus, the film industry or the record industry does not need to be subsidized from other areas of society—they can function in and of themselves. Control of the cultural realm is achieved not by subsidy but

> by extracting surpluses directly by means of economic processes. Thus the developments of the capitalist mode of production and its associated division of mental and manual labor has led to the development of the extraction of the necessary surplus for the maintenance of cultural production and reproduction directly via the commodity and exchange form. (Garnham, 1979, p. 142)

The real question that is posed by such a process is what happens to cultural activity within such a context? What constraints are imposed by the logic of commodity production on cultural and artistic activity?

In developing the argument thus far we have contrasted two different approaches to the study of culture. The *consciousness industry* approach stresses that the media are principally ideological institutions, whereas the *industrialization of culture* approach stresses the expansion of the commodity form that has little to do with ideology. This contrast is not oppositional but should be seen as complementary. Nicholas Garnham writes of this:

> One of the key features of the mass media within monopoly capitalism has been the exercise of political and ideological domination through the economic. What concerns us in fact is firstly to stress, from the analytical perspective, the validity of the base/superstructure model while at the same time pointing to and analyzing the ways in which the development of monopoly capitalism has industrialized the superstructure. Indeed Marx's own central insight into the capitalist mode of production stressed its generalizing, abstracting drive; the pressure to reduce everything to the equivalence of exchange-value. (1979, p. 133)

Advertising and Commodified Culture

Garnham, however, believes that there is something quite specific about cultural commodities that make it difficult for cultural industries to operate just like other industries. Problems of copyright, ease of duplication, control over consumption, etc., lead to pressure for financing either from advertising or the state. So, for instance, the videocassettes of the movie *Top Gun* had Pepsi ads on them at the start to defray costs. Indeed, in the United States, it is impossible to understand the media and cultural domain without recognizing the role of advertising revenues in the operation of the cultural industries. Broadcasting (television and radio) derive 100 percent of their revenues from advertisers. Magazines and newspapers draw a large majority of their revenues from advertisers. The movie, music, and sports industries increasingly are coming to rely on advertising expenditures for their profitability. In this section, we will examine the role that advertising expenditures play in the structure of our cultural forms.

What advertisers buy with their dollars is access to *audiences*. If we examined the broadcasting or printing industry in economic terms, we would see that what they produce as a commodity are not television programs or newspapers—what they sell are audiences to advertisers. Smythe was absolutely correct in maintaining, in advertising-supported media, audiences are produced as *commodities*. What cultural implications flow from this seemingly simple fact? The newspaper industry is a good example to highlight these issues. The 1970s and the 1980s have been characterized by two related trends. First, there has been an increasing concentration of ownership in which fewer and fewer corporate chains control large numbers of newspapers across the country. Second, there has been a growth in what are called *one-newspaper towns*, where old established newspapers with relatively large circulations are going out of business or are being bought up by their competitors and thus leaving many cities with only one newspaper. For example, in 1981, the *Washington Star* (with a daily circulation of 300,000), the *Philadelphia Bulletin* (with a daily circulation of 400,000), the *Minneapolis Star*, and the *Cleveland Press* all folded.

To understand these events, one has to understand the workings of the newspaper industry as an *industry*. Advertisers account for close to 80 percent of the revenue of newspapers. What they get for their dollars are the audiences and readerships of the newspapers in which they buy space. For advertisers, newspaper advertising is just one component of an integrated marketing strategy. They want to use their advertising dollars in the most cost-efficient manner, that is, to reach the greatest numbers of people for the least amount of money. Advertisers are not particularly concerned with how much it costs to run an ad in a newspaper, but they are concerned with whether it is a good buy. This is measured in cost per thousand, that is, how much it costs to reach one thousand people in the audience. Ben Bagdikian gives the following example from Washington, D.C. (1983). In 1970, there were three newspapers. The *Washington Post* had a circulation of 500,000 and charged $16,676 for a large ad. The *Washington Star* had a circulation of 300,000 and charged $12,634 for a large ad. The *Washington News* had a circulation of 200,000 and charged $9,676 for a large ad. It may seem from this that the *Washington Post* was the most expensive of the three papers, but, for advertisers, it was, in fact, the cheapest in terms of cost per thousand. Advertising in the *Washington Post* meant that each household could be reached for 3.34¢, whereas the *Washington News* cost 4.84¢ per household. In such a situation, even when two newspapers are relatively close in terms of circulation, a disproportionately large share of the available advertising dollars goes to the larger circulation newspaper. This puts intense pressure on the lower circulation paper. As a result, in 1972, the *Washington News* went out of business, and, in 1981, the *Washington Star* went out of business, leaving the *Washington Post* as the only newspaper in a one-newspaper town.[2] Monopoly newspapers are very profitable, for they pick up the audience of the demised competitor. In Washington, D.C., two years after the *Washington Star* folded, the *Washington Post*'s ad rates rose 58 percent.

The same logic of profit maximization has led to concentration of ownership within the field of media in general. It is more profitable to run a newspaper when you also own fifty others. There are large savings to be made in economies of scale in the buying of newsprint, in multiple uses of printing presses, and in the number of reporters needed to cover stories. This, of course, has serious implications in terms of the diversity of views that a democracy needs to survive as a democracy. Ben Bagdikian found that twenty-seven corporations controlled most of the American mass media. As he writes, "This is more than an industrial statistic. It goes to the heart of American democracy" (1983, p. 4). Similarly, Rohan Samarajiwa notes that

> public-information media are said to be organized in the framework of a private marketplace of ideas so that all viewpoints can be expressed without authoritative selection, especially by government. This system is said to ensure the availability of information from diverse and antagonistic sources. But this justification begins to wear dangerously thin when the last vestiges of choice are disappearing from the newspaper field; when the tentacles of massive conglomerates stretch across media boundaries; and when media content is drawn from an increasingly narrower range of sources reflecting a very limited number of viewpoints. (1983, p. 132)

The range of viewpoints is severely restricted as a result of treating culture as a commodity (especially within the newspaper field).

In addition to this, the actual content of media products is severely affected by their integration into a commodity marketplace. For instance, in television, most programs are produced by independent production companies that then sell their product to the networks. The networks recoup their expenses and derive profit by selling audience time to advertisers for spots within these programs. The content of television programs in this context is structured by at least three considerations. First, the program has been able to attract large numbers of people to watch it. It cannot therefore appeal to too narrow of a minority. Second, the program has to attract the right kinds of people. Not all parts of the audience are of equal value to the networks. The programming will have to attract those parts of the audience that advertisers wish to reach (such as appealing specifically to teenagers). The content of programs will have to reflect this targeting. Third, the programs not only have to deliver large numbers of the correct type of people to advertisers, but they also have to deliver them in the right frame of mind. Programs should be designed to enhance the effectiveness of the ads that are placed within them. They thus should emphasize the ethic of salvation through consumption and should encourage viewers to emulate lifestyles of the wealthy. Programs such as *Dallas*, *Dynasty*, and *Lifestyles of the Rich and Famous*—rather than programs that present the culture of and the real problems and issues facing working-class, lower-middle-class, and middle-class people (the bulk of the viewing audience)—predominate in broadcasting.

The logic of commodity production in this realm has another strange cultural effect. Todd Gitlin writes that "hits" are so rare in network television (evidenced by the huge turnover of series) that network executives think that "a blatant imitation stands a good chance of getting bigger numbers than a show that stands on its own" (Gitlin, 1983, p. 63). This leads to what he calls a *recombinant culture* in which the same old forms are endlessly repackaged in slightly different combinations. The networks are

> bureaucracies trying to capitalize on and mobilize demonstrable tastes. If the success rates of recombinants are not very good, what routine procedure stands a better chance of fabricating hits with minimum risk of embarrassing flops? Recombination and imitation seem like low-risk ways of getting by. . . . The pursuit of safety above all else makes economic sense to the networks, at least in the short run, but success anxiety reduces many a fertile idea to an inert object, which usually also turns out to be a commercial dud. For all the testing and ratings research and all the self-imitative market calculation in the world does not produce that originality or energy that makes for much commercial success, let alone truth, provocation, or beauty. (Gitlin, 1983, p. 77, p. 85)

One aspect of advertising's importance to the cultural realm, then, has to do with advertisers' revenues setting the context within which popular culture production takes place. In addition to this is, of course, the actual presence of the ads themselves within the contents of the media. In general, people turn on their televisions in order to watch programs (fictive stories, documentaries, sports events, news reportage, and so on) and editorial commentary. The time that is sold to advertisers, however, is neither program time nor editorial space. It is advertising time and space that is sold to be filled by ads. These ads are a central part of American culture. People talk about them to their fellow workers, children sing their jingles endlessly, and feminists complain about them. They are an all-pervasive element of modern culture. Often, they are much better produced and more creative than the non-advertising content that surrounds them, and, indeed, the advertising industry that creates them has concentrated within itself some of the best artistic talent of our society. But like all cultural products, advertising is constrained within the confines of a commodity system of production. For instance, the movement to shorter and shorter ads has resulted, in part, from the networks redividing the time available for them to sell advertisers in a new way (see Jhally, 1987). Faced with increasing costs for long ads, advertisers adapted to the shorter time-slots by creating a new type of advertising—what is called the *vignette approach* in which product information and reason why advertising are foregone in favor of a rapid succession of lifestyle images, meticulously timed with music, that sell feeling and emotion rather than products directly.

Indeed at every stage of the commercialization of a new media form through the nineteenth and twentieth centuries, advertising adapted itself to the changing commodity environment. One of the results of this has been the movement to *imagistic* modes of communication rather than verbal, audio, and textual ones. These images, many of them moving at an incredibly fast speed, are perhaps the most prominent aspect of modern culture. If advertising is a powerful form of social communication in modern society, then that influence is strongly mediated through the logic of a commodified cultural production (see Leiss, Kline, & Jhally, 1986).

The logic of the commodity form of culture is not limited to any one sphere of social life. Once unleashed, it can venture anywhere. For instance, the popular music industry is a commodified industry through and through. It produces and sells records, and the survival of musicians and artists is dependent on whether they can produce profit for record companies. This is dependent upon their success within the commodity marketplace, not just on the quality of their performances. Creativity then is constantly being juggled alongside commercialization, of how well one can fit into the existing radio formats that the marketing of records has created. There is nothing unique here as regards a sphere of the culture industry. However, in the 1980s, the popular music industry became inextricably linked with the advertising industry through the success of music video as a marketing tool. With the advent of MTV, a music video is indispensable to the success of a record album. Music videos are made by the advertising industry, utilizing techniques derived and learned from the marketing of products. (Through this century, these techniques have developed as a result of the interaction of the advertising industry with commercialized media forms dealing in the sale of audiences.) In many videos, there seems to be little link between the music and the visuals. The visuals are chosen because of their proven ability in another realm to *sell*. There seems to some phenomenological evidence that music videos strongly affect the interpretation that is given to the music when heard later without the visuals. The meaning becomes fixed rather than open to interpretation. The realm of *listening* here is subordinated to the realm of *seeing*, to the influence of commercial images. In this sense, popular music as a cultural form stands at the intersection of two realms of cultural commodity production that sets the context for the meaning that the audience derives from it. It does not determine it, but it sets the limits within which people can dream—a very powerful influence upon culture (see Jhally, 1987).

Similarly, professional sports are a cultural industry that has found it impossible to survive without substantial revenues from the media for the rights to televise their games. The sports industry has become dependent upon the media; the media, in turn, derive their revenues for the purchase of sports broadcast rights from advertisers who wish to reach the audiences that watch sports. Sports leagues then structure themselves and the rules of their sports to be able to offer the best television package. The sale of audience time as a commodity influences what actually gets defined as sports in a more general sense. The other way in which sports can derive additional revenue is to sell themselves directly to advertisers. The 1984 Olympic Games in Los Angeles are the best example of this commercialization taken to extreme lengths. Sports are undoubtedly a very important and powerful cultural force in contemporary America—they give meaning to the lives of many people. That meaning, though, is mediated through the commodity form of culture (Jhally, 1984).

Conclusion

Most critical discussions of the political economy of culture have taken as their starting point Marx's famous comment that

> the ideas of the ruling class are in every epoch the ruling ideas, i.e. the class which is the ruling *material* force of society, is at the same time its ruling *intellectual* force. The class which has the means of material production at its disposal, has control at the same time over the means of mental production, so that thereby, generally speaking, the ideas of those who lack the means of mental production are subject to it. (Marx & Engels, 1956, p. 64)

The vital issues concern how this control is established. How exactly does a ruling class establish control of the cultural realm? In this paper, I have pointed to the major ways in which culture can be materially organized. Nicholas Garnham summarizes the options that are open in a capitalist society. He writes,

> Under developing capitalism the means of cultural production may be provided either in commodity form as part of the accumulation process, e.g. records, or as part of the realization process of other sectors of the capitalist economy, e.g. advertising, or directly out of capitalist revenue, e.g. arts patronage . . . or through the State. (1979, p. 144)

In the United States, the major means of control have been organized around the first two options laid out by Garnham: producing culture directly as a commodity and through advertising support. Within this, also, there is a tendency toward relying more and more on advertising revenues. The third option, support through the state, has rarely been exercised as it has in other countries. What, then, are the implications of treating culture as a commodity? To answer that, we need to ask questions about the nature of commodities in general and to understand their constitutive features as commodities.

All commodities have two fundamental features: they have an *exchange-value* (that is, they are worth something and can be exchanged in the market-place), and they have a *use-value* (that is, they do something that makes them useful to human beings). What is the use-value of a cultural commodity? Its function and its importance stem from the *meaning* that it generates. Records, films, newspapers, paintings, and the like provide meaning for their consumers. If a cultural commodity did not provide this, then it would not be capable of being sold. People buy things for their use-value. Cultural commodities also have an exchange-value within the sphere of the marketplace—that is how profit is generated by the producers of the cultural commodities. The question is, what is the *relationship* between the use-value of a commodity and its exchange-value? Are they of equal importance or is one more important than the other? Within a capitalist economy, there is always an unequal balance between the twin features of the commodity in that exchange-value subordinates use-value. Producers of commodities are primarily concerned with the exchange-value of a product. The owner of a factory that makes tables and chairs does not produce them to use them, but produces them to sell them. If they cannot be sold, then they will not be produced. The use-values of things are affected by the dictates of exchange-value. This affects their use-value. Compare hand-crafted tables with mass-produced factory ones, for example.

The same is true in the realm of commodity culture. The system of exchange-value (worth) subordinates use-value (meaning). Television programs look like they do, not because this is the best that the American artistic community can come up with, but because programs have a role to play in the production and exchange of audiences. The exchange side dominates the use side. It does not determine in a one-dimensional way, but it sets the context within which television programs are produced. If you change the context, you change the nature of the programs. The BBC in Britain is a good example of what another context will produce.

Within the United States, there has never been any questioning of the domination of use-value by exchange-value. Unlike most other Western industrial democracies, there is no developed American debate concerning cultural policy. Indeed, the very term *cultural policy* seems anathema within an American context. (Compare this to the very developed and complex debate about culture that exists in Canada and France.) The rules of the marketplace have been accepted unquestioningly as also the rules of cultural activity. This should not be too surprising, given that it is these very assumptions that are enshrined in the First

Amendment. As we have seen, government is not the only enemy of freedom. The marketplace can work through different means toward the same ends. In the United States, we call government interference domination, and we call marketplace governance freedom. We should recognize that the marketplace does not automatically ensure diversity but that (as in the example of the United States) the marketplace can also act as a serious constraint to freedom. While I have concentrated on the material organization of culture, it is important to stress that all such formations are built upon a specific ideological understanding that accepts culture as an industrial issue. Capital is not powerful in and of itself. It requires the appropriate ideological context. It is only this conception of culture that makes possible the kind of political economy that I have described.

These are not simply academic questions, nor do they deal with a realm that is static. More and more areas are being drawn into the sphere of domination by exchange-value, so that the cultural realm (where healthy societies think about their past, present, and future) becomes more and more intertwined with narrow economic concerns. Capitalist interests are moving forcefully into the one area of society in which there may still exist alternate social visions—a process of increasing colonization and control. As Garnham notes, to understand the structure of our culture, to construct the first stages of an alternative cultural politics, we urgently need to confront these central questions.

Notes

1. There is a second newspaper in Washington today—the *Washington Times*. This is owned and operated (at a substantial loss) by the right-wing Moonies organization.

References

Adorno, T., & Horkheimer, M. (1977). The culture industry: Enlightenment as mass deception. In J. Curran, M. Gurevitch, & J. Wollacott (Eds.), *Mass communication and society* (pp. 349–383). London: Edward Arnold.
Bagdikian, B. (1983). *The media monopoly*. Boston: Beacon Press.
Bagdikian, B. (1985). The U.S. media: Supermarket or assembly line. *Journal of Communication, 35*(3, Summer) pp. 97–109.
Drier, P., & Weinberg, S. (1979). Interlocking directorates. *Columbia Journalism Review* (November/December) pp. 51–68.
Enzensberger, H. (1974). *The consciousness industry*. New York: Seabury Press.
Garnham, N. (1979). Contribution to a political economy of communication. *Media, Culture & Society, 1*. p.123–146.
Gitlin, T. (1983). *Inside prime time* (1st ed.). New York: Pantheon Books.
Held, D. (1980). *Introduction to critical theory*. Berkeley: University of California Press.

Jhally, S. (1984). The spectacle of accumulation: Material and cultural factors in the evolution of the sports/media complex. *The Insurgent Sociologist, 12*(3, Summer), 41–61.

Jhally, S. (1987). *The codes of advertising: Fetishism and the political economy of meaning in the consumer society.* New York: St. Martin's Press.

Jhally, S. (1989). Advertising as religion: The dialectic of technology and magic. In I. Angus & S. Jhally (Eds.), *Cultural politics in contemporary America* (pp. 217–229). New York: Routledge.

Leiss, W., Kline, S., & Jhally, S. (Eds.). (1986). *Social communication in advertising.* London: Methuen.

Marx, K. (1976). *Capital: A critique of political economy* (B. Fowkes, Trans., Vol. 1). London: Penguin.

Marx, K., & Engels, F. (1956). *The German ideology.* New York: International Publishers.

Owen, B. (1975). *Economics and freedom of expression.* Cambridge, MA: Ballinger.

Samarajiwa, R. (1983). The Canadian newspaper industry and the Kent Commission: Rationalization and response. *Studies in Political Economy, 12*(Fall). p. 125–134.

Smythe, D. W. (1981). *Dependency road: Communications, capitalism, consciousness, and Canada.* Norwood, NJ: Ablex.

Swingewood, A. (1977). *The myth of mass culture.* London: Macmillan.

Communications and the Materialist Conception of History

Marx, Innis, and Technology[*]

Why do societies periodically undergo radical, structural changes? Why have modes of thought changed over time and space? These two questions have occupied the thoughts and writings of social theorists for at least the last two hundred years. The first question has been posed around the idealist *versus* materialist debate, while the second has been around a binary *versus* development position. Within the tradition of Marxism, these two questions have been addressed more specifically as (a) the problems of explaining the *transition* between modes of production and (b) the problem of *ideology*.

In this paper, I would like to bring these two related sets of questions together under one framework—specifically around a materialist/development synthesis focusing on the role of communication technology. In relation to this, I will argue that those who wish to explore these long-standing problematic aspects within Marxism can find much of value in the work of Canadian theorist Harold Innis. More specifically, I will argue two main points: first, that a discussion of communication technology is a required addition to the materialist theory of history and, second, that Innis's concept of *bias* has many similarities with Marx's concept of *fetishism,* and that the problem of ideology may be fruitfully addressed

[*] This essay first appeared in *Continuum: The Australian Journal of Media & Culture* 7, no. 1 (1993). Reprinted by permission.

from this direction rather than exclusively from the well-traversed terrain of the base/superstructure debates.

The Materialist Conception of History

The materialist theory of history was first developed by Karl Marx and Frederick Engels in *The German Ideology* in 1846 but was given its clearest summary and formulation in Marx's 1859 "Preface" to *A Contribution to the Critique of Political Economy* (1968). In this, he writes that a mode of production is constituted by the material productive forces and the relations of production. The relations "correspond to a definite stage of development" of the material forces (1968). Additionally, the relations of production constitute

> the economic structure of society, the real basis, on which rises a legal and political superstructure, and to which correspond definite forms of social consciousness. The mode of production of material life conditions the social, political and intellectual life process in general. It is not the consciousness of men that determines their being, but, the reverse, their social being that determines their consciousness. (Marx and Engels, 1968, p. 181)

Thus, in a highly compressed expression, we have four major connected (and it seems hierarchical) domains: (a) the material forces of production, to which correspond (b) the relations of production, on which is erected (c) a legal and political superstructure and to which correspond (d) forms of social consciousness.

The transition between modes of production (Marx lists the Asiatic, the ancient, the feudal, and the modern bourgeois) is brought about by a conflict between the forces and relations of production. "From forms of development of the productive forces these relations turn into their fetters. Then begins an epoch of social revolution. With the change of the economic foundation the entire immense super-structure is more or less rapidly transformed" (Marx and Engels, 1968, p. 182). That is, at a certain stage, the development of the productive forces is held back by the existing property relations. This necessitates a change in the relations of production, which correspondingly results in transformations in the superstructures and the forms of social consciousness.

Here, Marx introduces an approach to two key concepts—mode of production and social consciousness. He then proceeds to systematically develop the first, especially the correspondence between the forces and relations of production as it pertains to the capitalist, social formation. However, Marx does not examine communication technology as an essential part of the mode of production. The second issue is only obliquely addressed in his subsequent work.

Subsequently, twentieth-century Western Marxism has been mostly concerned with filling out the undeveloped side of the radical tradition. Cultural studies has been at the leading edge of this attempt to understand the ways in which societies move subjectively. Some of the key terms in this attempt have been those of *ideology*, *hegemony*, and *subculture* and have mostly concerned operating on the terrain of the base/superstructure model, as outlined in the "Preface." Recent attempts to overcome this model (see Laclau and Mouffe, 1985; Hall, 1986b) have introduced the new terms of *discourse* and *articulation* to the debate. What is significant about cultural studies is that the concern has mostly focused around issues of meaning and content and has not addressed, in any useful way, issues connected with communication technology, aside from the important issues of ownership and control.

In this paper, I wish to argue that both the *orthodox* and *Western* wings of Marxism have much to gain for their respective concerns by rethinking the role that communication media have played in the transition *between* modes of production, as well as the role that they play *within* modes of production. Such a perspective will be a valuable addition to the recent concern with *representation*, for communication technologies play a key role in determining the limits and potentialities of possible social relations. In addition, a focus on communication technology adds an important understanding to the necessary process whereby societies and individuals come to *understand* the meaning of social relations. The development of a new conceptual tool, the *mode of communication*, is key to this attempt. As Jack Goody says, "only to a limited extent can the means of communication, to use Marx's terminology from a different context, be separated from the relations of communication, which together form the mode of communication" (1977, p. 46). Marxian-inspired communication studies have concentrated almost exclusively on the *relations of communication* (ownership and control) and have thus developed a one-sided approach to the question of the *mode of communication*.

An Ecology of Information

Key to filling out the undeveloped side of this conceptual model is the work of Harold Innis, who, in an implicit critique of Marxism, noted that, for too long, the study of the success or failure of *empires* (power structures) has been dominated by economic considerations (1972, p. 4). "Obsession with economic considerations illustrates the dangers of monopolies of knowledge and suggests the necessity of appraising its limitations" (p. 4). An alternative emphasis that would prove more profitable was an analysis of the role of communication media in the organization and administration of various social formations. Innis was particularly concerned with the effects of communication media in emphasizing a *bias* of *space* administration and/or the *temporal* survival of structures of power. The material *form* of communication media is argued by Innis to be powerfully connected with the ability of social formations (such as empires) to reproduce themselves based on both force (administration over a wide geographical area) and ideology (survival and maintenance of social relations over a period of time based on legitimation and consensus). It is also connected in important ways to the historical transformation and fall of empires.

For Jack Goody in *The Domestication of the Savage Mind* (1977), the study of communications technology enables us to bridge the gap between various contemporary disciplines and also allows the complex problem of the general effects of technology to be discussed in more manageable terms. Innis similarly argues that a focus on communication media is important because advances in technology are *first* applied to the communication apparatus of society. Unlike other theorists who see a radical break between historical periods (and consequently between the modes of thought of those periods), Innis and Goody suggest that human history should be viewed in a more continuous manner and that a study of communications media gives us an instrument both for the analysis of distinct periods and an explanation for the process of change from primitive to modern.

Vitally, however, Goody and Innis do not discuss communication media in an isolated manner, but rather as being integrated within wider socioeconomic frameworks. In this regard, it is especially instructive to examine the relation between the mode of communication and the mode of production—to see the development of communication media as responding to changes in the broader set of social relations. Raymond Williams (1974) in his analysis of television argues for a view of technology as neither determined (where technology is seen as developing and initiating changes, abstracted from the social processes that surround it and mould it) nor symptomatic (where the technology is viewed as a symptom of some other changes, so that it becomes a by-product of the process). For Williams, these views are so powerfully entrenched that it becomes difficult to think past them to *intention*:

> To change these emphases would require prolonged and cooperative intellectual effort. . . . Such an interpretation would differ from technological determinism in that it would restore *intention* to the process of research and development. The technology would be seen, that is to say, as being looked for and developed with certain purposes and practices in mind. At the same time the interpretation would differ from symptomatic technology in that these purposes and practices would be seen as *direct*: as known social needs, purposes and practices to which the technology is not marginal but central. (Williams, 1974, p. 14)

In this view, the media are not neutral technology, but rather are seen as *practices* responding to the dominant tendencies of societies (and especially powerful groups within societies) and, in turn, by mediating and translating social relations, acting as forces within the society itself. As Herbert Schiller remarks, "Technology is a social construct and serves the prevailing system of social power, though it often contributes to changes in the organization and distribution of that power" (1976, p. 51).

Within these concerns, the work of Innis is vital in the attempt to understand how communication technology creates an "ecology of information" (Kuhns, 1971). For Innis, the most critical factor in society is the way in which the means of communication provide a framework of possibilities and parameters—the limits and boundaries within which social power (as well as modes of cognition) operates.

For Innis, social power is measured along two axes—space and time. Different communication technologies will *bias* the particular form of power operative in any society. Media that are durable but that make transportation difficult will emphasize a bias of time and will tend to be controlled by religious groups. Media that are easily transportable but less durable will emphasize a bias of space and will tend to be controlled by political and class groups. Thus, different communication technologies encourage different structures of *monopolies of knowledge*.

Innis always locates communications within a rich, societal web. William Kuhns (1971) argues that Innis views society as an organism whose skeleton is comprised of its chief institutions (politics, religion, law, economics, and so on), and whose *lifeblood* (the form of connection between institutions) is the movement of information. It is the information (mediated through the form of communication technologies) that allows the pattern to connect. For Innis, the form of this connection is vital to issues of stability and change. Societies dominated by only *one* kind of bias are inherently unstable and susceptible to the changes introduced by new media. Societies with a balance between time and space technologies are more likely to experience stability and provide a healthy environment for creative and cultural innovations. Innis's favorite example is ancient Greece and the balance between oral and written media. The rise and fall of empires is thus studied by Innis from the viewpoint of communication technology, bias, and the monopoly of knowledge built around this pattern. The dynamic interplay between these factors is held to be the key to history.

Hence, the introduction of a new medium threatens the established relationships and patterns and provides a range of possibilities for new ones. The precise form of the new arrangements will depend upon specific history and the unique social, economic, and cultural configurations on which it is acting. There is little doubt that, at times, Innis overstates the case for a communications perspective on history, but the general framework that can be extracted from his gallop through history provides a rich field of possibilities for the proper integration of a communication approach within a materialist theory of history.

As well as being sources of power, media and their interrelationships also affect modes of *cognition* within particular historical periods. Following in Innis's tradition, Jack Goody (1977) has looked at how changes in the means of communication led to the emergence of a whole host of phenomena (the development of logic, a sense of history, mathematics, and so on), that traditionally have been ascribed as products of the mind in different periods. While Goody adopts a carefully documented approach to these issues, the most famous popularizer of these ideas, Marshall McLuhan, throws caution (and specificity) to the wind and deals only in generalities. As David Crowley (1981) has noted, McLuhan's crude popularization of the more measured approach of Innis and Goody has meant that it is now viewed as "a theory of technological effects and perception where the problem of authority and its deeper constraints on social order gave way to the less complicated surface of events and more painless reformations of the moment" (Crowley, 1981, p. 239). It is this abstraction of media from their societal context that has led most critical analysts to dismiss not only McLuhan, but also the view of historical change from this perspective. This is unfortunate and has prevented adequate theorization in this area.

The understandable rejection by critical thinkers of McLuhan's general, celebratory thesis has had unfortunate consequences—the baby was thrown out with the bathwater. As Jean Baudrillard argues about this, "*The medium is the message* is not a critical proposition . . . but it has analytic value" (1981, p. 172). If the post-structuralist insight that subjects should not be essentialized but are always in a process of social formation is valid, then it is incumbent upon us to examine the total overall ecology within which such subjects are constructed. A great deal of attention has been paid to content from this perspective, with less focus on form. However, if subjects' experience of themselves and the world is always a social process, then the forms of our connections to the world are also part of that construction.

For McLuhan, human experience is mediated through the senses (sound, sight, smell, taste, and touch), and the most effective means of communication are those that utilize the most of these senses. In this respect, speech is said to activate the entire human sensorium. The introduction of writing, especially printing, has broken the organic unity of the senses and has imposed the domination of the visual on the complex totality of human experience. The literate human is argued to be logical, visual, linear, and literal. The regimentation of the mind that writing involves is reflected in mass submission to the tyranny of mechanical life. Above all, imagination and creativity have been submerged beneath the need for order and discipline. As such, McLuhan sees great hope in the development of modern, electronic media that he hopes will once again emphasize the rich totality of human experience. While McLuhan's stress on the means of communication by itself leads him to ignore the relations of production (and thus to an incomplete understanding of the mode of communication), it is possible to take that stress as showing the *range of possibilities* that various media offer for communication. Raymond Williams's insight that all media are at once selected and controlled by existing social authorities should not blind us to the possibility that the uses to which such technologies can be put may be limited by their material structure. The material limits of technology also limit the range of possibilities of social organization. This is the dialectic *between* the means and relations of communication that is encapsulated by the notion of mode of communication.

Innis's importance resides in his linking of communication technology and social control. The discussion of the cognitive effects of modes of communication needs to be similarly theorized. The cultural and ideological effects of media are related to the *monopolies of knowledge* that arise in any period and the uses to which the technology is put. As David Crowley (1981) notes, a communication theory of knowledge should address the manner in which monopolies of knowledge are related to more complicated divisions of labor and more complex, social orders. Specifically, this suggests that media do not have a simple blanket effect on societies. Especially after the introduction of writing, the means of communication were restricted to specific classes and specific functions. The mass of the population experienced these media as instruments of domination, administration, and social control, rather than as instruments of enlightened communication. The broader effects of the technology here are mediated through the structure of social relations.

It is only with printing that we can begin, however tentatively, to talk about mass effects based upon the spread of literacy beyond a narrow, elite class; but, even here, the situation is complicated by the mediation of social power. As Raymond Williams perceptively notes in relation to this,

> It is interesting that at the beginning of the industrial revolution in Britain, when education had to be reorganized, the ruling class decided to teach working people to read but not to write. If they could read, they could understand new kinds of instructions and, moreover, they could read the Bible for their moral improvement. They did not need writing, however, since they would have no orders or instructions or lessons to communicate. . . . The full range of writing came later, with further development of the society and the economy. (1974, p. 131)

With the development of electronic communication, it was precisely the contact with a mass audience for specific purposes of economic, social, and ideological integration and control that led to more general effects. This suggests that bias does not only derive from the technology (the means of communication), but is also related importantly to the functions to which it is put and the manner in which it is organized (the relations of communication).

In summary, then, an adequate, materialist theory of history from a communications perspective would see the wider mode of production incorporate the mode of communication into itself. The development of the mode of communication is dependent on needs generated by shifts in the wider social formation. However, once mobilized, the mode of communication then becomes one of the defining characteristics of the mode of production, importantly connecting to the lifeblood or the patterns that connect, changing its form, and adding to the set of overdetermined contradictions that lead to qualitative change. Apart from this study of historical change, an emphasis on the mode of communication also allows us to see the way that a particular structure of power achieves domination based on both force (control of space) and ideology (time) and how the precise integration of the mode of communication into the wider mode of production can affect modes of thought and subjectivity (of at least some members). The notion of *monopolies of knowledge* wedded to the concept of bias helps us to see the precise forms of domination and administration.

Precedents, Examples, and Applications

In this section, I wish to offer some concrete examples of the gain that may be expected from the integration of Innisian themes into subjects that have traditionally interested Marxist thinkers.

A Marxian Precedent: Engels and the Labor Theory of Human Communication

I have argued that communication technology is not integrated very fully into present Marxist writing on the transition between modes of production and that this is an important and damaging omission. However, there is evidence that one of the inventors of the materialist theory of history was very conscious of the role that communication can play in historical transition. Frederick Engels, in an unfinished 1876 essay entitled *The Part Played by Labor in the Transition from Ape to Man* (1975), specifically relates labor and communication. In this section, I will present Engels's argument (fleshed out with contemporary sources) as an indication of the importance of integrating communication into the discussion of the mode of production.

In tracing the chain of events that produced the *human revolution*, Hockett and Ascher start their study with the protohominids of the middle and lower Miocene period: primate-like beings living in the trees of the jungle. The first form of communication that is posited is a primitive call system. Hewes also posits an *emotional* call system that is not propositional, with the calls not under close, voluntary control but used as responses to other stimuli (1973). There were also other physical aspects of communication, such as patterns of body motion, pushing and prodding, changes of body odor, and so forth. Thus, the earliest form of communication we can posit for our primate ancestors is nominally vocal, physical, and gestural.

How then are we to explain the development of a complex, open system of language from this crude, closed call system? Hockett and Ascher suggest that the decisive step in the next stage of human evolution was the forcing out of some of these bands of protohominids from the trees, as climatic changes thinned the forest and created more open savanna with scattered clumps of trees. The more powerful of the bands, the ones that stayed in the trees, were the ancestors of today's gibbons and siamangs. The less powerful bands who were forced to abandon the shrinking forest environment were *our* ancestors. "We did not abandon the trees because we wanted to but because we were pushed out" (Hewes, 1973, p. 30). The forcing into open savanna led to the *bipedalism* of these groups. In the trees, the hands were used for climbing. But traveling and scavenging for food in open land encouraged the freeing of the hand for other functions. Frederick Engels writes the following:

> Presumably as an immediate consequence of their mode of life which in climbing assigns different functions to the hands than to the feet, these apes began to lose the habit of using their hands when walking on level ground and to adopt a more and more erect gait. This was the decisive step in the transition from ape to man. (1975, p. 2)

The hand was thus left free for other functions—carrying, using weapons, and so on. In short, *tool use*. This, in conjunction with a new, hominid population increasingly dependent upon *social* production is viewed by Ruyle (1974) as the distinctive feature that separates hominoid from hominid, and, on it, he bases, following Engels, a *labor* theory of human development. Hockett and Ascher (1968) also point out how hunting developed into a collective enterprise that stressed a more complex form of social organization. It was the development of tool use especially that led to increased brain size and the *need* for language. As Engels notes, the hand does not develop in isolation from the rest of the organism:

> The mastery over nature which began with the improvement of the hand, with labor, widened man's horizon at every new advance. He continually discovered new, hitherto unknown, properties of natural objects. On the other hand, the progress of labor necessarily helped to bring the members of society closer together by multiplying cases of mutual support and joint activity, and by giving each individual a clearer consciousness of the advantage of this joint activity, in short men arrived at the point where they *had something to say* to one another. The need created its organ. (1975, p. 5)

Thus, as a result of environmental and material changes in the mode of life and production of certain groups of hominids, and as a result of their adaptation to the new material conditions, a need was created for a change in the means of communication, as well as the material possibilities for its satisfaction.

Obviously, speech did not develop overnight, and there were many intermediate stages corresponding to changes in biology and social organization in the development of speech and language. Hockett and Ascher (1968) write that, as the mouth was freed from carrying, so it was possible to use it for other things—like chattering. At the same time, as the hand grew more skilled and flexible, so it became possible to use it as an instrument of communication. Hewes (1973) argues that the archaeological evidence suggests that the early hominids were probably incapable of producing human speech sounds. However, there are also indications that these same hominids also made tools to a pattern and used fire, both of which have been theorized to have been impossible without the existence of language. Hewes suggests that a *gestural* language would have been sufficient for these purposes. The kinds of environmental information that would have been needed here (pointing, directing) could have been accomplished by gestures. Similarly, tool use could have depended not on speech but on visual observation and gestural imitation. The success of teaching sign language to chimpanzees would indicate that early humans were at least capable of internalizing and using a gestural language.

However, it seems unlikely that gestural developments would have proceeded in isolation. The freeing of the mouth also gave it increased possibilities of expression. As social organization, tool use, and culture became more complex, so the need was created for the development of language proper, as gestural language stretches the limits of memory with a collection of about one hundred signs. Hewes suggests that this occurred at about the end of the lower Paleolithic period and that speech subordinated, but did not destroy, gesture.

This example suggests that changes in the mode of production create possibilities for new uses of old technologies (the hand) and the development of new technologies (vocal chords) and that the communication was vital to new modes of social existence, pushing it in new directions.

Once language develops, cultural struggle over the meanings it shapes also becomes a factor. As Ruyle argues,

> Religion cannot appear until after labor and language develop hominid mental abilities to the point where it is *possible* to begin to conceive on non-existent supernatural beings. . . . Labor and language raise humanity to the level where it can begin to create the sacred and supernatural world. Once this world is created, those individuals who can operate in it are reproductively favored over those who cannot, because the sacred and the supernatural world helps to give people the strength to operate in the world of social production. (1974, p. 161)

As soon as language develops, so too do *monopolies of knowledge*, and we are into the age of contestation and control over the signification systems that map out social life.

An Example: Exchange and the Development of Writing— the Prehistory of Printing

The work of both Goody and Innis on early forms of graphic representation suggests that, as the expansion of local production leads to the possibilities of exchanging goods with other geographical markets, a possibility and need is created for some sort of permanent record of supplies, transactions, and iden-tifications of goods. At the same time, and as a result, large-scale bureaucratic organizations (empires) arise, also necessitating new forms of graphic communi-cation.

Goody (1977) notes that early forms of representation were not alphabetic but graphic. They were representations not of speech but of words. Thus, the first use of writing was mainly pictographic, taking the form of tables and lists.

> But what is the topic of the bulk of the written material? Even in Assyrian times, it is not the main "stream of tradition," either in the form of literary cre-ations or the recording of myth and folktale, but rather the administrative and economic documents found in temples and palaces throughout Babylonia and covering a wider geographical and chronological extent than the more aca-demic records. (p. 79)

The earliest forms of writing were *lists*. Goody suggests that the earliest written forms developed in Sumer in about 3000 BC. Clay tags with personal seals were attached to objects being transported. In time, a more secure method of identifi-cation was developed that consisted of a list of the objects represented by pictures and the corresponding written signs of the senders.

> The tablets bearing details of names and objects led to the development of led-gers. . . . It is a system which . . . owes its origins to the needs arising from public economy and administration. With the rise in productivity of the coun-try, resulting from the state controlled canalization and irrigation systems, the accumulated agricultural surplus made its way to the depots and granaries of the cities, necessitating the keeping of accounts of goods coming to the town, as well as of manufacturing goods leaving for the country. (p. 82)

Thus, early written forms were used for administrative and economic purposes within an evolving bureaucratic structure that emphasized systemization and for-malization. However, the use of lists expanded from its purely bureaucratic and accounting function to the listing of events and the emergence of the concept that we understand as *history*. Also, lexical lists were extensions of this, leading to a growth of classification and knowledge. While the initial impetus for the development of written forms was economic, once introduced, the technology advanced autonomously into new forms and new effects.

Goody argues that the written word obviously did not replace speech, but rather added an important dimension to social action. The existence of a plural-ity of forms within a social formation suggests that attention also has to be paid to the relationship between these forms within a mode of communication. So, for example, the earliest, written forms thus fall under the control of those groups who dominate the monopolies of knowledge of oral culture and religious groups.

The first forms of written communication media (stone and hieroglyphics in Egypt; clay and cuneiform in Sumer; and stone, clay, and cuneiform in Babylon) emphasized the preoccupation of these groups—the control of time. The early forms of graphic writing set in motion by economic considerations were adapted to fit the needs of religious orders.

It is important to note here that Innis does not merely focus on communication technology, but also on the forms of writing with which they existed. It is the relation between them that gives rise to bias, one way or the other. For instance, when papyrus was introduced into Egypt, it existed in conjunction with a complex system of hieroglyphics that ensured that specialist knowledge was needed to participate in the communication process, which was dominated by religion. It was only once simpler forms of script were introduced that the full use of the potentialities of papyrus could be made.

The use of papyrus undoubtedly did much to help the spatial control of territory by military groups. Just as gesture gave way to language, so the phonetic alphabet developed in succession to a system of closed signs and pictographs. The increasing complexity of state organizations necessitated a corresponding change in the means of communication. The use of papyrus with the phonetic alphabet was thus extremely effective in controlling large territories.

However, the supply of the material of media is always framed within broader, socioeconomic structures. Innis argues that the spread of Mohammedanism reduced exports of papyrus from Egypt and that, by 719 AD, it had practically disappeared. Its place was taken by parchment, which in turn led to new monopolies of knowledge based in the monasteries and gave the church its monopoly in the Middle Ages.

The monopoly also invited competition from a new medium—paper. The spread of paper manufacturing from China to the West supported the growth of trade and cities and extended education beyond the influence of the monasteries. It also led, in turn, to the growth of local and vernacular literature. The demands of trade also led to the influx of new supplies of paper and the development of clerks skilled in writing. As parchment was displaced, albeit slowly, in the university and the church, there also developed, for the first time, a number of booksellers catering to an expanded *market* in written materials. This latter factor was to lie at the root of the most important change in communications since the introduction of writing—printing and the well-established revolution in thinking that it precipitated (the Enlightenment)—paving the way for the development of capitalist industry (see Eisenstein, 1979).

Such a perspective also allows us to negotiate a truce in the Marx/Weber debate about the transition to capitalism. Rather than pitting the *Protestant ethic* against *material forces* as an explanatory factor in the rise of capitalism, a focus on the mode of communication allows us to see the relation between material and cultural factors in historical transitions.

An Application: Advertising and Culture

In addition to examining transitions between modes of production, a focus on communication is important for looking at transitions within a particular period also. For example, advertising has been a key aspect of capitalist, consumer societies since the second half of the nineteenth century. However, its general role of distributing goods has gone through a number of specific and different forms and frameworks. In this section, I will report on an approach to the historical study of advertising that centrally integrates discussion of the issues connected to the means of communication into its analysis.

Social Communication in Advertising (1986) by William Leiss, Stephen Kline, and Sut Jhally develops an *institutional* approach to the study of "the discourse through and about objects" (advertising). In seeking to analyze this discourse and its historical evolution, Leiss et al. draw upon and attempt to synthesize elements from a number of different perspectives.

First, Leiss et al. focus on broad economic changes that characterize the transition from agricultural to industrial modes of production that necessitated the development of new mechanisms for the distribution and circulation of goods. Second, they draw upon sociocultural perspectives in seeking to understand how economic shifts influenced the way in which people related to goods, especially the growing influence of marketplace institutions in everyday life. Third, and most importantly for the concerns of this paper, a focus on the means of communication is key to their historical argument about the transition between the *cultural frames* that characterize North American, consumer society. Leiss et al. (1986) pay special attention to the specific manner in which these economic and sociocultural shifts were *institutionally* mediated by the emergence and development of two key, symbiotically related industries: the commercial mass media and advertising agencies. Of special importance was the way in which the successive integration of newspapers, magazines, radio, and television into the sphere of marketplace communications that deal with the discourse through and about objects profoundly influences the nature of that discourse. Different media offer different potentialities for advertising formats and strategies. The commercial media are the delivery system for advertisements, which are actually planned and created by advertising agencies who act on behalf of their manufacturing clients. Leiss et al. focus on how the agencies and advertisers thought about consumers and ways to appeal to them. Fourth, Leiss et al. examine advertisements from all periods of the century to see how the economic, sociocultural, and institutional contexts influence their form and content. Lastly, they ask how this framework impacts upon the general understanding of goods and the ways in which they are integrated into the process of satisfaction and communication in consumer society throughout the twentieth century. In focusing on the predominant set of images, values, and forms of communication in any period, Leiss et al. develop the notion of *cultural frames for goods* and identify four of these frames that historically have given some definition to the relationship between people and things.

This is a very complex framework, and I wish here simply to draw attention to the third aspect of this project—the role that the progressive integration of different forms of media into the institutional arrangements of commercial culture played in the process whereby North American consumer society came to understand itself.

The first of the commercial media are the print media, with their reliance on columns of text. In seeking to extend commercial messages beyond merely the announcements of previous years, the agencies had to invent new, persuasive, informational discourses arguing the merits of the product. The appeals were predominantly rationalistic, and the written text was the core of this explanation. Slogans resembled newspaper headlines. However, as new technologies of printing (in magazines and then newspapers) emerged, there was an increasing use of illustration and visual layout in the development of arguments about the qualities of products. In magazines, photography and art allowed for innovations in the associational dimension of argumentation. Products were presented less and less on the basis of a performance promise and more on the basis of making them resonate with qualities desired by the consumer—status, glamour, reduction of anxiety, happy families—as the social motivations of consumption. The world of goods became more abstract.

The integration of radio into the commercial framework added a dramatically new possibility to the world of goods—speech. The agencies did not merely create the ads on radio; they also controlled the programming. People could not listen to selling messages all day, so the agencies began to explore styles of communication and the production values that would draw and hold listeners. Music, humor, stars, pathos, tragedy, excitement, and human relationships became familiar terrain for advertising agencies and opened up new ideas about how to improve advertising. For instance, soap operas were written by agencies and usually revolved around emotionally excruciating, family dilemmas. A whole new domain of human interest and human interaction was being added to the agencies' repertoire as they experimented with storyline, characterization, dramatic impact, and emotional tone and then applied what they had learned to the construction of ads. As a result, advertising became rooted in a distinctly human-interest environment. One important consequence was that products began to speak—to tell their own story. Although the full anthropomorphizing of goods had to await the use of animation on television, radio took a preliminary step in dialogue. Products, through ads, began to tell stories, and the writing styles incorporated allusions to real social situations and a variety of settings.

After the heyday of radio advertising in the late 1940s, much of the experience and talent accumulated from radio production was turned to developing advertising modes suited for television. As a medium of communication, television, like radio before it, offered new possibilities to advertising strategists. Products had been woven into a broad range of simulated and fictional settings since the turn of the century, but television simply could do everything so much better. Magazines had displayed goods amid Doric columns or Greek statues, thus positioning them within an associational matrix of images and styles; radio had opened up dialogue and social interaction as contexts within which appeals were made; television swept all earlier forms into its orbit and added others, ultimately offering the whole range of cultural reference systems to advertisers as aids in selling products.

Since television was best at simulating interpersonal communication either directly or as observed in drama, it seemed natural for television commercials to focus on these elements, and, thus, the testimonial and the minidrama became important elements of television advertising. Television offered a whole new range to the uses of people and dialogue that had been explored during the 1930s and 1940s, but it personalized it more intensely. The development of cable television in the 1970s has enabled advertisers to draw audiences together in specific segments and to appeal to them on the basis of lifestyle.

The four cultural frames used by Leiss et al. (1986)—*idolatry, iconology, narcissism, totemism*—to categorize commercial culture through the twentieth century are importantly connected to the development of new media forms that allowed experimentation with new, associational relationships between people and things. While certainly not sufficient explanations, the focus on the new potentialities offered by media forms as they became integrated into the institutional structure of commercial culture has helped to make sense of the direction and shape of frameworks of understanding and action that people live in and through. That is, a purely economic focus on advertising as a distributive mechanism *par excellence* would simply not offer as much as the framework outlined.

Bias and Fetishism

Innis's notion of *bias* is concerned with highlighting the issue of *form* in the study of societies from a communication perspective. In this regard, it is illuminating to consider that the idea of forms also seems to be important to the way that Marx approached the analysis of social problems. Richard Johnson, a former director of the Centre for Contemporary Cultural Studies at the University of Birmingham, remarks how, in his own thinking about cultural studies, the notion of *forms* repeatedly arises, and that this is partly connected to Marx's framing and usage of terms such as *social forms* or *historical forms* when he is examining the various moments of economic circulation: for example, the money form, the commodity form, and the form of abstract labor. In the 1959 "Preface," Marx also talks about the "ideological forms in which men become conscious" of their social actions (Marx and Engels, 1968). Johnson writes of the implication of this view of forms in the following way with regard to cultural studies:

What interests *me* about this passage is the implication of a different project to Marx's own. His preoccupation was with those forms through which human beings produce and reproduce their material life. He abstracted, analyzed and sometimes reconstituted in more concrete accounts the economic forms and tendencies of social life. It seems to me that cultural studies too is concerned with whole societies (or broader social formations) and how they move. But it looks at social processes from another complimentary point of view. *Our* project is to abstract, describe and reconstitute in concrete studies the social forms through which human beings "live," become conscious, sustain themselves subjectively. (Johnson, 1986–7, p. 45)

The clearest example of Marx's own stress on *form* as a structuring principle of social life is in his analysis of the fetishism of commodities. The opening lines of *Capital* announce that capitalism presents itself as an "immense accumulation of commodities" (1976). Marx is specifically concerned with delving beneath this "appearance" (the market) to the "hidden abode" (production) that is the dynamic element of the process. To do so, he starts with a focus on the surface, what we can all see, the commodity, and distinguishes between its use-value and exchange-value. So far as the former is concerned, there is no disjuncture between appearance and essence. The mystery of the commodity, the making of it into a fetish, arises from its form, its exchange-value.

There is not room here for a thorough explication of the theory of fetishism, except to say that some writers have claimed that the search for a Marxist theory of ideology may have no better starting point than this, for the theory is essentially a story of how the realm of exchange—the market—comes to structure how we *understand* society and also to legitimate the *status quo* as natural and unchanging. In this, the exchange of labor power for wages is held to be key. "The relation of exchange between capitalist and worker becomes a mere semblance belonging only to the process of circulation, it becomes a mere form, which is alien to the content of the transaction itself, and merely mystifies it" (Marx, 1976, pp. 729–730). The wage-form also gives rise to other appearances—that workers are free to dispose of their own labor power as they see fit.

> All the notions of justice held by both worker and capitalist, all the mystifications of the capitalist mode of production, all capitalism's illusions about freedom, all the apologetic tricks of vulgar economics, have as their basis the form of appearance . . . which makes the actual relation invisible and indeed presents to the eye the precise opposite of that relation. (Marx, 1976, p. 680)

Marx's argument is not about trickery and manipulation but about viewing social life through the lens of *exchange only,* especially commodities themselves, which become material bearers of the ideology of the marketplace.

In this regard, Stuart Hall (1986b) has recently suggested that the perennial problem of Marxist cultural studies, the base/superstructure model and determination in the last instance by the economic, may be more fruitful if we reverse the normal equation and think of "determination by the economic in the *first* instance." This is based upon the construction of a different causal model in which *the economic* structures *the ground* on which we move, live, and *become conscious*. We live through the forms offered by our social life. Central to this is the market:

> It is the part of the capitalist circuit which everyone can plainly *see*, the bit we all experience daily. . . . So the market is the part of the system which is universally encountered and experienced. It is the obvious, the visible part: the part which constantly *appears*. (Hall, 1986b, pp. 34–35)

It is through this sphere that we experience, make sense of, and become conscious of our social lives. This is an active process that takes place under specific conditions of determinacy—the generative set of categories of market exchange that may be extended to other spheres of social life. The hegemonic ideas of freedom, equality, property, individualism,

> the ruling ideological principles of the bourgeois lexicon, and the key political themes which, in our time, have made a powerful and compelling return . . . may derive from the categories we use in our practical commonsense thinking about the market economy. This is how there arises, out of daily, mundane experience the powerful categories of bourgeois legal, political, social and philosophical thought. (p. 35)

For Hall, such a model of "determination" based on

> a setting of limits, the establishment of parameters, the defining of the space of operations, the concrete conditions of existence, the "givenness" of social practices, rather than in terms of the absolute predictability of particular outcomes, is the only basis of a "Marxism without final guarantees." (p. 43)

The notion of *bias* in Innis shares much in common with this model of determination but is grounded in the operation of a specific, key, communication technology that becomes the medium through which social action is conducted and understood. Unlike McLuhan's fundamentalist extensions, Innis would find much in common with Hall's more measured and more precise discussion of limits, pressures, parameters, and emphases. It is *through* these forms that we live and become conscious of ourselves and our lives. These forms structure the ground *on* which we operate and on which we actively construct meanings—they are the conditions "not of our own choosing."

Conclusion

This paper has argued that both the *orthodox* and the *nonorthodox* variants of Marxism have much to gain from an investigation, entanglement, and conversation with the issues raised by the work of Harold Innis. I have attempted to show the value of such a theoretical collaboration by charting some of the main themes in Innis's work, showing how that work has a precedent within classical Marxism itself, giving an example of how the addition of a communication technology perspective might aid the discussion of transition, describing an application of such a perspective to the study of advertising within a social formation, and, finally, suggesting that the concepts of *bias* and *fetishism* may be alternative ways of thinking about the problem of ideology. If we accept Richard Johnson's argument that cultural studies is a parallel project to Marx's economic project, then we also need to recognize that such an endeavor is a massive undertaking that will require the collaboration of analysts in many different fields of investigation. We also need to recognize that we are in the beginning stages of such a project and that our best chance of advance will be dependent upon remaining open to the contributions of others working on similar issues, albeit within different frameworks. The work of Harold Innis is just such an opportunity and should not be missed.

References

Baudrillard, J. (1981). *For a critique of the political economy of the sign*. St. Louis, MO: Telos Press.

Crowley, D. (1981). Harold Innis and the modern perspective of communications. In W. Melody, L. Salter, & P. Heyer (Eds.), *Culture, communication, and dependency: The tradition of H. A. Innis*. Norwood, NJ: Ablex.

Eisenstein, E. (1979). *The printing press as an agent of change*. Cambridge, UK: Cambridge University Press.

Engels, F. (1975). *The part played by labor in the transition from ape to man*. New York: International Publishers.

Goody, J. (1977). *The domestication of the savage mind*. Cambridge, UK: Cambridge University Press.

Hall, S. (1986a). *The hard road to renewal*. London: Verso.

Hall, S. (1986b). Marxism without guarantees: The problem of ideology. *Journal of Communication Inquiry, 10*(2). pp. 28–44

Hewes, G. W. (1973). Primate communication and the gestural theory of language. *Current Anthropology, 14*(1–2) pp. 5–24.

Hockett, C. F., & Ascher, R. (1968). The human revolution. In M. F. A. Montagu (Ed.), *Culture: Man's adaptive dimension*. New York: Oxford University Press.

Innis, H. (1972). *Empire and communication*. Toronto: University of Toronto Press.

Johnson, R. (1986–1987). What is cultural studies anyway? *Social Text, 16* (Winter). pp. 38–80.

Kuhns, W. (1971). *The post-industrial prophets.* New York: Weybright & Talley.

Laclau, E., & Mouffe, C. (1985). *Hegemony and socialist strategy.* London: Verso.

Leiss, W., Kline, S., & Jhally, S. (Eds.). (1986). *Social communication in advertising.* London: Methuen.

Marx, K. (1976). *Capital: A critique of political economy* (B. Fowkes, Trans., Vol. 1). London: Penguin.

Marx, K., & Engels, F. (1968). *Karl Marx and Frederick Engels: Selected works in one volume.* New York: International Publishers.

Ruyle, E. (1974). Labor, people, culture: A labor theory of human origins. *Yearbook of Physical Anthropology.* New York: Wiley-Liss.

Schiller, H. (1976). *Communication and cultural domination.* White Plains, NY: International Arts and Sciences Press.

Williams, R. (1974). *Television, technology and cultural form.* London: Fontana.

Advertising and Culture

Advertising as Religion

The Dialectic of Technology and Magic[*]

The Magic of the Marketplace

In contemporary America, we are immersed most of our waking hours in a world and a discourse where all normal physical and social arrangements are held in abeyance.

- From deep in the ocean depths, swimming alongside sleek and dangerous sharks, taking on their shape and form, emerges "a new species" of automobile—a Chevrolet Beretta.

- As a woman passes behind him, a man is overcome with desire and immediately starts to pursue her in a blind passion, pausing only to snatch up some flowers that he presents to her when he catches her. We are told that the spell is cast because the woman uses Impulse body spray.

- A young male adolescent stares in horror at his pimpled complexion in a bathroom mirror. As he applies a magical lotion, his pimples immediately disappear, even as we watch.

* This essay first appeared in *Cultural Politics in Contemporary America*, ed. S. Jhally I. Angus (New York: Routledge, 1989), pp. 217–229. Reprinted by permission.

- A young attractive woman boldly enters a pool room where she announces that she has had enough of Mr. Wrong and that it is time for Mr. Right. As she sings this, she throws a can of Right Guard antiperspirant to individuals with the faces of grotesque monsters. They are immediately transformed into handsome young men who crowd around the woman.

- A young woman walks by groups of men; a "sea breeze" is unleashed by her that envelops the young males.

In advertising, the commodity world interacts with the human world at the most fundamental of levels: It performs magical feats of transformation and bewitchment, brings instant happiness and gratification, captures the forces of nature, and holds within itself the essence of important social relationships (in fact, it substitutes for those relations).

What is noteworthy about such scenes is not that they are concerned with the role of objects in the social lives of people. Such a relationship is one of the defining features of what it means to be human; the relationship between people and things is a universal one. What is noteworthy in the modern period, however, is the *extent* to which goods enter into the arrangements of everyday life. Much more so than in previous societies, in the consumer culture it seems that every aspect of life is permeated by the presence of objects. Karl Marx, writing in the middle of the nineteenth century and in the early phases of the development of industrial capitalism, perceptively pointed to what would become the main features of the developing system. In the opening lines of *Capital*, he states that "the wealth of societies in which the capitalist mode of production prevails appears as an 'immense collection of commodities'" (Marx, 1976, p. 125). Unlike all previous modes of production, capitalism discovered the secret of material production and proceeded to install it as its central and defining activity. While Marx did not witness the emergence of the institution of national advertising, he was able to penetrate to what would become its essential feature:

> It is nothing but the definite social relation between men themselves which assumes here, for them, the fantastic form of a relation between things. In order, therefore, to find an analogy, we must take flight into the misty realm of religion. There the products of the human brain appear as autonomous figures endowed with a life of their own, which enter into relations both with each other and with the human race. So it is in the world of commodities with the products of men's hands. I call this the fetishism which attaches itself to the products of labor as soon as they are produced as commodities, and is therefore inseparable from the production of commodities . . . the labor of the private individual manifests itself as an element of the total labor of society only through the relations which the act of exchange establishes between the product, and, through their mediations, between the producers. To the producers, therefore, the social

relations between their private labors appear as what they are, i.e. they do not appear as direct social relations between persons in their work, but rather as material relations between persons and social relations between things. (1976, pp. 125–126)

Marx was able to predict the supernatural world that advertising would create, in which relationships between people are mediated through things and in which things themselves come alive and interact with each other and with human beings. This prediction was based upon his understanding that capitalism as a system of production and consumption entails a very different relationship between people and the world of goods than had existed previously—that the *discourse* about society that takes place through the medium of things has a different content and structure. For him, it came down to the difference between market and nonmarket exchange.

In older, nonmarket societies, there was a much more direct connection between people and the goods that they used in everyday life. Most of the goods they consumed were produced by themselves or were produced by persons and processes that they knew, so that people had a great deal of information about the world of goods. The social relations of production were visible to all and, furthermore, they were, in a sense, *embedded* in goods as part of their meaning. Indeed, in many traditional societies, the exchange of goods was literally an exchange of people, in that people had embedded something of themselves in the goods that they produced. In giving a good that you produced, you were giving a part of yourself. Inherently, goods are communicators of social relations.

Marx recognized this fundamental feature of goods and installed it as part of his methodological framework for the analysis of capitalism. He starts *Capital* by saying that his investigation will begin with the analysis of the commodity, because he thought that if one could understand how the commodity was produced, exchanged, and consumed, then one would have the basis for an understanding of the entire system of capitalist relations—like goods in any social system, contained within them are the social relations of their production. However, in capitalism, and unlike previous societies, there is a problem in terms of trying to read goods for the social information they contain. Their origins are hidden from us. There are two dimensions to this.

First, in the world of production, the work process is increasingly subdivided and specialized so that workers only work on part of a product. In addition, there is a separation between the planning process for the production of goods and the actual process of production itself—a split between mental and manual labor such that those people who actually physically produce the product (wage-laborers) have no overall sense of the production process or its relationship to other aspects of social life. (Of course, increasingly smaller numbers of people are actually involved in industrial production itself.) Second, most of us use goods that come to us through the marketplace. As such, we have little information about them beyond what manufacturers choose to tell us through media advertising or packaging. The social relations of production embedded in goods are systematically hidden from our eyes. The real meaning of goods, in fact, is *emptied* out of them in capitalist production and consumption. Marx labeled this the *fetishism of commodities*, a disguise whereby the appearance of things in the marketplace masks the story of who fashioned them and under what conditions.

The Development of the Consumer Society

Of course, the implementation of capitalist production methods meant more than merely a new way to produce goods—it entailed a revolution in the cultural arrangements of traditional society. Traditional preindustrial society was based around agriculture, and there was little separation between work and leisure. The extended family and religion were hugely important influences on the conduct of everyday life. The meaning of goods in such a context was intimately tied up with local production and was integrated within the structure of ethnic cultural forms. Ethnicity, family, religion, and community structured the discourse surrounding goods.

The coming of capitalist industrial society shattered these bonds. City living, factory labor, and the separation between work and leisure destroyed the vitality of the older traditions that could not be sustained within the new urban context. T. Jackson Lears argues that, in the early years of the twentieth century, American society was going through a major crisis of meaning in which an older culture of Puritanism, self-denial, and work was dissolving under the strains brought on by modernism. Feelings of unreality, depression, and loss accompanied the experience of anonymity associated with urbanization. Religious beliefs waned in strength as traditional Protestant theology underwent a process of secularization. The feelings of unreality that arose in this period could not be dealt with by the traditional institutions that had previously fulfilled this role. Indeed, it was the loosening of their influence that led to the feelings of unreality. These feelings were reflected in a concern for physical and emotional health. Whereas before the quest for health had been part of a larger communal, ethical, and religious framework, by the twentieth century this had become almost entirely a *secular* process. Lears argues that advertisers picked up on these movements and began to exploit the emotional needs of advertisers:

> A dialectic developed between America's new emotional needs and advertiser's strategies; each continually reshaped and intensified the other. . . . By the 1920s the symbolic universe of national advertising markedly resembled the therapeutic world described by Philip Rieff—a world in which all overarching structures of meaning had collapsed. . . . It is important to underscore the role of advertising in accelerating this collapse of meaning. (1983, pp. 4, 21)

Industrial society is a transitional society, which can neither draw on the past nor construct its own structures of meaning. It is a cultural void in which old and new ways of living collide.

In addition to this crisis of meaning, industrial capitalism also faced the potential problem of a severe and debilitating economic crisis. The immense collection of commodities that capitalism produces also has to be *sold*. Without the consumption of these commodities, capitalism would be in a state of permanent depression and would quickly die. This crisis was especially acute in the early years of this century. Stuart Ewen refers to this complex of relations as the *social crisis of industrialization* and argues that the developing institutions of the consumer society (such as advertising) offered to solve both problems simultaneously. The consumer society resolves the tensions and contradictions of industrial society as the marketplace and consumption take over the functions of traditional culture. Into the void left by the transition from traditional to industrial society comes advertising, the most prominent aspect of the "discourse through and about objects," and the reconstitution of the population not into social classes as the primary mode of identification, but into consumption classes (Leiss, Kline, & Jhally, 1986; Jhally, 1987).

Advertising: The Theft and Reappropriation of Meaning

How precisely does advertising fit into this scenario? I argued earlier that in non-market societies there is a unity between people and goods, but that in capitalism there is a separation between object and producer. The world of goods in industrial society offers no meaning; meaning has been emptied out of these goods. The function of advertising is to refill the emptied commodity with meaning. Indeed, the meaning of advertising would make no sense if objects already had an established meaning. The power of advertising *depends* upon the initial emptying out. Only then can advertising refill this void with its own meaning. Its power comes from the fact that it works its magic on a blank slate. The fetishism of commodities consists, in the first place, of emptying them of meaning, of hiding the real social relations objectified in them through human labor, to make it possible for the imaginary and symbolic social relations to be injected into the construction of meaning at a secondary level. Production empties. Advertising fills. The real is hidden by the imaginary. The social significance of the marketplace is only possible after the social significance of production disappears beneath the structure of capitalist property relations. The hollow husk of the commodity-form needs to be filled by some kind of meaning, however superficial. This is why advertising is so powerful. People need meaning for the world of goods. The traditional institutions that provided this have been weakened. Thus, advertising derives its power from providing meaning that is not available elsewhere.

If what I have just described is the broad social role that advertising plays, what specific strategies does it use to accomplish this? Looked at historically, there is no single set of strategies that advertising utilizes. Instead, we can identify a number of different strategies that are developed through the course of the twentieth century in response to changing market and social conditions (see Leiss et al., 1986).

In the initial stage of the development of national advertising, the consumer society responds to the appearance of the immense collection of commodities in a celebratory mode. What is celebrated is the great productive capacities of industrial society as reflected in products. Advertising has a strong theme of veneration of products, almost worshipping the fruits of industrial technology. Commodities are idols in early advertising.

> Huge refrigerators towered above tiny towns of consumers; silhouetted against the starry sky, they stood guard over communities like giant sentinels. Immense cars straddled the rivers and towns of miniaturized countrysides below, symbolizing the command over the landscape obtainable through the automobile. (Marchand, 1985, p. 264)

Such images "conveyed impressions of the product as dominant or transcendent, if not awesome" (Marchand, 1985, p. 267). The initial development of national advertising can then be labeled as the stage of *idolatry*.

Such a development is not an accident or a clever creation by the advertising industry alone. Advertisers sought to mediate between the needs of manufacturers to sell products and the changing context of meaning for consumers. Advertising had to reflect some real needs in the consuming public. What advertisers recognized was the nostalgia for the world that was passing, for a stable world of religious, family, and community life. The early stages of national advertising are characterized both by a veneration for the immense collection of commodities and a linking back to traditional themes. The transcendental religious realm provided a rich, deep resource from which to draw, although its influence was weakening throughout the society. Advertisers recognized that the public yearned to experience moments of enhancement, awe, and rapture.

Advertisers, though, could not be too explicit with this for fear of negative public reaction. Roland Marchand points out that instead they used visual clichés

> that employed vague forms of sacred symbolism rather than specific religious figures. . . . Such visual strategies sought to transform the product . . . into a "surrogate trigger" for producing those life-enhancing feelings that consumers avidly pursued. As an ad in *Printers' Ink Monthly* offhandedly noted in 1926, advertisements were "beginning to occupy the place in inspiration that religion did several hundred years ago." (1985, p. 265)

Consumers were shown entranced before the power of the object. Refrigerator ads featured women who looked as though they had glimpsed through the open door "a secular revelation as spellbinding as any religious vision" (Marchand, 1985, p. 272). The visual cliché of radiant beams that came from outside the picture and highlighted the product was another often used strategy suggesting some divine intervention in the world of commodities. In other versions, the beams radiated from the product itself, suggesting a kind of halo effect around the product. Marchand argues that, through such strategies, advertisers were secularizing images without losing their original spiritual overtones. Such imagery "represented a final step in the successful, though largely unconscious adaptation of religious imagery to the advertising tableaux, the modern icons of a faith in mass consumption" (p. 282).

The idolatrous stage of advertising predominates from the 1890s and into the 1920s. The second stage of religious adaptation starts in the 1920s and can be labeled the stage of *iconology*. Icons are symbols; they mean something. Advertising in this stage moves from the worship of commodities to their meaning within a social context. As the traditional customs and behavioral codes became unglued in the cultural void of industrial society, marketplace communication stepped in to provide consumers with the needed advice. Goods became powerful not only through what they could do, but also through what they could mean. Consumption here becomes explicitly a social activity, and goods are intimately connected with social relations. There is a shift away from the product alone and toward the consumer, but the movement stops halfway. In the stage of iconology, both products and persons are embodiments of reigning social values, and the world of advertising is neither wholly thing-based or person-based—instead, it is meaning-based. Commodities are the icons of the marketplace.

From the 1940s and into the 1960s, advertising completes the shift toward the consumer. The product is seen as powerful, but now its power is put at the disposal of individuals. Furthermore, these individuals are presented in so-called real terms rather than the abstract depictions of the second stage. This is the stage of *narcissism*, in which the product reflects the desires of the individual. Advertisements show the fantasized completion of the self, of how the product can transform individual existence. The power of the product can be manifested in many ways, but, predominantly, it is through the strategy of *black magic*, in which persons undergo sudden physical transformations or in which the commodity can be used to entrance and enrapture other people. The world of objects here enters the everyday world of people and performs in magical ways.

From the 1960s to the present, the focus shifts yet again into the stage of *totemism*. *Totemism* in older societies refers to the correlation between the natural world and the social world, where natural differences stand for social differences. In modern advertising, goods take the place of natural species. In this last phase, the predominant themes of the previous stages are drawn together and remixed into a unique form: commodities are freed from being merely utilitarian things (idolatry), or abstract representations of social values (iconology), or intimately connected with the world of personal and interpersonal relations (narcissism). In the totemic stage, utility, symbolization, and personalization are mixed and remixed under the sign of the *group*. In lifestyle advertising, products are badges of group membership. Through consumption, one has access to and participates in a very specific consumption community that is defined through that very consumption activity. Products give magical access to a previously closed world of group activities.

Although these stages have been presented as an historical progression, they should not be thought of as being exclusive of each other: rather, they should be viewed as cumulative. The labels apply to the dominant tendency within any period. The particular forms that arise in different periods do not disappear, but rather are segregated as a mode of representation for particular products and audiences. In the contemporary marketplace, the person-object relation is articulated psychologically, physically, and socially. Some goods seem to serve primarily for display and social judgment, some goods seem to serve for personal enhancement, some goods seem to serve for locating us within the nexus of group relations, and some goods seem to serve just for simple utility in everyday life.

Furthermore, commodities appear as miraculous products of an invisible process of production. In the marketplace, they enter into unique and changing relations with each other, jostling for position to satisfy the needs of the consumer. In some instances, products explicitly take on animate features and come alive. Advertising truly reflects the world that Marx described as being characteristic of capitalism—an enchanted kingdom of magic and fetishism in which goods are autonomous, in which they enter into relations with each other, and in which they appear in fantastic forms in their relations with humans.

The Fetishism of Commodities

The economic and business literature on advertising is dominated by the concept of *information*—advertising is supposed to provide consumers with marketplace information about goods, so that there is some rational basis for choice. Unless one has a very broad definition of what constitutes information, this is clearly not a very fruitful way to understand this institution. (The installation of the concept of information is, of course, an ideological strategy to deflect debate away from the really important features of advertising.) The real function of advertising is not to give people information but to make them feel good. Ad maker Tony Schwartz explicitly articulates this when he tells advertisers not to make claims that could be proven false but to concentrate instead on creating pleasurable experiences (1974). T. Jackson Lears points out that *feeling* replaced information very early on in the development of advertising. In the most sophisticated version of this *feeling good* theory, Staffan Linder claims that it is unreasonable to expect consumers to gather full information to inform their purchasing decisions—there simply is not enough time to collect all the information that would be needed to make truly rational purchasing decisions. In such a context, what consumers require is to have *some* justification for their purchasing decisions, however irrational. Advertising provides this and makes consumers feel that they have made decisions at least on some basis rather than on some totally arbitrary criteria (Linder, 1975).

I argued previously that one of the most important functions that advertising performs is to provide meaning for the world of goods in a context in which true meaning has been stolen. It helps us to understand the world and our place in it, and it accomplishes this through integrating people and things within a magical and supernatural sphere. If this function were attributed to an institution in non-capitalist society, we would have no trouble seeing it for what is was—*religion*. Indeed, if the basis of advertising is to make us feel good, and it has surrendered any objective basis for this feeling, in what way is it different from religion? Why not also tea leaves, Ouija boards, black cats, dice, sounds that go bump in the night? Why not God? All these too can "satisfy" us, can "justify" our choices! Advertising here becomes a secular version of God! When couched in the context of religion, our four-stage developmental model of advertising history takes on new meaning. For instance, is it an accident that advertising messages have moved from focusing on physical functions to focusing on desires, personal and small-group lifestyles, and the form of being in the world of a whole social formation? Is it an accident that the messages have moved from the verbal to the visual (see Livant, 1983)?

Indeed, representatives of established religious faiths have recognized with alarm the manner in which this new religion threatens their own existence. Believing that a

> gospel is a book of revelation, an ultimate source of reference wherein we find ourselves revealed . . . a response to questions of who we are, what we may hope for, how we may aspire to act, what endures, what is important, what is of true value (Kavanaugh, 1981, p. 15),

the Jesuit scholar John Kavanaugh argues that advertising is part of a gospel based upon the *commodity form*—a world in which people are identified through the things they consume as well as being dominated by them. Kavanaugh compares this to a life based on more human values, such as justice and spirituality—a gospel based upon the *personal form*. These two kinds of gospels

> serve as ultimate and competing "forms" of perception, through which we filter our experience. Each form, moreover, provides a controlling image for our consciousness in apprehending our selves and our world. . . . Each has its own "church," you might say, its own cults and liturgical rites, its own special language, and its own concept of the heretical. (p.16)

We should hesitate in accepting the notion of advertising as religion, however, until we have asked one additional question: What *kind* of religion is it? Is it the same as Christianity, Hinduism, Judaism, Islam, etc.? If it is different, how is it different? Clearly, it is different from the established religions in that there is no moral core at its center that is articulated in a ritualized form. We may be able to read the entire set of advertisements for this moral order, but that is not the same as having an articulated moral code already in existence. In established religions, the icons that are used reflect a central system of beliefs—they are ritualized expressions of it. In advertising, the icons of the marketplace themselves are this religion. I will come back to this point later.

The *levels* at which the different religions operate are also important. Advertising operates not at a spiritual level but at a mundane, everyday level. In this, it resembles systems of belief that have existed in other societies. Early anthropological accounts of nineteenth-century West Africa tribes describe practices whereby objects were believed to be possessed by some kind of supernatural spirit, which, if worshipped and appeased, could have a beneficial influence on the worldly existence of the owner. The control of the power of the fetish was associated with black magic and was used for personal ends. It could guard against sickness, bring rain, catch fish, make the owner brave, bring the owners good fortune, protect against other evil spirits, cure the ill, sexually attract persons, and capture the power of some aspect of the animal kingdom. This system of belief was labeled by anthropologists as *fetishism*. Like the world of advertising, fetishism operated at the level of everyday activity; its effects were short-term and immediate and concerned the practical welfare of the fetish's possessor. It was not, in and of itself, a *total* spiritual belief system, but rather a *part* of a much larger one (see Jhally, 1987).

In all societies in which the term *fetishism* has been applied, there are different levels of spiritual belief: Acceptance of the powers of the fetish should not blind us to the possibility that its user may also have belief in a higher spiritual power, such as a supreme being. There is no denial of God but merely an *indifference* to God as regards the conduct of everyday life. The fetish does not operate at a higher spiritualistic or vague futuristic level, for which other spheres of religion are more appropriate. In fetishism, it is to the vast number of spirits in the air, which affect physical, social, and psychological human conduct, that attention is directed. Advertising, then, can more closely be compared to this fetishistic religion.

> The moral universe . . . is essentially that of a polytheistic religion. It is a world dominated by a sheer numberless pantheon of powerful forces, which literally reside in every article of use or consumption, in every institution of daily life. If the winds and waters, the trees and brooks of ancient Greece were inhabited by a vast host of nymphs, dryads, satyrs, and other local and specific deities, so is the universe of the TV commercial. The polytheism that confronts us here is thus a fairly primitive one, closely akin to animistic and fetishistic beliefs. (Esslin, 1976, p. 271)

Technology and Magic

Raymond Williams notes that advertising is "a highly organized and professional system of magical inducements and satisfactions, functionally very similar to magical systems in simpler societies, but rather strangely coexistent with a highly developed scientific technology" (1980, p. 185). If, functionally speaking, the broad purpose of a religion is to provide a confused population with answers to the problems of existence, why does advertising focus so much attention on the use of magic rather than on some other, more spiritual system of beliefs? To answer this question, we need to recontextualize advertising within the broader parameters of seeing it as an institution of a developing capitalist society. Judith Williamson defines magic as "the production of results disproportionate to the effort put in (a transformation of power—or of impotence *into* power)" (1978, p. 141). How does this fit into the cultural framework of advanced capitalist society?

For Raymond Williams, the fundamental choice that emerges in a modern industrial society is between seeing people as producers or as consumers. A society that encourages a view of people as producers highlights the political dimensions of industrial activity and recognizes that different ways of organizing material production entails debates about the distribution of power and who benefits within any social system. Such a society recognizes that the important decisions made about the structure of society are made in the realm of production—for it is the economic sphere that structures the distribution of valuable and scarce social resources. To the extent that a society wants democratic discussion about the proper uses of social resources, a view of people as producers is absolutely vital.

On the other hand, to the extent that a society wants to divert attention away from the political consequences of economic structures, it encourages people to regard themselves as consumers of industrial products rather than as their producers. Democratic activity in this perspective is equated with the different options that the marketplace is able to offer. Consumption is democracy, in as much as people have so-called choices about the products that they can buy but not the productive arrangements under which they live. To the extent that a society is successful in this type of definition of people, we have a deflection of consciousness away from the real areas of social life (production) and toward those that are secondary (consumption). As Raymond Williams writes,

> The fundamental choice that emerges, in the problems set to us by modern industrial production, is between man as consumer and man as user. The system of organized magic which is modern advertising is primarily important as a functional obscuring of this choice. (1980, p. 186)

It obscures this choice because it both recognizes our reality and then offers a false interpretation of it. It recognizes the reality that modern forms of capitalist production strip away from us any notion of control of our productive activity. At work, we are not in control. It gives a false interpretation of this in that it naturalizes the loss of control and instead offers us control in another realm—consumption. Judith Williamson writes the following:

> In advertising, it is essential to compensate for the inactivity forced on us; hence advertising's Romanticism and its emphasis on adventure and excitement. But the only thing we can *do* in fact is to buy the product, or incant its name—this is all the action possible as *our* part of the excitement offered. Such minimal action inevitably creates a "magical spell" element: from a little action we get "great" results (or are promised them). . . . Magic allows us to feel that we may not be producers of meaning but of *material* effects. . . . This creates a never ending exchange between passivity and action, a translation between technological action and magical action with our own inactivity as the turning point. Technology deprives us of a control which we are given back in the surrogate form of spells and promises. (1978, pp. 140, 142)

In modern industrial society, the link with nature has been shattered: Nature is viewed only as a resource that is there for human consumption. Our defining relationship is with technology. Rather than the spirits of nature invading the body of objects (as in older fetishistic belief systems), in the mythical universe of advertising, it is the spirits of technology that invade the body of the commodity and supply the basis for a belief in its power. In modern capitalist society, the technological fix is a deeply rooted way of approaching (and obscuring) *social* problems, and it would not surprise us to see this pattern everywhere we look, from the Strategic Defense Initiative (SDI) to car commercials, cloaked in magical and supernatural modes of representation.

References

Esslin, M. (1976). Aristotle and the advertisers: The television commercial considered as a form of drama. In H. Newcombe (Ed.), *Television: The critical view.* New York: Oxford University Press.

Jhally, S. (1987). *The codes of advertising: Fetishism and the political economy of meaning in the consumer society.* New York: St. Martin's Press.

Kavanaugh, J. (1981). *Following Christ in a consumer culture.* New York: Orbis.

Lears, T. J. (1983). From salvation to self-realization: Advertising and the therapeutic roots of consumer culture. In T. J. Lears & R. Fox (Eds.), *The culture of consumption.* New York: Pantheon.

Leiss, W., Kline, S., & Jhally, S. (Eds.). (1986). *Social communication in advertising.* London: Methuen.

Linder, S. (1975). *The harried leisure class.* New York: Columbia University Press.

Livant, B. (1983). *On the religion of use-value*. Paper presented at the University of Regina, Regina, Saskatchewan, Canada. (unpublished)

Marchand, R. (1985). *Advertising the American dream*. Berkeley: University of California Press.

Marx, K. (1976). *Capital: A critique of political economy* (B. Fowkes, Trans., Vol. 1). London: Penguin.

Schwartz, T. (1974). *The responsive chord*. New York: Anchor.

Williams, R. (1980). *Problems in materialism and culture*. London: New Left Books.

Williamson, J. (1978). *Decoding advertisements: Ideology and meaning in advertising*. London: Boyars.

Advertising at the Edge of the Apocalypse*

In this essay I wish to make a simple claim: Twentieth century advertising is the most powerful and sustained system of propaganda in human history, and its cumulative cultural effects, unless quickly checked, will be responsible for destroying the world as we know it. As it achieves this, it will be responsible for the deaths of hundreds of thousands of non-Western peoples and will prevent the peoples of the world from achieving true happiness. *Simply stated, our survival as a species is dependent upon minimizing the threat from advertising and the commercial culture that has spawned it.* I am stating my claims boldly at the outset, so that there can be no doubt as to what is at stake in our debates about the media and culture as we enter the new millennium.

Colonizing Culture

Karl Marx, the preeminent analyst of nineteenth-century industrial capitalism, wrote, in 1867, in the very opening lines of *Capital*, that "The wealth of societies in which the capitalist mode of production prevails appears as an 'immense

* This essay first appeared in *Critical Studies in Media Commercialism*, ed. R. Anderson & L. Strate (New York: Oxford University Press, 2000), pp. 27–39. Reprinted by permission.

collection of commodities'" (1976, p. 125). In seeking to initially distinguish his object of analysis from preceding societies, Marx referred to the way that the society showed itself on a surface level and highlighted a *quantitative* dimension—the number of objects that humans interacted with in everyday life.

Indeed, no other society in history has been able to match the immense productive output of industrial capitalism. This feature colors the way in which the society presents itself—the way it *appears*. Objects are everywhere in capitalism. In this sense, capitalism is truly a revolutionary society, dramatically altering the very landscape of social life, in a way in which no other form of social organization had been able to achieve in such a short period of time. (In *The Communist Manifesto*, Marx and Engels would coin the famous phrase "all that is solid melts into air" to highlight capitalism's unique dynamism.) It is this that strikes Marx as distinctive as he observes nineteenth-century London. The starting point of his own critique therefore is not what he believes is the dominating agent of the society, *capital*, nor is it what he believes creates the value and wealth, *labor*—instead, it is the *commodity*. From this surface appearance, Marx then proceeds to peel away the outer skin of the society and to penetrate to the underlying essential structure that lies in the hidden abode of production.

It is not enough, of course, to only produce the immense collection of commodities—they must also be *sold*, so that further investment in production is feasible. Once produced, commodities must go through the circuit of distribution, exchange, and consumption, so that profit can be returned to the owners of capital, and value can be realized again in a money form. If the circuit is not completed, the system will collapse into stagnation and depression. Capitalism therefore has to ensure the sale of commodities on *pain of death*. In that sense, the problem of capitalism is not mass production (which has been solved), but is instead the *problem of consumption*. That is why, from the early years of this century, it is more accurate to use the label *the consumer culture* to describe the Western industrial market societies.

So central is consumption to its survival and growth that, at the end of the nineteenth century, industrial capitalism invented a unique new institution—the advertising industry—to ensure that the immense accumulation of commodities is converted back into a money form. The function of this new industry would be to recruit the best creative talent of the society and to create a culture in which desire and identity would be fused with commodities—to make the dead world of things come alive with human and social possibilities (what Marx would prophetically call the *fetishism of commodities*). And, indeed, there has never been a propaganda effort to match the effort of advertising in the twentieth century. More thought, effort, creativity, time, and attention to detail has gone into the selling of the immense collection of commodities than any other campaign in human history to change public consciousness. One indication of this is simply the amount of money that has been exponentially expended on this effort.

Today, in the United States alone, more than $175 billion a year is spent to sell us things. This concentration of effort is unprecedented.

It should not be surprising that something this central and with so much being expended on it should become an important presence in social life. Indeed, commercial interests intent on maximizing the consumption of the immense collection of commodities have colonized more and more of the spaces of our culture. For instance, almost the entire media system (television and print) has been developed as a delivery system for marketers—its prime function to produce audiences for sale to advertisers. Both the advertisements it carries, as well as the editorial matter that acts as a support for it, celebrate the consumer society. The movie system, at one time outside the direct influence of the broader marketing system, is now fully integrated into it through the strategies of licensing, tie-ins, and product placements. The prime function of many Hollywood films today is to aid in the selling of the immense collection of commodities. As public funds are drained from the noncommercial cultural sector, art galleries, museums, and symphonies bid for corporate sponsorship. Even those institutions thought to be outside of the market are being sucked in. High schools now sell the sides of their buses, the spaces of their hallways, and the classroom time of their students to hawkers of candy bars, soft drinks, and jeans. In New York City, sponsors are being sought for public playgrounds. In the contemporary world, everything is sponsored by someone. The latest plans of Space Marketing, Inc., call for rockets to deliver mile-wide Mylar billboards to compete with the sun and the moon for the attention of the earth's population.

With advertising messages on everything from fruit on supermarket shelves, to urinals, to, literally, the space beneath our feet (Bamboo lingerie conducted a spray-paint pavement campaign in Manhattan telling consumers that "from here it looks like you could use some new underwear"), it should not be surprising that many commentators now identify the realm of culture as simply an *adjunct* to the system of production and consumption.

Indeed, so overwhelming has the commercial colonization of our culture become that it has created its own problems for marketers who now worry about how to ensure that their *individual* message stands out from the clutter and the noise of this busy environment. In that sense, the main competition for market-ers is not simply other brands in their product type, but all the other advertisers who are competing for the attention of an increasingly cynical audience that is doing all that it can to avoid ads. In a strange paradox, as advertising takes over more and more space in the culture, the job of the individual advertisers becomes much more difficult. Therefore, ever greater care and resources are poured into the creation of commercial messages—much greater care than the surrounding editorial matter designed to capture the attention of the audience. Indeed, if we wanted to compare national television commercials to something equivalent, it would the biggest budget movie blockbusters. Second by second, it costs more to produce the average network ad than a movie like *Jurassic Park*.

The twin results of these developments are that advertising is everywhere and that huge amounts of money and creativity are expended upon it.

If Marx were writing today, I believe that he would be struck not only by the presence of even more objects, but also by the ever-present "discourse through and about objects" that permeates the spaces of our public and private domains (Leiss, Kline & Jhally, 1990, p. 1). This commercial discourse is the *ground* on which we live, the *space* in which we learn to think, and the *lens* through which we come to understand the world that surrounds us. In seeking to understand where we are headed as a society, an adequate analysis of this commercial environment is essential.

Seeking this understanding will involve clarifying what we mean by the power and effectiveness of ads, and being able to pose the right questions. For too long, debate has been concentrated around the issue of whether ad campaigns create demand for a particular product. If you are Pepsi Cola or Ford or Anheuser Busch, then it may be the right question for your interests. But, if you are interested in the social power of advertising—the impact of advertising on society—then that is the wrong question.

The right question would ask about the *cultural* role of advertising, not its marketing role. Culture is the place and space where a society tells stories about itself, where values are articulated and expressed, where notions of good and evil, of morality and immorality, are defined. In our culture, it is the stories of advertising that dominate the spaces that mediate this function. If human beings are essentially a storytelling species, then to study advertising is to examine the central storytelling mechanism of our society. The correct question to ask from this perspective is not whether particular ads sell the products they are hawking, but rather, what are the consistent stories that advertising spins, as a whole, about what is important in the world, about how to behave, and about what is good and bad? Indeed, it is to ask what *values* does advertising consistently push?

Happiness

Every society has to tell a story about happiness, about how individuals can satisfy themselves and feel both subjectively and objectively good. The cultural system of advertising gives a very specific answer to that question for our society. *The way to happiness and satisfaction is through the consumption of objects through the marketplace.* Commodities will make us happy (Leiss, 1976, p. 4). In one very important sense, that is the consistent and explicit message of every single message within the system of market communication.

Neither the fact of advertising's colonization of the horizons of imagination nor the pushing of a story about the centrality of goods to human satisfaction should surprise us. The immense collection of goods has to be consumed (and even more goods produced), and the story that is used to ensure this function equates goods with happiness. Insiders to the system have recognized this obvious fact for many years. Retail analyst Victor Liebow said, just after the Second World War,

> Our enormously productive economy . . . demands that we make consumption our way of life, that we convert the buying and the selling of goods into rituals, that we seek our spiritual satisfaction, our ego satisfaction in commodities. . . . We need things consumed, burned up, worn out, replaced, and discarded at an ever-increasing rate. (Durning 1991, p. 153)

So economic growth is justified not simply on the basis that it will provide employment (after all, a host of alternative nonproductive activities could also provide that), but because it will give us access to more things that will make us happy. This rationale for the existing system of ever-increasing production is told by advertising in the most compelling form possible. In fact, it is this story—that human satisfaction is intimately connected to the provisions of the market and to economic growth—that is the major motivating force for social change as we start the twenty-first century.

The social upheavals of Eastern Europe were pushed by this vision. As Gloria Steinem described the East German transformation, "First we have a revolution then we go shopping" (Ehrenreich, 1990, p. 46). The attractions of this vision in the third world are not difficult to discern. When your reality is empty stomachs and empty shelves, no wonder the marketplace appears as the panacea for your problems. When your reality is hunger and despair, it should not be surprising that the seductive images of desire and abundance emanating from the advertising system should be so influential in thinking about social and economic policy. Indeed, not only happiness but also political freedom itself are made possible by access to the immense collection of commodities. These are very powerful stories that equate happiness and freedom with consumption—and advertising is the main propaganda arm of this view.

The question that we need to pose at this stage (that is almost never asked) is, is it true? Does happiness come from material things? Do we get happier as a society as we get richer, as our standard of living increases, as we have more access to the immense collection of objects? Obviously, these are complex issues, but the general answer to these questions is no (see Leiss et al., 1990, chap. 10 for a fuller discussion of these issues).

In a series of surveys conducted in the United States starting in 1945 (labeled the happiness surveys), researchers sought to examine the link between material wealth and subjective happiness and concluded that, when examined both cross-culturally as well as historically in one society, there is a very weak correlation. Why should this be so?

When we examine this process more closely, the conclusions appear to be less surprising than our intuitive perspective might suggest. In another series of surveys (*the quality of life surveys*) people were asked about the kinds of things that are important to them—about what would constitute a good quality of life. The findings of this line of research indicate that if the elements of satisfaction were divided up into social values (love, family, and friends) and material values (economic security and success), the former outranks the latter in terms of importance. What people say they really want out of life is autonomy and control of life, good self-esteem, warm family relationships, tension-free leisure time, and close and intimate friends, as well as romance and love. This is not to say that material values are not important. They form a necessary component of a good quality of life. But above a certain level of poverty and comfort, material things stop giving us the kind of satisfaction that the magical world of advertising insists that they can deliver.

These conclusions point to one of the great ironies of the market system. The market is good at providing those things that can be bought and sold, and it pushes us—via advertising—in that direction. But the real sources of happiness—social relationships—are outside the capability of the marketplace to provide. The marketplace cannot provide love, it cannot provide real friendships, and it cannot provide sociability. It can provide other material things and services—but they are not what makes us happy.

The advertising industry has known this since at least the 1920s and, in fact, has stopped trying to sell us things based on their material qualities alone. If we examine the advertising of the end of the nineteenth century and in the first years of the twentieth century, we would see that advertising talked a lot about the properties of commodities—what they did, how well they did it, etc. But starting in the 1920s, advertising shifts to talking about the relationship of objects to the social life of people. It starts to connect commodities (the things they have to sell) with the powerful images of a deeply desired social life that people say they want.

No wonder then that advertising is so attractive to us, so powerful, so seductive. What it offers us are images of the real sources of human happiness—family life, romance and love, sexuality and pleasure, friendship and sociability, leisure and relaxation, independence and control of life. That is why advertising is so powerful; that is what is real about it. The cruel illusion of advertising, however, is in the way that it links those qualities to a place that, by definition, cannot provide it—the market and the immense collection of commodities. The falsity of advertising is not in the *appeals* it makes (which are very real) but in the *answers* it provides. We want love and friendship and sexuality—and advertising points the way to it through objects.

To reject or to criticize advertising as false and manipulative misses the point. Ad executive Jerry Goodis puts it this way: "Advertising doesn't mirror how people are acting but how they are dreaming" (Nelson, 1983). It taps into our real emotions and repackages them back to us as connected to the world of things. What advertising really reflects, in that sense, is what I call the the *dreamlife of the culture.* Even saying this, however, simplifies a deeper process, because advertisers do more than mirror our dreamlife—they help to create it. They *translate our desires* (for love, for family, for friendship, for adventure, and for sex) *into our dreams.* Advertising is like a fantasy factory, taking our desire for human social contact and reconceiving it, reconceptualizing it, connecting it with the world of commodities and then translating into a form that can be communicated.

The great irony is that as advertising does this, it draws us further away from what really has the capacity to satisfy us (meaningful human contact and relationships) to what does not (material things). In that sense, advertising *reduces* our capacity to become happy by pushing us, cajoling us, to carry on in the direction of things. If we really wanted to create a world that reflected our desires, then the consumer culture would not be it. It would look very different—a society that stressed and built the institutions that would foster social relationships, rather than endless material accumulation.

Advertising's role in channeling us in these fruitless directions is profound. In one sense, its function is analogous to the drug pusher on the street corner. As we try to break our addiction to things, it is there, constantly offering us another hit. By persistently pushing the idea of the good life being connected to products, and by colonizing every nook and cranny of the culture where alternative ideas could be raised, advertising is an important part of the creation of what Tibor Scitovsky (1976) calls "the joyless economy." The great political challenge that emerges from this analysis is how to connect our real desires to a truly human world, rather than the dead world of the immense collection of commodities.

"There Is No Such Thing as 'Society'"

A culture dominated by commercial messages that tell individuals that the way to happiness is through consuming objects bought in the marketplace gives a very particular answer to the question of what society is—what it is that binds us together in some kind of collective way; what concerns or interests we share. In fact, Margaret Thatcher, the former conservative British Prime Minister, gave the most succinct answer to this question from the viewpoint of the market. In perhaps her most (in)famous quote, she announced, "There is no such thing as 'society.' There are just individuals and their families." According to Mrs. Thatcher, there is nothing solid we can call society—no group values, no collective interests—society is just a bunch of individuals acting on their own.

Indeed, this is precisely how advertising talks to us. It addresses us not as members of society talking about collective issues, but as individuals. It talks about our individual needs and desires. It does not talk about those things that we have to negotiate collectively, such as poverty, healthcare, housing and the homeless, the environment, among other things.

The market appeals to the worst in us (greed and selfishness) and discourages what is the best about us (compassion, caring, and generosity).

Again, this should not surprise us. In those societies in which the market-place dominates, what will be stressed is what the marketplace can deliver—and advertising is the main voice of the marketplace—so discussions of collective issues are pushed to the margins of the culture. They are not there in the center of the main system of communication that exists in the society. It is no accident that, politically, the market vision associated with neoconservatives has come to dominate at exactly that time when advertising has been pushing the same values into every available space in the culture. The widespread disillusionment with government (and, hence, with thinking about issues in a collective manner) has found extremely fertile ground in the fields of commercial culture.

Unfortunately, we are now in a situation, both globally and domestically, in which solutions to pressing nuclear and environmental problems will have to take a collective form. The marketplace cannot deal with the problems that face us at the turn of the millennium. For example, it cannot deal with the threat of nuclear extermination that is still with us in the post–cold war age. It cannot deal with global warming, the erosion of the ozone layer, or the depletion of our nonrenewable resources. The effects of the way we do business are no longer localized, they are now global, and we will have to have international and collective ways of dealing with them. Individual action will not be enough. As the environmentalist slogan puts it, "we all live downstream now."

Domestically, how do we find a way to tackle issues, such as the nightmares of our inner cities, the ravages of poverty, and the neglect of healthcare for the most vulnerable section of the population? How can we find a way to talk realistically and passionately of such problems within a culture in which the central message is "don't worry, be happy"? As Barbara Ehrenreich says,

> Television commercials offer solutions to hundreds of problems we didn't even know we had—from 'morning mouth' to shampoo build-up—but nowhere in the consumer culture do we find anyone offering us such mundane necessities as affordable health insurance, childcare, housing, or higher education. The flip side of the consumer spectacle . . . is the starved and impoverished public sector. We have Teenage Mutant Ninja Turtles, but no way to feed and educate the one-fifth of American children who are growing up in poverty. We have dozens of varieties of breakfast cereal, and no help for the hungry. (Ehrenreich, 1990, p. 47)

In that sense, advertising systematically relegates discussion of key societal issues to the peripheries of the culture and talks in powerful ways instead of individual desire, fantasy, pleasure, and comfort.

Partly, this is because of advertising's *monopolization* of cultural life. There is no space left for different types of discussion, no space at the center of the society where alternative values can be expressed. But it is also connected to the failure of those who care about collective issues to create alternative visions that can compete in any way with the commercial vision. The major alternatives offered to date have been a gray and dismal *stateism*. This occurred not only in the Western societies, but also in the former so-called socialist societies of Eastern Europe. These repressive societies never found a way to connect to people in any kind of pleasurable way, relegating issues of pleasure and individual expression to the nonessential and distracting aspects of social life. This indeed was the core of the failure of Communism in Eastern Europe. As Ehrenreich reminds us, not only was it unable to deliver the material goods, but it was also unable to create a fully human "ideological retort to the powerful seductive messages of the capitalist consumer culture" (1990, p. 47). The problems are no less severe domestically.

> Everything enticing and appealing is located in the (thoroughly private) consumer spectacle. In contrast, the public sector looms as a realm devoid of erotic promise—the home of the IRS [Internal Revenue Service], the DMV [Department of Motor Vehicles], and other irritating, intrusive bureaucracies. Thus, though everyone wants national health insurance, and parental leave, few are moved to wage political struggles for them. "Necessity" is not enough; we may have to find a way to glamorize the possibility of an activist public sector, and to glamorize the possibility of public activism. (p. 47)

The imperative task for those who want to stress a different set of values is to make the struggle for social change fun and sexy. By that I do not mean that we have to use images of sexuality, but that we have to find a way of thinking about the struggle against poverty, against homelessness, for healthcare and child care, and to protect the environment in terms of *pleasure and fun and happiness*.

To make this glamorization of collective issues possible will require that the present commercial monopoly of the channels of communication be broken in favor of more democratic access, where difficult discussion of important and relevant issues may be possible. While the situation may appear hopeless, we should remind ourselves of how important capitalism deems its monopoly of the imagination to be. The campaigns of successive United States governments against the Cuban revolution and the obsession of our national security state with the Sandinista revolution in Nicaragua in the 1980s demonstrate the importance that capitalism places on smashing the alternative model. Even as the United States government continues to support the most vicious, barbarous, brutal, and murderous regimes around the world, it takes explicit aim at those governments that have tried to redistribute wealth to the most needy—who have prioritized collective values over the values of selfishness and greed. The monopoly of the vision is vital, and capitalism knows it.

The End of the World as We Know It

The consumer vision that is pushed by advertising and that is conquering the world is based fundamentally, as I argued previously, on a notion of *economic growth.* Growth requires resources (both raw materials and energy), and there is a broad consensus among environmental scholars that the earth cannot sustain past levels of expansion based upon resource-intensive modes of economic activity, especially as more and more nations struggle to join the feeding trough.

The environmental crisis is complex and multilayered, cutting across both production and consumption issues. For instance, just in terms of resource depletion, we know that we are rapidly exhausting what the earth can offer and that, if the present growth and consumption trends continue unchecked, the limits to growth on the planet will be reached sometime within the next century. Industrial production uses up resources and energy at a rate that has never before even been imagined. Since 1950, the world's population has used up more of the earth's resources than all the generations that came before (Durning, 1991, p. 157). In fifty years, we have matched the use of thousands of years. The West and especially Americans have used most of these resources, so we have a special responsibility for the approaching crisis. In another hundred years we will have exhausted the planet.

But even more than that, we will have done irreparable damage to the environment on which we depend for everything. As environmental activist Barry Commoner says,

> The environment makes up a huge, enormously complex living machine that forms a thin dynamic layer on the earth's surface, and every human activity depends on the integrity and proper functioning of this machine. . . . This machine is our biological capital, the basic apparatus on which our total productivity depends. If we destroy it, our most advanced technology will become useless and any economic and political system that depends on it will flounder. The environmental crisis is a signal of the approaching catastrophe. (1971, pp. 16–17)

The clearest indication that the way we produce is having an effect on the ecosphere of the planet is the depletion of the ozone layer, which has dramatically increased the amount of ultraviolet radiation that is damaging or lethal to many life forms on the planet. In 1985, scientists discovered the existence of a huge hole in the ozone layer over the South Pole that is the size of the United States, illustrating how the activities of humans are changing the very makeup of the earth. In his book *The End of Nature*, Bill McKibben reminds us that "we have done this ourselves . . . by driving our cars, building our factories, cutting down our forests, turning on air conditioners" (1989, p. 45). He writes that the history of the world is full of the most incredible events that changed the way we lived, but they are all dwarfed by what we have accomplished in the last fifty years:

> Man's efforts, even at their mightiest, were tiny compared with the size of the planet—the Roman Empire meant nothing to the Artic or the Amazon. But

now, the way of life of one part of the world in one half-century is altering every inch and every hour of the globe. (p. 46)

The situation is so bad that the scientific community is desperately trying to get the attention of the rest of us to wake up to the danger. The Union of Concerned Scientists (representing 1,700 of the world's leading scientists, including a majority of Nobel laureates in the sciences) recently issued this appeal:

Human beings and the natural world are on a collision course. Human activities inflict harsh and irreversible damage on the environment and on critical resources. If not checked, many of our current practices put at serious risk the future that we wish for human society and the plant and animal kingdoms, and may so alter the living world that it will be unable to sustain life in the manner we know. Fundamental changes are urgent if we are to avoid the collision our present course will bring. (World Scientists Warning to Humanity, 1992)

It is important to avoid the prediction of immediate catastrophe. We have already done a lot of damage, but the real environmental crisis will not hit until sometime in the middle of the next century. However, to avoid that catastrophe we have to take action *now*. We have to put in place the steps that will save us in seventy years' time.

The metaphor that best describes the task before us is of an oil tanker heading for a crash on the shore. Because of its momentum and size, to avoid crashing the oil tanker has to start turning well before it reaches the coast, anticipating its own momentum. If it starts turning too late, it will smash into the coast. That is where the consumer society is right now. We have to make fundamental changes in the way in which we organize ourselves, in what we stress in our economy, if we want to avoid the catastrophe in seventy years' time. We have to take action *now*.

In that sense, the present generation has a unique responsibility in human history. It is literally up to us to save the world, to make the changes we need to make. If we do not, we will be in barbarism and savagery toward each other in seventy years' time. We have to make short-term sacrifices. We have to give up our nonessential appliances. We especially have to rethink our relationship to the car. We have to make *real* changes—not just recycling but also fundamental changes in how we live and produce. And we cannot do this individually. We have to do it collectively. We have to find the political will somehow to do this—and we may even be dead when its real effects will be felt. The vital issue is how we identify with that generation in the next century. As the political philosopher Robert Heilbroner says,

A crucial problem for the world of the future will be a concern for generations to come. Where will such concern arise? . . . Contemporary industrial man, his appetite for the present whetted by the values of a high-consumption society and his attitude toward the future influenced by the prevailing canons of self-concern, has but a limited motivation to form such bonds. There are many who would sacrifice much for their children; fewer would do so for their grandchildren. (1980, pp. 134–135)

Forming such bonds will be made even more difficult within our current context that stresses individual (not social) needs and the immediate situation (not the long term). The advertising system will form *the ground* on which we think about the future of the human race, and there is nothing there that should give us any hope for the development of such a perspective. The time frame of advertising is very short term. It does not encourage us to think beyond the immediacy of present sensual experience. Indeed, it may well be the case that, as the advertising environment gets more and more crowded, with more and more of what advertisers label as *noise* threatening to drown out individual messages, the appeal will be made to levels of experience that cut through clutter, appealing immediately and deeply to very emotional states. Striking emotional imagery that grabs the gut instantly leaves no room for thinking about anything. Sexual imagery, especially in the age of AIDS, where sex is being connected to death, will need to become even more powerful and immediate to overcome any possible negative associations—indeed to remove us from the world of connotation and meaning construed *cognitively*. The value of a collective social future is one that does not, and will not, find expression within our commercially dominated culture. Indeed, the prevailing values provide no incentive to develop bonds with future generations, and there is a real sense of nihilism and despair about the future and a closing of ranks against the outside.

Imagining a Different Future

Over one hundred years ago, Marx observed that there were two directions that capitalism could take: toward a democratic *socialism* or toward a brutal *barbarism*. Both long-term and recent evidence would seem to indicate that the latter is where we are headed, unless alternative values quickly come to the fore.

Many people thought that the environmental crisis would be the linchpin for the lessening of international tensions as we recognized our interdependence and our collective security and future. But as the Persian Gulf War made clear, the new world order will be based upon a struggle for scarce resources. Before the propaganda rationale shifted to the struggle for freedom and democracy, George Bush Sr. reminded the American people that the troops were being dispatched to the Gulf to protect the resources that make possible our way of life. An automobile culture and commodity-based culture such as ours is reliant upon sources of cheap oil. And if the cost of that is one hundred thousand dead Iraqis, well so be it. In such a scenario, the peoples of the third world will be seen as enemies who are making unreasonable claims on our resources. The future and the third world can wait. Our commercial-dominated cultural discourse powerfully reminds us everyday that we need *ours* and we need it *now*. In that sense, the Gulf War is a preview of what is to come. As the world runs out of resources, the most powerful military sources will use that might to ensure access.

The destructive aspects of capitalism (its short-term nature, its denial of collective values, its stress on the material life), are starting to be recognized by some people who have made their fortunes through the market. The billionaire turned philanthropist George Soros (1997) talks about what he calls "the capitalist threat"—and, culturally speaking, advertising is the main voice of that threat. To the extent that it pushes us toward material things for satisfaction and away from the construction of social relationships, it pushes us down the road to increased economic production that is driving the coming environmental catastrophe. To the extent that it talks about our individual and private needs, it pushes discussion about collective issues to the margins. To the extent that it talks about the present only, it makes thinking about the future difficult. To the extent that it does all of these things, advertising becomes one of the major obstacles to our survival as a species.

Getting out of this situation, coming up with new ways to look at the world, will require enormous work, and one response may just be to enjoy the end of the world—one last great fling, the party to end all parties. The alternative response, to change the situation, to work for humane, collective, long-term values, will require an effort of the most immense kind.

And there is evidence to be hopeful about the results of such an attempt. It is important to stress that creating and maintaining the present structure of the consumer culture takes enormous work and effort. The reason that consumer ways of looking at the world predominate is because there are billions of dollars being spent on it every single day. The consumer culture is not simply erected and then forgotten. It has to be held in place by the activities of the ad industry and, increasingly, the activities of the public relations industry. Capitalism has to try really hard to convince us about the value of the commercial vision. In some senses, consumer capitalism is a house of cards, held together in a fragile way by immense effort, and it could just as soon melt away as hold together. It will depend on whether there are viable alternatives that will motivate people to believe in a different future, whether there are other ideas as pleasurable, as powerful, as fun, as passionate with which people can identify.

I am reminded here of the work of Antonio Gramsci, who coined the famous phrase, "pessimism of the intellect, optimism of the will." "Pessimism of the intellect" means recognizing the reality of our present circumstances, analyzing the vast forces arrayed against us, but insisting on the possibilities and the moral desirability of social change—that is "the optimism of the will," believing in human values that will be the inspiration for us to struggle for our survival

I do not want to be too Pollyannaish about the possibilities of social change. It is not just collective values that need to be struggled for, but collective values that recognize individual rights and individual creativity. There are many repressive collective movements already in existence—from our own homegrown Christian fundamentalists to the Islamic zealots of the Taliban in Afghanistan. The task is not easy. It means balancing and integrating different views of the world. As Ehrenreich writes,

> Can we envision a society which values—not "collectivity" with its dreary implications of conformity—but what I can only think to call *conviviality*, which could, potentially, be built right into the social infrastructure with opportunities, at all levels for rewarding, democratic participation? Can we envision a society that does not dismiss individualism, but truly values individual creative expression—including dissidence, debate, nonconformity, artistic experimentation, and in the larger sense, adventure . . . [T]he project remains what it has always been: to replace the consumer culture with a genuinely *human* culture. (1990, p. 47)

The stakes are simply too high for us not to deal with the real and pressing problems that face us as a species—finding a progressive and humane collective solution to the global crisis and ensuring for our children and future generations a world fit for truly human habitation.

References

Commoner, B. (1971). *The closing circle: Nature, man and technology*. New York: Knopf.
Durning, A. (1991). Asking how much is enough. In L. Brown (Ed.), *State of the world, 1991*. New York: Norton. pp. 153–169.
Ehrenreich, B. (1990). Laden with lard. *Zeta*, July/August.
Heilbroner, R. (1980). *An inquiry into the human prospect: Updated and reconsidered for the 1980s*. New York: Norton.
Leiss, W. (1976). *The limits to satisfaction*. London: Marion Boyars.
Leiss, W., Kline, S., & Jhally, S. (1990). *Social communication in advertising* (2nd ed.). New York: Routledge.
Marx, K. (1976). *Capital: A critique of political economy*. (B. Fowkes, Trans., Vol. 1). London: Penguin.
McKibben, B. (1989). *The end of nature*. New York: Random House.
Nelson, J. (1983). As the brain tunes out, the TV ad-men tune in. *Globe and Mail*.
Scitovsky, T. (1976). *The joyless economy*. New York: Oxford University Press.
Soros, G. (1997, February). The capitalist threat. *The Atlantic Monthly, 45*.

On Advertising

Sut Jhally versus James Twitchell[*]

Carrie McLaren, editor of Stay Free! *magazine, moderated a debate between Sut Jhally and James Twitchell, Professor of English and advertising at the University of Florida in the summer of 1999. Twitchell's books include* Adcult USA: The Triumph of Advertising in America *(1995),* Lead Us into Temptation: The Triumph of American Materialism *(1999),* Twenty Ads that Shook the World: The Century's Most Groundbreaking Advertising *(2000), and* Living It Up: America's Love Affair with Luxury *(2002). He is an articulate defender of advertising and commercial culture.*

STAY FREE!: What's your agenda? What are you trying to accomplish?

JHALLY: As a social scientist, I am interested in the question of determination—what structures the world and how we live in it. To understand the modern world requires some perspective on advertising. For me, the function of knowledge is to provide people with tools to see the world in different ways and to be able to act and to change the world. I work with Marx's aphorism: philosophers help us understand the world, but the point is to change it. If that's not the function of universities, I don't know why we exist. If it's simply to reproduce knowledge about the world or train people for jobs, why bother?

TWITCHELL: I agree with most of that. Advertising is the lingua franca by which we communicate our needs and desires and wants. Not to take it seriously is not to do our job. I was intrigued by advertising first as a scholar of language

[*] This interview first appeared in *Stay Free!* 16 (Summer 1999), http://www.stayfreemagazine.org/archives/16/twitchell.html. Reprinted by permission.

and literature. I was amazed by how little my students knew about literature compared to advertising. Almost in a flash, I realized I was neglecting this great body of material while the material I was teaching seemed, to them, unimportant. I jumped tracks then and moved from high culture to commercial culture. These are tracks, incidentally, not just in American culture but in world culture as well. We are now living in a world informed by language about things. It's not the world that I knew and studied—the world about thoughts and feelings in terms of literature—or the world that preceded that one, which was a world about language and religion.

JHALLY: So do you use advertising as a way of doing literary analysis?

TWITCHELL: I look at it like this: We've turned up our noses at the material world and pretended it was not really important. Clearly, for most people, most of the time, the material is the world. They live in terms of mass-produced objects. How we understand those objects is, to a great degree, what commercial interests decide to say about them. So I'm not just looking at linguistic aspects. I'm interested in why the material world has been so overlooked. Why has it been so denigrated? Why are we convinced that happiness can't come from it? Why do those of us in our fifties warn the generation behind us to stay away from this stuff?

JHALLY: The material world was, for many years, ignored, but not by Marxists. In fact, Marx starts off *Capital* with an analysis of the material world. He says that capitalism has transformed the material world, and, in that sense, it's a revolutionary society. Marx thought that capitalism had a lot of very literary and progressive things, because it blew away the repression of feudalism. The Left has often been criticized for not looking at the material world, but they focus almost entirely on production. What they've really left out is culture. They've regarded it as secondary, and so Western Marxism has tried to redress that imbalance. The reason that I am interested in advertising, coming out of that tradition, is that advertising links those two things together. It allows us to speak about both the material world and the world of symbolism and culture.

Jim, you were saying that we are always preaching that happiness doesn't come from things and we should be less moralistic. My view is driven by political factors, not moral ones. I think we should ask empirical questions. Does happiness come from things? Has more happiness given us more things? If it has, what are the costs of that? The evidence is that material things do not deliver the type of happiness that the system says they should deliver.

TWITCHELL: Is there a system that does deliver more happiness? If so, why hasn't it elbowed its way through and pushed this system aside?

JHALLY: The other systems don't exist. I certainly couldn't point to anything based on what is called the Marxian tradition. The Soviet Union was a dungeon. China is not quite the same dungeon but . . . a better system lies in the future.

The whole point of doing this type of analysis is to imagine what a system would look like that catered to human needs. That's why I look at advertising. What does advertising stress as a system? What are the values? Advertising doesn't say happiness comes only from things. It says that you can get friendship through things. You can get family life through things. Things are used as a medium. Advertisers are really smart. They've realized since the 1920s that things don't make people happy, that what drives people is a social life.

TWITCHELL: In that case, maybe they are doing what most people want, loading value into things. You may not like the amount of money they make or you may think the process is environmentally wicked, but aren't they delivering what people want and need?

JHALLY: No! Advertisers are delivering images of what people say they want connected to the things advertisers sell. If you want to create a world focused on family, focused on community, focused on friendship, focused on independence, focused on autonomy in work, then capitalism would not be it. In fact, what you have in advertising, I believe, is a vision of socialism. And that vision is used to sell these things called commodities. If you wanted to create the world according to the values advertising focuses on, it would look very different. That's where a progressive movement should start. It should take the promises of advertising seriously and say, "Look, if you want this world, what do we have to do to ensure that these values are stressed instead of the values of individualism and greed and materialism?"

TWITCHELL: But advertising doesn't stress greed and materialism.

JHALLY: Well, it's about individual desires.

TWITCHELL: Maybe advertising excludes communal desires because they are not as high on most people's agendas as they are for those of us in our fifties. Maybe most people are not as interested in the things we say we are interested in, such as family and community. Maybe they are more interested in individual happiness.

JHALLY: That's a fair question. We can't answer it yet, though, because advertising dominates so much that it leaves little room for alternative visions. My major problem with advertising is not the vision that it gives out. There are many positive things within that, and that's what attracts people. Part of my problem with advertising is its monopolization of the cultural field. The questions that you are asking can only be answered when you have a space in the culture where alternative values can be articulated. Then perhaps we can see what people's real values and preferences are, because, at that point, they've had some choice. They have the alternative values expressed in as powerful and creative a form as the values that advertisers express.

TWITCHELL: Why aren't there enough people like you in positions of cultural power? Why haven't these people, these silent but passionate people, been able to make their concerns known? Is it because the advertising culture is so powerful that it squeezes them into silence?

JHALLY: It's the way power operates. Some of us have more power and visibility than others. It depends to what degree your values link up with the people who control the cultural system.

TWITCHELL: Don't we control part of that system, the schools? Why have we done such a poor job?

JHALLY: I don't think we've done a poor job. The academy is the one place where there is independent thinking. That's why the Right and business have targeted it. The universities are the only place where these discussions take place. The Right complains about how the universities have been taken over by Leftists. To some extent, that's nonsense, because most academics are fairly innocuous conservatives.

TWITCHELL: They are? Not at the schools I've been at.

JHALLY: There's a visible minority, but most of my colleagues are quite ordinary people. And the tendency is to focus on liberal academics and leave out the larger academic community: the scientists and business schools. . . . But when there is a choice, students will choose those ideas. Our ideas are popular on campuses, because it is one place where they can be expressed. It is one of the few places where there is competition between ideas.

TWITCHELL: Then why do these ideas lose their steam when students leave the campus?

JHALLY: When people leave school, they have to figure out what they're going to do. They're $30,000 in debt. That's one of the great tricks of American capitalism; to get loyalty is to get people into debt early.

TWITCHELL: So this is the indenture system simply made more modern? You and I have completely different views of the same nest. My view is that these ideas don't really hold sway with our students, only our colleagues.

JHALLY: That's not my experience at all. When people are exposed to this, they have a couple of responses. The main one is, "Wow, this is overwhelming. I don't know what to do." So when people ask me what to do, I say, "That's not my job." Education provides the tools to think and understand the world. It is up to them to figure out what to do with that. Of course, once outside the university, you've got to have some community working in the same ways, otherwise you are indirectly isolated. This is not strictly evil capitalism; this is also the Left not building the kinds of institutions that provide people support. They don't exist, and you can either be an active or passive participant in building them.

TWITCHELL: So you are part of the solution, or you're the problem.

JHALLY: Well, I don't think there is any such thing as being innocent in a world that is being constantly constructed.

TWITCHELL: Do you feel marginalized?

JHALLY: Sure. To some degree.

TWITCHELL: You have books that have been published.

JHALLY: Do I have as much power as Peter Jennings?

TWITCHELL: No. Should you? Do you have a pretty face? Can you read well?

JHALLY: Should that matter?

TWITCHELL: In television, absolutely.

JHALLY: Well, it matters in a system that's built on television ratings and keeping advertisers happy. But why must debate and media always be along those lines?

TWITCHELL: All these media are driven by the same machinery—the audience that can be delivered to advertisers. So it's skewed away from certain kinds of people who do not consume, and it's pushed toward people who are massive consumers. It's pushed away from Sut and myself. We feel, Sut especially, marginalized.

JHALLY: Actually, in that sense, I feel targeted.

TWITCHELL: You're not targeted in the way that an eighteen-year-old is.

JHALLY: I have a lot of disposable income.

TWITCHELL: I'm not concerned about money. The point is that you've already made your brand choices. You probably use the same toothpaste. You probably have a highly routinized consumptive life. You're not as interesting to an advertiser as an eighteen-year-old who has not made these choices. We see this when we look around. We see this great dreck of vulgarity that is being pumped out of Hollywood and the television networks and even in books. It's clear that this is not making me feel important, but I sometimes think, well, maybe that's the price you pay in a world where getting Nielsen ratings or getting on the bestseller list is crucial. Now, we're back to Peter Jennings. Peter Jennings's ideas—if those can be called ideas—are more alluring to more people than what Sut and I have to say. We may think our ideas are great, but the prime audience is saying no.

JHALLY: I totally disagree. It doesn't have anything to do with ideas. It's got to do with access. Americans gave away the broadcast system to advertisers in 1934, which meant that everything was going to be dependent on advertising revenues rather than public service.

TWITCHELL: What about PBS?

JHALLY: Public broadcasting is a great idea. I wish that we could have it. PBS was always envisioned as entertainment for the elite rather than as an alternative to commercial TV. It's possible to do public interest programming and be popular. Look at England. The BBC is driven by a different set of economic logics and produces different types of programs. That's why *Masterpiece Theatre* looks so different than the dreck that comes out from the networks. It's not because the Brits are more artistic. The BBC operates within a system of public service.

TWITCHELL: Is the BBC the most popular of the networks?

JHALLY: I don't have the latest figures, but I would imagine yes.

TWITCHELL: Is American dreck popular on English television?

JHALLY: Some. But if you're saying public service stuff is not popular, you're wrong.

TWITCHELL: What do you think should be on PBS?

JHALLY: There is a whole slew of independent filmmakers who don't get their work onto television or into Hollywood. The products of the Media Education Foundation, which are distributed mostly in classrooms . . . there is no shortage of stuff.

TWITCHELL: And there's an audience for this?

JHALLY: Sure. The question is whether you want to encourage diversity. Let's say it's not popular: So what! Why must popularity drive everything? Why shouldn't minority views be heard? Why is that so radical?

TWITCHELL: It's a great idea. But when I hear this argument, I always think: Why are the people saying it so powerless? Why do they always seem to be saying, "We should have this delivered to us?" Why don't they essentially force it through the system? I think it's because, if you observe what they consume, you'll see that it's not what they say they want but is really the popular stuff that other people like.

JHALLY: Well, there are two issues here. One is diversity. Do you think diversity is a good thing to have in American media? The other issue is why hasn't this happened? That is an issue of power. Those are two separate questions. One is a question of value; the other is how you make it come about. There are more and more people who are starting to participate in collective movements and trying to bring about a different kind of culture. And I think education is the first step of that.

TWITCHELL: Well, I say more power to them. That is exactly what should be happening.

JHALLY: And that is what is happening. But do you recognize such a thing as power operating in the public sphere? Do you see that some people have more power than others and that not everyone can have their voice heard?

TWITCHELL: Here's where we differ. You see it as power coming from outside in. As if these corporate interests are over there doing things to us. I see it in a contrary way. I see a great deal of advertising and commercialism as being the articulated will of consumers rather than the air pumped out by commercial interests. Let's take an example where you seem to hold all the cards. Take De Beers' diamonds advertising campaign. What is more ridiculous than the browbeating of men into buying utterly worthless hunks of stone to make Harry Oppenheimer and his descendants wealthy? Here's this company saying that if you want to be successful in courting women, it requires two months of your salary. Isn't this an example, from your point of view, of power from the outside compressing human freedom and desire? Yet, as hideous as it is—and I think it the most hideous of advertising campaigns—there is something in it that speaks deeply to human beings in moments of high anxiety—namely, how to stabilize a frantic period of time. You stabilize it by buying something that all logic tells you is ridiculous and stupid, at a time in your life when you are the least able to afford it, when it is the most wasteful expenditure and the cruelest exploitation in terms of how these stones are mined. And they're completely worthless. I mean, at least Nike makes good shoes! You would say, "Boy, I rest my case," but I say, "Is there any other explanation?" The explanation, I think, is the need to make ceremony, to fetishize moments of great anxiety. You can actually see them colonizing these moments later in life; now they're saying the ten-year anniversary or the twenty-year anniversary demands a whole new panoply of these otherwise worthless stones.

JHALLY: Sure, I agree with all of that. Advertising caters to deep human needs. People's relationship with objects is what defines us as human beings. The diamond example illustrates the power of advertising, but it's ultimately about how many goods are sold, which I don't think is a good way of measuring. Advertising can be powerful even if it never sells a product. The De Beers campaign means something to people who may never buy a diamond because it gives a particular vision of what love and courtship are about. I use this example in my class and people become outraged. In fact, I've had students say, "God, that's it, I'm never going to buy a diamond. They've tricked me into thinking that I've gotta have this." The De Beers example points to a number of things. One is how advertising works, by reaching deep-seated human needs. I don't call this manipulation. Capitalism works because, in one sense, it talks about real needs that drive people.

TWITCHELL: It's doing the work of religion.

JHALLY: Partly, yes. But it takes real needs and desires and says that they are only satisfied by purchasing products. So what's real about advertising is its appeals. What's false about advertising is the answers it provides to those appeals.

TWITCHELL: But why not through objects?

JHALLY: We can argue about this in terms of moralistic standards or whatever, but I prefer an empirical question: Do people become happier when they have more things? There's quite a bit of literature on this. Robert Lane and Fred Hirsch have talked about it. And Tibor Scitovsky, in his wonderful book *The Joyless Economy*. There's a wonderful article by Richard Easterlin, who examined all the cross-cultural data on subjectivity and happiness and found that there is no correlation cross-nationally and historically between things and happiness. More things do not bring you more happiness. Although things are connected to happiness, it is always in a relative state. It is always in terms of what other people also have at that time. And so happiness in that sense is a zero-sum game. I think you can make a fine argument for a system of production that says, "We are going to make the most number of people the most happy, and we will do this more and more over time." But capitalism is not that system. Advertising people don't want to be selling this stupid stuff; they want to be making films and writing novels. If you really wanted to make more people happy (which I think should be the goal of a political movement, because that notion of subjectivity is incredibly important), then what is it that actually makes people happy? What institutions will cater to those things? Secondly, if it's having this incredible effect on the environment, then we need alternative ways of thinking about it.

TWITCHELL: I'm with you. We agree. But I'm going to be Johnny One-Note and ask, "What are those things?" I'm very suspicious of those things and how powerful they really are. The great con game when we had very few things was the promised pie in the sky. In other words, a life after death. Really, what's happened is that we've moved all those promises down here into this world. I don't know if this works or not. But who cares whether it works. We believe it works. We think things make us happy. My personal view is that probably 0.0001 percent of that is true.

JHALLY: I want to go back to your question, "What are those things?" Those things aren't what I say they are. The social scientific literature reveals that what people talk about is social things. They want good family life . . .

TWITCHELL: Yeah, I never listen to what people say. I always listen to what people do.

JHALLY: That's a strange line for a democrat to be taking. [*laughs*]

TWITCHELL: No, not at all.

JHALLY: In democracies, shouldn't you pay some attention to what people say they want?

TWITCHELL: Here's my idea for an independent film. I want to set a camera on the head of my colleagues. And then I want to see what they do when they're left alone, to study the difference between saying and doing. It seems to me that reaching into the wallet is a much more powerful articulation of desire and belief than delivering the lecture. In that area, I think that the market essentially shows this. What is being consumed is what people really do think is entertaining them, satisfying them, making them happy. It may not be what you and I like, but it is the illusion, perhaps, that is so powerful. And this illusion seems to be making American culture incredibly attractive to others and making other cultures essentially mimics of American popular culture. Whatever this stuff is in advertising, it's incredibly powerful. It's pushed all these other things aside. Literature, art, religion. It's eating everybody's lunch. Maybe that's because most people most of the time want that for lunch. Maybe it really is resolving the concerns that they have, as hard as that is for us to believe.

JHALLY: Or maybe it's that the environment within which people make decisions is so dominated by one very narrow segment of the population.

TWITCHELL: Exactly.

JHALLY: That's where the issue of power comes in.

TWITCHELL: Even in countries where these commercial interests were put not just on the back burner but on no burner at all, all it took was just a momentary crack in the wall—Berlin or wherever—to come tumbling down.

JHALLY: It's the major motivating force transforming the world.

TWITCHELL: Could it also be because partly it is resolving what most people consider to be their concerns?

JHALLY: I go back to Marx on this. He starts off *Capital* by saying that, if you can understand the world of commodities, then you can understand the entire system in which we live. The other thing I always use from Marx is his statement that "People make their own history [or meaning] . . . but not in conditions of their own choosing." If you only look at the "conditions not of their own choosing," then all you focus on is power and manipulation. If you only look at "people make their own meanings," then all you see is individual freedom and choice. If you only look at one or the other, you get a distorted view. Advertising is the conditions not of your own choosing, because it has dominated everything. If you give me a monopoly, I can sell you anything. That's what De Beers did.

TWITCHELL: And, of course, communist countries essentially had a monopoly on media and on the production of objects and what happened to them? Why weren't they strong enough, powerful enough, to make the dream of Marx come to reality?

JHALLY: Well, they weren't Marxist countries. The Soviet Union never dealt with people's individual needs. The Soviet Union fell apart because no one believed it. It fell apart partly because they could see these images coming out of the West, the most glamorous images of an alternative. When your reality is hunger and despair, no wonder this advertising model should be so powerful.

TWITCHELL: You seem to see advertising as a trick. I see the trickery not as them pulling a trick on us but as us actively collaborating in this process. Like the audience observing the magician, we know that the lady is not being sawed in half. We can't quite understand how it works, but we suspend disbelief, and give ourselves over to it. Even though we know that the claims of Alka-Seltzer are not true, we give ourselves over to it.

JHALLY: I agree. Advertising is an active process of creating meaning in which people and advertisers interact. But that is not devoid of power. Again, people make their own messages and meanings, but not in conditions of their own choosing. Jim always wants to stress the first part.

TWITCHELL: Yes, I do.

JHALLY: I stress both. I don't stress the second part, but I don't forget the second part. If you don't have the second part, then you don't have the context within which things are taking place. You have abstract analysis, literary analysis. That's why I asked you if you view your work as literary analysis, because that would explain our different takes.

TWITCHELL: Yes, and I think the context to which Sut refers is so close to the water in which all us fish are swimming that we're begging the question if we think we can ever come to any understanding of it.

JHALLY: Oh, but we have to try, otherwise, what are we here for? One more thing. It's a little bit annoying to me, because you used your colleagues as evidence, but I agree, I think most academics don't think about knowledge in the way that you and I do, actually. I think most people view this as a relatively simple, easy job that allows you to teach six hours a week, and, once you've got tenure, you don't have to do very much.

STAY FREE!: Jim, where does morality figure into advertising?

TWITCHELL: It doesn't. Advertising has one moral: buy stuff. Not very sophisticated. There are certain areas where I think we should pull the cord and say, "No advertising." I'm vehemently against Channel One. I despise billboards. They are in my opinion immoral. I am distraught that the state has gone into not only the lottery business but also advertising. Other than that, I think that the application of moral concerns to advertising is feckless.

JHALLY: I think there is a morality in advertising. It may not be totally systematic, everyone may not adhere to the same thing, but there is a sort of story about what is good and bad and what values should be stressed. That is a moral system.

And I think that you can evaluate that as you can evaluate any moral system. I think that whether advertising tells the truth or not is actually the last thing you should evaluate it for.

TWITCHELL: It does not tell the truth.

JHALLY: Advertising doesn't even make any claims. That's one of the great tricks of the ad industry in terms of how it's regulated. You can only take legislative action against an ad if you can prove that it is deceptive. But you can't evaluate most ads on that basis, because there is nothing to evaluate.

TWITCHELL: I think when most people consume advertising, they know that they have to filter it because it's not going to be telling them the truth. But it's not the truth that they're after. They're after these patterns that have to do with belonging, with ordering, with making sense. So put the truth meter on Nike and you'll say, "My God, who would pay an extra 50 percent for something that is fungible with another product?" Put the truth meter on De Beers, and you'd see that, "My God, what are we doing?" It's not put on these things, because, clearly, they're addressing concerns that are not susceptible to normal reasoning. Ask somebody who has just bought a Lexus SUV, "Was that a sensible purchase?" And they'll almost always tell you that it was a ridiculous purchase. Ask them why they bought it, and they'll say, "I dunno . . . I just like the idea that I have this." Why would somebody have a Polo pony on their shirt when they know that they're just paying an exorbitant amount for the pony? Why would they do that unless somehow the pony was a badge or some kind of a token through which they magically thought they could understand and fit into the world? I am as susceptible as anyone. Sut teaches at the University of Massachusetts. Down the road is Amherst College, which charges triple what the University of Massachusetts charges. I, and my colleagues, go into voluntary indenture sending our kids to schools like Amherst rather than the University of Massachusetts. Why do I, one who is inside this system and knows that U. Mass is not four times worse than Amherst, go and borrow money to send my kids to this school? I do it because, within the system that I move, that is one of the Polo ponies. It doesn't go on my shirt; actually, it's a decal that goes on the back of my Volvo. It violates every sensible bit of behavior. But in so doing it gives me what I want, which is this other sense of, "I'm doing well, I'm raising my child properly, I'm with the community that I feel values what I do." We are willing and conscious participators in a process that is hyperirrational.

STAY FREE!: Is advertising art?

TWITCHELL: Art is whatever I say it is, and I mean that quite literally. There is a group of people whose job is to make claims about certain things and, in making those claims, essentially to apply the label *art*. We are to high culture what advertisers, in some ways, are to mass-produced objects. Art really is what the people who teach literature, who teach art, who run galleries, and who edit magazines say it is. It is not immutable, it is not timeless, and it is not free of space. It's a community of critics who, in order to trade, teach, and communicate, say certain works need special treatment and that they're art. Is advertising art? No. Could it become art? Absolutely. The next generation may very well look at Bernback's Volkswagen ads and say, "Oh, that's art!" But, right now, advertising is in the position of photography back in the 1930s, where it was treated as a kind of whimsical, not-very-serious study. You can see it happening in movies. Movies which were thought to be entertainment, now thanks to the Academy, are considered works of enduring art.

JHALLY: There is a famous article by Theodore Levitt that essentially equates advertising with art. It's a defense of advertising that says, "People have always interpreted the world. What's the problem?" It suggests that as long as advertising doesn't lie, it should be evaluated by the same criteria with which we've always evaluated art. I think that's a sort of self-serving argument.

TWITCHELL: But you wouldn't think that advertising currently is thought of that way, would you?

JHALLY: It depends what you mean by *art*. Art in elite standards, no. But advertising has always been popular art. Even early on, people stuck ads on their walls. And, in one sense, that's a good indication of what people regard as art.

TWITCHELL: Except it's the wrong people. If you were to take your camera around to your colleagues' cubicles, what you'd see there would be more intriguing. I think that, if you were to take a camera around to my colleagues' offices, you would find a lot of advertising.

STAY FREE!: [*At this point, I asked them to comment on a fan letter to Nike, which was printed in* Stay Free!, *Issue 14. The letter writer, like many Nike devotees, has a Nike tattoo; she thanks Nike for helping turn her life around and offers an idea for a commercial.*]

TWITCHELL: Listen, Carrie, I've been terribly depressed in my life. I've been an alcoholic, I freebased cocaine for most of my childhood, and then I found Jesus . . . and, look, I have a cross tattooed on my forearm.

Of course, I'm distressed over someone who attributes redemption to a sneaker company. I've been conditioned not to be distressed at a born-again Christian . . .

JHALLY: I'm more distressed by the born-again Christian [*laughs*]. . . . Your analogy is right on. I'd like to ask her exactly what about Nike made a great difference in her life. Part of it I can understand because the culture tells us that redemption comes through objects, and she just happened to choose the one that, for the moment, is everywhere. Her reaction is not totally off the wall, although it is extreme.

TWITCHELL: What separates her and the yuppie with his Polo pony?

JHALLY: Not much. There's a wonderful new book out called the *Overspent American* by Juliet Schor . . .

TWITCHELL: [*laughing*] Don't tell me you liked that!

JHALLY: I thought is was great. It talked about how people go into debt for these things without the satisfaction that is supposed to go along with it. Goods have always been used to demarcate groups. A lot of defenses of advertising come from that notion, "Oh, people have always used products in this way, products have always had symbolic dimensions, what's wrong with advertising as long as we don't lie, etc." Part of being human is connecting through objects. That in itself is not what's interesting. What's interesting is the context within which these things appear. That's what analysis is for. . . . Advertising says that you are what you buy. Religions offer other conceptions of identity . . .

TWITCHELL: Where do you see power existing in a religious world? If power in the consumer world is with the producer or corporation . . .

JHALLY: In the religious world, power comes from the church.

TWITCHELL: I see the power more from the congregation than behind the pulpit. And the analogy with advertising is a valid one: Consumers travel through ads looking for meaning and purpose; so, too, the congregation forces the pastor to behave in certain ways. You say the power is with the Vatican or Madison Avenue, whereas the power really is in the supermarket aisle or church pew.

JHALLY: I think power is in both places. You can't look at one or the other.

STAY FREE!: [*I asked Sut to state briefly, in closing, what he thinks can and should be done about advertising's monopoly of the culture.*]

JHALLY: Cultural change takes time. The Left needs to see culture as a place where we have to battle. And we have to build new institutions that will be able to battle in that field. I'm trying to do it through the Media Education Foundation as one start. Of course, there's a risk in engaging in advertising, because the language may take you over. But there's no other choice right now; that is the language of the modern world, and we've got to use it.

Sports and Culture

Cultural Studies and the Sports-Media Complex[*]

Men make their own history, but not in conditions of their own choosing.

—Karl Marx

The Critical Legacy: Circuses, Opiates, and Ideology

On September 26, 1987, *The Nation* magazine, one of the leading voices on the American Left, editorialized against the decisions by both the *New York Times* and CBS to give priority to sports coverage over the coverage of "real" (political, economic, and social) events. While recognizing that the coverage of politics by these organizations leaves a great deal to be desired, the editors nonetheless reflected what has been the Left's attitude toward sports in noting that sports have come to usurp the role that politics had occupied in American public life and in noting disapprovingly that "it's more important for a paper of record to report ball scores than to analyze the week's events." Sports spectating is a deflection, an activity that channels potentially critical political activity into a safe and neutral realm. Sports have taken over the function in advanced capitalist societies that Marx believed religion fulfilled in the nineteenth century—an opiate of the masses—providing the basis for spectacular shows and circuses that narcotize large segments of the population. An unimportant area of life obscures a more fundamental and important one.

[*] This essay first appeared in *Media, Sports, & Society*, ed. L. Wenner (Newbury Park, CA: Sage Publications, 1989), pp. 70–93. Reprinted by permission.

Gary Whannel (1983) notes, however, that, at the same time that social-ists decry the importance that sports have achieved in social life, they are also attracted to the possibilities it opens up, of what could happen if that energy were directed to political activity instead. But that vision is a fantasy. The challenge for a cultural studies approach to sport is to use the fantasy creatively, to under-stand the context within which sports spectating, as a cultural activity, takes place, so that the domain of sport becomes not merely something to be deplored, but rather a site on which to fight for definitions of the social world. Such a proj-ect involves moving beyond the predominant circuses-and-opiates position. It also means moving beyond much of the work that has tended to characterize and define critical approaches to sport. Although simplifying an increasingly complex field, it is possible to identify two major themes in this literature: sports spectat-ing as (a) ritual and ideology and (b) compensatory fulfillment.

Much of the tacit background to critical work on sport as ideology and ritual is based upon a search for those factors that have prevented the economic con-tradictions of capitalism from being expressed in revolutionary movements. The orthodox argument runs that the ideological sphere of capitalism has prevented workers from seeing the reality of their exploitation and has convinced them to identify with the system that dominates them. Sport is a key institution in this process. Sports function as a form of celebration of the dominant order. Other writers have extended the analysis beyond the notion of ideology to that of rit-ual. Noting that all societies require ritualistic celebration of their central value systems, these writers focus on the role of sports in these processes. Michael Real (1975) labels sport a form of mythic spectacle and argues that

> in the classical manner of mythical beliefs and ritual activities, the Super Bowl is a communal celebration of and indoctrination into specific socially domi-nant emotions, life styles, values . . . all functional to the larger society. . . . Rather than mere diversionary entertainment, it can be seen to function as a "propaganda" vehicle strengthening and developing the larger social structure. (pp. 36, 42)

Richard Lipsky (1981) argues that the ability of sports to function as a social-izer of dominant values, as well as providing a form of refuge, is derived from its existence as a "dramatic life-world" in which the values of the larger society are highlighted and celebrated by being inserted into a different (human) context.

In a different vein, John Alt (1983) argues that, while, traditionally, Western sport has functioned as a ritual of liberal values, recent changes in the productive sphere of a corporate and bureaucratic society have led to a new role for spectator sports: that of compensatory fulfillment. Arguing that liberalism and its atten-dant ideologies of fair play and moral order have broken down in the face of the increasing bureaucratization of social life and its ends-oriented organization, Alt contends that sports now have to cater to the "new cultural-emotional needs of the masses." In short, as one part of the social world robs people of meaning and emotional gratification, another part offers it to them in the form of commodified spectacles. Sport offers excitement and emotional gratification denied to the citizens of a corporate society. We are back once again in the world of opiates.

This, then, is the legacy of a critical approach to sport. I do not want to deny the utility of such analyses or their many considerable insights into the role that sport plays in advanced capitalist societies. Indeed, later in this chapter, I hope to fill out in more detail the specifics of this ritualistic, escapist ideology. I do, however, want to insist that terms such as *ideology* are necessary but ultimately insufficient for a full understanding of the role that sports play in modern society and that the task now is to build on this base while, at the same time, overcoming the obstacles that it throws up.

The New Direction: Cultural Studies

One of the problems with the approaches outlined previously is that they have a tendency to treat the people involved in these ideological and ritualistic processes as largely passive, internalizing, and accepting the definitions of the situations presented to them. They also tend to be static and functionalist in their modes of explanation. While terms such as *power* (and even *manipulation*) are vital to a proper understanding of sport, we must treat them as dialectical notions, rather than as unidirectional and one-dimensional concepts.

The most ambitious attempt at this kind of reworking of the ideological and cultural sphere has been connected with British cultural studies, specifically with the writers associated with the Center for Contemporary Cultural Studies (CCCS) at the University of Birmingham in England (especially under the directorships of Stuart Hall and Richard Johnson). It is part of an attempt to shift the focus of debate from a concentration on ideology to one on *culture* and to focus on power from the viewpoint of contestation. Richard Johnson (1986–1987) stresses the following three premises as the minimum basis of critical cultural studies: (a) "Cultural processes are intimately connected with social relations, especially with class relations and class formations, with sexual divisions, with the racial structuring of social relations and with age oppressions as a form of dependency"; (b) "culture involves power and helps to produce asymmetries in the abilities of individuals and social groups to define and realise their needs"; (c) "culture is neither an autonomous nor an externally determined field, but a site of social differences and struggles" (p. 39).

Now, certainly, *culture* as a term cannot be used unproblematically in the sense that there is wide agreement as to what it means—there is not. Raymond Williams (1976) argues that it is one of the two or three most complicated words in the English language. Johnson recognizes this and suggests instead that cultural studies should focus on the terms *consciousness* and *subjectivity*, "with the key problems now lying somewhere in the relation between the two, . . . cultural studies is about the historical forms of consciousness or subjectivity, or the subjective forms we live by, or, in a rather perilous compression, perhaps a reduction, the subjective side of social relations" (1986–1987, p. 43).

For the study of sport, these are highly pertinent and relevant organizing terms. First, *consciousness* refers to the way in which we cognitively make sense of the world, the knowledge that we have of it, of how it works, and of our place in it. It is largely a conscious, known process. *Subjectivity*, on the other hand, refers to the absences in consciousness, or to the possibility that some things that move us (such as aesthetic or emotional life) remain consciously unknown to us. For Johnson, subjectivity "focuses on the 'who I am' or, as important, the 'who we are' of culture, on individual and collective identities" (1986–1987, p. 44). Sports certainly offer a mapping of the world, a way of understanding the social relations within which we live our lives, but, unlike other media messages (e.g., the news), sports also involve us in other ways. There are passions involved, emotional entanglements with the events that we witness that cannot simply be explained under terms such as *consciousness* and *ideology*. They are a part (for many people, heretofore largely male) of how social identity is formed.

Raymond Williams has coined two key terms (*way of life* and *structure of feeling*) that can describe this tension between consciousness and subjectivity. Williams (1961) stresses that a simple description of cultural phenomena will not be sufficient to understand those forms:

> Cultural history must be more than the sum of the particular histories, for it is with the relations between them, the particular forms of the whole organization, that it is especially concerned. I would then define the theory of culture as the study of relationships between elements in a whole way of life. . . . A key word, in such analysis, is pattern: it is with the discovery of patterns of a characteristic kind that any useful cultural analysis begins, and it is with the relationships between these patterns, which sometimes reveal unexpected identities and correspondences in hitherto separately considered activities, sometimes again reveal discontinuities of an unexpected kind, that general cultural analysis is concerned. (pp. 46–47)

Connected with this *way of life* is a *structure of feeling* that refers to the

> felt sense of the quality of life at a particular place and time: a sense of the ways in which particular activities combined into a way of thinking and living. . . . It is as firm and definite as "structure" suggests, yet it operates in the most delicate and least tangible parts of our activity. (p. 48)

Sports, perhaps more than any other cultural phenomenon, lie at this tension between consciousness and subjectivity, between *way of life* and *structure of feeling*.

While Williams has made an immense contribution to the development of cultural studies, I think it is fair to say that the very fierce critique of his work by E. P. Thompson has yielded just as valid contributions. In his now classic review of Williams's *The Long Revolution*, Thompson (1961) stresses (at least) three things in opposition. The first is with a concern to break with the literary tradition when talking of culture and to include within a *whole way of life* the terrain of everyday, concrete, practical cultural processes that are cut through and through with power. Second, while Williams coined the term *way of life*, Thompson insists on a corrective to a "whole way of conflict . . . a way of struggle." Third, uniting the first two, Thompson wants to substitute for Williams's abstract historical forces the idea that it is people who make history, rather than vice versa. Quoting Marx, he argues, "History does nothing, it possesses no immense wealth, fights no battles. It is rather *man*, real living *man* who does everything, who possesses and fights." (p. 33)

However, while Thompson is undoubtedly a key figure in the development of cultural studies, the inclusion of his concerns into an evolving theoretical framework depended, in part, on the appropriation by critical scholars of the newly translated work of the Italian Marxist Antonio Gramsci, whose key contribution to Western Marxism has clearly been the notion of *hegemony*. In many appropriations, this has simply been taken as a slightly more complex form of ideological domination. In contrast, Gramsci insisted that power and domination are always exercised in a combination of force and consent and that the two never operate in isolation. Hegemony consists, in part, of a class asserting intellectual and moral leadership in a particular period. This is not done in a way that simply *imposes* ideology on a passive and accepting subordinate class; instead, the hegemonic process is one of negotiation, compromise, and struggle in which the ruling class, or, more precisely, the ruling bloc, gives concessions in one area so that it may receive them in another.

Similar to Thompson, Gramsci (1971) also insists that, if and when hegemony is won, it operates not solely at the level of coherent philosophies, but at the level of everyday consciousness or common sense. To the extent that hegemony operates at this level, it becomes far easier to *naturalize* a particular way of defining things, because common sense is not coherent and does not have to be. It has been "inherited from the past and uncritically absorbed" (p. 333). It is the "way things are." Raymond Williams (1977) notes that, for Gramsci, hegemony

> is a lived system of meanings and values—constitutive and constituting—which as they are experienced as practices appear as reciprocally confirming. It thus constitutes a sense of reality for most people in society, a sense of absolute because experienced reality. (p. 110)

Similarly, John Hargreaves (1982b) argues the following:

It is easy to see how, from this point of view, popular culture, and specifically sport, could be given their proper share of attention alongside other cultural constituents of civil society, like language usage, formal and informal education, the media, habits and customs, etc., as resources out of which a class fashions its hegemony. (p. 115)

It was undoubtedly Gramsci's discussion of these issues that led Louis Althusser to his seminal redefinitions of the field of Marxist ideology studies and his reworking of the base/superstructure metaphor. Although, for many different reasons, Althusser's work, in recent years, has been much criticized and sometimes simply ignored, there is much of value that can be drawn from his writings. For example, Stuart Hall (1985) paraphrases Althusser's formulation of ideology in *For Marx* in the following way: as "systems of representation—composed of concepts, ideas, myths or images—in which men and women . . . live their imaginary relations to the real conditions of existence" (p. 103). Althusser (1977) argues that all societies (even socialist ones) require ideology, because the understanding of real conditions does not occur in any simple or direct way—there is no one understanding or experience of social existence that imposes itself in our minds in a direct, unmediated way: "It [ideology] is a structure essential to the historical life of societies" (p. 232). Our understanding of our conditions is always socially constructed. This does not mean that social relations are not real, that they do not exist separate from our understanding of them. As Hall says,

Social relations do exist. We are born into them. They exist independent of our will. They are real in their structure and tendency. . . . Social relations exist, independent of mind, independent of thought. And yet, they can only be conceptualized in thought, in the head. (1985, p. 105)

These real relations, however, do not declare their meanings directly and unambiguously. That is why Althusser calls ideology an *imaginary relation*. Ideology is *the* way that people live the relation between themselves and their conditions of existence. Moreover, this is not simply *false consciousness*, as in the traditional Marxist sense of ideology, because people have to *live* these imaginary relations; they have to survive and operate practically in the material world according to these imaginary relations. Ideology must then bear some relationship to real conditions, otherwise it could not work; it would fall apart as obviously false. This is the sense in which Althusser (1971) is able to talk about ideology not simply as abstract representations but as having a *material* existence in that ideas are lived out in practices:

The "ideas" of a human subject exist in his actions. . . . I shall talk of actions inserted into *practices*. . . . And I shall point out that these practices are governed by the *rituals* in which these practices are inscribed, within the *material existence of an ideological apparatus,* be it only a small part of that apparatus: a small mass in a small church, a funeral, a minor match at a sports' club, a school day, a political party meeting, etc. (p. 158)

From this context, it becomes easier now to make sense of Althusser's central claim that "ideology interpellates individuals as subjects." It is through ideology defined in this way that we recognize ourselves as socially constituted individuals in our own particular culture. We are again back to our starting terms of *consciousness* and *subjectivity.* Althusser writes the following:

> In truth, ideology has very little to do with "consciousness," even supposing this term to have an unambiguous meaning. It is profoundly *unconscious.* . . . Ideology is indeed a system of representations, but in the majority of cases these representations have nothing to do with "consciousness": they are usually images and occasionally concepts, but it is above all as *structures* that they impose on the vast majority of men, not via their "consciousness": They are perceived-accepted-suffered cultural objects and they act functionally on men via a process that escapes them. (1977, p. 233)

This formulation again has a great deal of relevance for the study of sport, precisely because it is viewed as separate from the rest of social life, it is viewed as neutral when it comes to issues of power and politics, and it works at multiple levels of social existence in a very powerful and profound way.

While Althusser tends to collapse the distinction between ideology and culture, other writers who have been influenced by his work insist on the analytic separation. For example, Clarke et al. (1976) define culture as "that level at which social groups develop distinct patterns of life and give *expressive form* to their social and material life-experience" (p. 10), distinguishing among the dominant culture, the class culture, and the youth subculture. It is the *relation* among them that is important to investigate. There is no straightforward passage from culture to ideology in this perspective. Paul Willis (1977) argues that the cultural level is a mediation through which wider structural determinants (class, gender, race, and so on) need to pass to reproduce themselves in distinct social ways. Moreover, the cultural level is not determined but is open for contestation. In relation to the key terms I have been working with here, perhaps the best formulation of this relation is to say that *ideology* is the form that *culture* takes in conditions of *hegemony.*

I have spent a good deal of time and space elaborating on some of the main features of cultural studies, because I believe that critical scholars of sport *must* address these issues, which have redefined the field. It is a framework that insists upon the cultural level as a place where people actively seek to understand the conditions of their existence, where social groups battle and struggle over the definitions given to social life, and where unequal access to the resources to accomplish this lead to the privileging of some groups' views over those of others. The production of culture (or cultural production) is an active process with no predetermined result that can be read from its relation to other levels of the social formation.

While insisting on the analytic necessity of terms such as *struggle* and *contestation*, we should take care not to privilege them in situations in which they are not to be found. Sports may be one of those arenas that is relatively free from real contestation. As Chas Critcher says,

> Sport is no longer, if it ever was, a major area of cultural contestation. . . . Change and tension are always evident but these are principally within rather than over sport. Understanding how and why this has happened remains an important question to those interested in understanding how capitalist culture works. (1986, p. 343)

The vital question then becomes, in what ways are some cultural forms taken out of the play of overt struggle?

Cultural Studies, the Media, and Cultural Commodities

These issues have specific reference to the study of sports. In the remainder of this chapter, I address the task of cultural studies in understanding sport, paying special attention to the role of the media.

I have not dealt specifically with the sports-media relation as yet, because I was concerned to establish the proper theoretical background that is necessary with regard to the broader field of cultural studies. However, as soon as we concentrate specifically on the subject of sports in capitalism, it becomes apparent that we can talk *only* about a *sports-media complex* (see Jhally, 1984). This can be (briefly) justified in two fundamental ways: (a) Most people do the vast majority of their sports spectating via the media (largely through television), so that the cultural experience of sports is hugely mediated, and (b) from a financial point of view, professional point of view, and, increasingly, collegiate point of view, sports are dependent upon media money for their very survival and their present organizational structure.

Within the tradition of cultural studies that I have been examining, there are a couple of models of media analysis that can be readily adapted for the study of mediated sport and that I will use in the following sections. Stuart Hall (1980) lays out what has become a very influential approach to media studies with his *encoding/decoding* model. Drawing upon Marx's model of the circuit of capital (production, circulation, distribution/consumption, and reproduction), and criticizing traditional mass communication sender/message/receiver models, Hall encourages us to think of the different moments of the communication process as "a 'complex structure in dominance,' sustained through the articulation of connected practices, each of which, however, retains its distinctiveness and has its own specific modality, its own forms and conditions of existence" (p. 128).

Richard Johnson (1986–1987) also draws upon Marx's model of the circuit of capital to suggest his own *circuit of culture* model, which bears many resemblances to Hall's, as well as exhibiting important differences (such as being able to be applied to cultural products in general and not simply media forms). The model

> represent[s] a circuit of the production, circulation and consumption of cultural products. Each box represents a moment in this circuit. Each moment or aspect depends upon the others and is indispensable to the whole. Each, however, is distinct and involves characteristic changes of form. It follows that if we are placed at one point of the circuit, we do not necessarily see what is happening at others. The forms that have most significance for us at one point may be very different from those at another. Processes disappear in results. (p. 46)

There are four moments of the process: (a) a focus on the production of cultural products, (b) a focus on the texts that are produced, (c) a focus on how these texts are read by ordinary people, and (d) a focus on *lived cultures* and *social relations* that relate to the *uses* made of the readings of texts, as well as being materials that new forms of cultural production can draw upon. It is with these types of understanding about the nature of this circuit of culture and the relations among the different moments that I shall proceed with the specific discussion of mediated sports.

Production: The Commodity Context

The cultural and ideological role of sport in advanced capitalism (especially in the United States) is impossible to understand without locating the centrality of commodity relations to the framework of which it is a part. If we follow through the political economy of professional and college sports, we will see that each stage is dominated by a concern with commodities. The overall *logic* is provided by the processes concerned with the circulation of commodities in general.

Corporations directly sponsor teams and events in the hope of attaching their names to the meaning of the particular activities. The auctioning off of the Los Angeles Olympics was perhaps the most spectacular example to date of this linking of the spheres of commerce and sports. (Its blatancy led some commentators to describe them as the "hamburger Olympics.") Indeed, given the prevalence of brand names in the athletic events themselves and the use made of sporting themes in the advertisements that appeared between the events, the blurring of the line between the two realms was so complete that, at times, it was difficult to tell exactly what one was watching.

In addition to the direct sponsorship of events, corporations also buy advertising time on broadcast media during sports programming. This is connected to the very elusive and concentrated audience that sports programming is able to capture. Sports constitute a very important part of the schedule of the major television networks, which sell the time of particular audience segments to corporations that wish to reach those people with advertising messages. The material importance of this relationship between sports and the media will vary from society to society, depending in large part on the extent of private versus public control of the broadcasting sphere. Where there is private control (with revenues being drawn largely from advertising), it will be very difficult to separate media from sports. Where there is public control of broadcasting (through the state), the relationship will be less important, because the media are not governed by the same criterion of programming *having* to create audience segments that advertisers want. There is thus, at present, a major difference between the United States and Western Europe when it comes to defining this relationship, although, as broadcasting in the latter increasingly falls into private hands, we can expect that difference to decrease (see Seifart, 1984). In the United States, not only does sports programming generate a great deal of revenue for the media, but the media can also advertise their own upcoming programs during sports events and thus increase ratings and advertising revenues for nonsports programming. This is what ABC was able to accomplish through its coverage of the 1984 Olympics.

Following from this, there is an argument that, because media revenues are so important to their functioning, professional sports have been *transformed* and changed, that something pure has been lost in their commercialization (Altheide & Snow, 1978). Such an argument detracts from the fact that sports have *always* been based on commercial relations. Professional sports depend on two kinds of commodity sales, the relative importance of which has shifted historically. First, they sell tickets to fans who come to see the live event. For the first thirty years of this century, the role of the media was basically to act as publicity agents for sports, to get people into the stadiums. (This is still largely the role of newspapers today.) Second, professional sports sell the rights to broadcast events to the media. Historically, this has become far more important (contracts can now run into the billions of dollars) and is the basis of the claim that the broadcast media have transformed sports. While this is undoubtedly a valid observation, it seems to imply that, before the influence of the media, there was something that was pure sports. But sports have always been tied into a commodity sphere of one kind or another, their shape and organization always dependent upon their level of profitability. In the latter period, the major commodity that sports sell has changed; it is not that sports have suddenly been inserted into a commercial realm. The question is to what extent these historical transformations constitute a qualitatively new stage for the domain of professional sports. This is a very interesting question that we have not yet really begun to answer. The field awaits a detailed historical study of the political economy of professional sports, as well as data on the extent of cross-ownership among the spheres of sports, media, and commerce.

While the commodity structure is an indispensable way of understanding the interlocking of sports, media, and commerce, it is also a useful way of looking at the role of individual players within this framework. The advertising revenues that manufacturers provide to media, who in turn buy broadcasting rights, is at the root of the sizable increases in player salaries over the last thirty years. The players then are able, like other workers, to sell their specialized labor power to employers for its market value. In addition to this, however, players are also trying to create a commodity that they can, in turn, sell—celebrity. In this way, players can obtain revenues directly from manufacturers that are interested in having famous players endorse their products. For many players, this may be of even greater value than higher sports salaries, in that they can trade in their celebrity for many years after they have finished playing.

The last major actor that needs to be understood in this commodity structure is the state. Although the state itself, in the United States, is not involved in the production and sale of commodities, it performs a vital function for the whole structure—it defines the *conditions* within which the other activities take place. With specific regard to the media and sport, we can identify three important areas. First, the state provides an exemption from antitrust legislation for sports leagues in their negotiations with television networks. This leads to far higher prices that networks have to pay, although they are guaranteed a nonfractioned audience (see Horowitz, 1978). Second, advertising expenditures by manufacturers are tax deductible as business expenses. If they were not, the whole structure of the sports-media complex would be altered, as the proportion of advertising revenues directed toward broadcast media would be much smaller. Third, the state can impose (or lift) restrictions on the types of products that can be advertised and the media that they can be advertised on and thus again can affect the amount of advertising dollars that the sports-media complex can attract.

There has been a great deal written about the effect that this commodity structure has had on the organization and nature of professional sports. It has led to sports leagues changing the rules of the game to provide a better television package; clubs moving from one city to another based not upon stadium support, but upon the television audience; the flow and momentum of the game being interrupted as the game is stopped for time-outs that are called so that television can show commercials; the creation and destruction of entire sports leagues based upon whether or not television support could be found; and the ability (or inability) of teams to sign players, depending on the size of the television market a team controls.

A corresponding view treats the process of the increasing commercialization of sports (largely through the media) as leading to a *massification* of sports, as the search now is for new mass audiences for advertisers, rather than the appeal to the so-called cultivated minority who really understand what sports are about. John Alt writes the following:

> The form of the spectacle—commodity rationalization—comes to envelop the structure of sports performances, shaping, changing, and altering the game to meet market and technical criteria. . . . Packaging the game, altering the rules and action, is undertaken to create special effects, usually in the form of visual-audial images. . . . In the extreme, the spectacle form reduces sport to its most banal and sensational elements as standards of excellence are repressed by commercial norms. (1983, p. 98)

Additionally, the increasing commercialization of professional sports has led to players' paying more and more attention to individual rather than team accomplishments and has changed the way that sports are played. Community and team loyalty are jettisoned in favor of self-identification in the building of celebrity.

Production: Encoding the Message

The last section looked at the wider constraints that are produced by the commodity-logic of the market selling on the way that sports appear to us in this society. In this section, I wish to focus on the more immediate and practical factors that affect the nature of the mediated sports message on television. The first point that needs to be made is simple but vital: Television does not present us with a sports event but with a sports event (already highly structured by the commodity-logic) that is *mediated* by television. A sports event is live and unscripted, and television is forced to provide its own structures and ideological viewpoints in a unique way. Directors, producers, camera operators, editors, and commentators are inserted between the live event and the home audience. As Stuart Hall notes,

> The production process is not without its "discursive" aspect: it, too, is framed throughout by meanings and ideas; knowledge-in-use concerning the routines of production, historically defined technical skills, professional ideologies, institutional knowledge, definitions and assumptions, assumptions about the audience frame the constitution of the programme through this production structure. (1980, p. 129)

Gary Whannel (1984) provides an illuminating example from the coverage of the 1980 Moscow Olympics of what happens when this hidden production process loses its internal unity. Soviet television provided the video pictures of the events, to which British television could add its own commentary. The agendas of these two institutions, however, were very different. While Soviet television wanted to present the games as being unaffected by the U.S.-led boycott, British television wished to emphasize their abnormal character. This led to an "enthralling television battle—a struggle between Soviet television and the British channels to define the meaning of the Games" (p. 36). As this example illustrates, the mediating production process is not a closed system. "They draw topics, treatments, agendas, events, personnel, images of the audience, 'definitions of the situation' from other sources and other discursive formations within the wider socio-cultural and political structure of which they are a differentiated part" (Hall, 1980, p. 129). In this sense, the encoding process involves precisely what it says—using *codes* (technical, organizational, social, cultural, and political) to produce a *meaningful discourse*. Wren-Lewis and Clarke (1983) offer a reading of the television coverage of the 1982 soccer World Cup from the perspective of the surrounding political context (the Malvinas/Falklands War). From the perspective of the Johnson model mentioned previously, this wider context from which materials are drawn would constitute the moment of lived cultures and social relations.

The existing research on this production moment of the circuit of culture is very sparse. The few studies that do exist tend to work back from the encoded messages to a reading of motives and practice. Peters (1976), Buscombe (1974), and Williams (1977) have conducted these kinds of studies. Whannel also works backward from the message to come up with four important aspects of television sports production:

> First, hierarchization, the process of signalling that some things are more important than others. Second, personalization, the presentation of events from an individualized perspective. Third, narrative, the telling of events in the form of stories. Fourth, the placing of events in the context of frames of reference. (Cantelon & Gruneau, 1988, p. 183)

In Canada, Rick Gruneau and Hart Cantelon are attempting at the present time the most ambitious and thorough analysis of TV sports from the viewpoint of production of which I am aware. This involves, among other things, a focus on the organizational structures of the sports commentators' booth through both ethnographic and interview research methods (in addition to content analysis of the actual encoded messages). Such a project is urgently required for the American situation also. Todd Gitlin (1983) has shown how this can be accomplished for the understanding of prime-time television. The time is ripe for an *Inside Sports Time* companion to his work.

The Texts of Mediated Sport

Within critical analyses of sports, the reading of sports (through the media or directly) for their ideological meanings has been very prominent, and these readings are very important follow-ups to the focus on production and encoding—a shift from process to product. As we have seen, there is no natural meaning of sport. The meaning of mediated sport is the outcome of a complex articulation of technical, organizational, economic, cultural, political, and social factors. There is nothing accidental about this process, and we should not forget, for all the stress on complexity, negotiation, and struggle, that this cultural production takes place within a *capitalist* context, where access to resources is differentially distributed. As Whannel notes,

> Sport offers a way of seeing the world. It is part of the system of ideas that supports, sustains and reproduces capitalism. It offers a way of seeing the world that makes our very specific form of social organization seem natural, correct and inevitable. (1983, p. 27)

Many writers have focused on this general ability that sports discourses have, because of the seeming separation of sport from other areas of life, to *naturalize* forms of organization that have a social and political basis. Despite increasing evidence to the contrary (boycotts, kidnappings, player strikes, and so on), the refrain to keep politics out of sport is still constantly heard. In the remainder of this section, I wish to highlight briefly some of the major tenets of this naturalized and ideological version of the world.

Militarism and Nationalism

Many major sports telecasts are saturated with militaristic values that start with the presentation of the colors or the flying overhead of fighter airplanes as "The Star-Spangled Banner" is sung. Again, I need to stress that this is simply not *showing* what is going on at the game: the television presentation of these events is normally *highly* technically mediated, with elaborate camera angles; overlapping pictures of players, flags, and weapons; and careful use of juxtaposition and dissolves. The Super Bowl especially seems to be inextricably tied up with this militaristic ideology. Writers have also noted the manner in which the very language of sports commentators embodies the vocabulary that one would actually expect of a society that houses the military and industrial complex at its heart. For example, in football, phrases such as "the bomb," "the aerial attack," "advancing into enemy territory," "the bullet pass," and "the offensive arsenal" are common ways of describing and interpreting the ostensibly sporting action (see Hoch, 1971).

A theme accompanying the militaristic one is, of course, the nationalistic one. This takes place in two related movements. First, "we" are separated from "them," the foreigners, through the use of stereotypical representations. "They" are different from us culturally and psychologically. Second, "we," who are separated from them, are drawn together under the mythical sign of the nation. This itself involves a two-step procedure. In the initial step, our real differences (of class, ethnicity, religion, and so on) are dissolved to create a false unity of nation (Americanness, Englishness, and so on). As Clarke and Clarke write of the English situation regarding this, the unity is not simply a sum of the different parts, but

> is structured in a particular direction. It draws its conceptions of Englishness from a specific set of social images and practices—those of the dominant social groups. Nationalism as an ideology works in two directions. One is to mark us off from the "others"—foreigners, strangers, aliens—it identifies and values what is unique to us. The other is to draw us together, to unite us in the celebration, maintenance and furtherance of "our" way of life. (1982, p. 80)

Competition and the Rules of the Game

At the heart of all sports is competition. The definition given to the form of the competition found in sports is thus an important dimension to their understanding. As for most factors involved in the analysis of cultural products, there is no single definition that holds cross-culturally. Joan Chandler (1983) argues that there are important differences between the United States and Britain in terms of the relationship between competition and social mobility and that these are reflected in the structures of competition found in their respective sports and the meanings given to them by the media.

In the United States, competition in sport is viewed essentially as competition between equals, without differential access to resources playing an important role. Moreover, the rules of the game are clear and neutral, so that the basis of the competition is unobscured. It is essentially *fair* competition, with the individual being the prime unit of action, so that failures become individual rather than social or class failures. The relationship of this kind of definition of competition to the way in which dominant groups would like to define competition in the wider economic, social, and cultural world is an important issue to discuss (see Jhally, 1988).

Labor, the Team, and Authority

One of the major themes in the critical analysis of sport is that sports reflect and celebrate the basic features of the capitalist labor process by presenting them in an idealized form. John Hargreaves summarizes this approach in the following terms:

> In their organization and functioning the major popular sports are seen as replicating all the fundamental features of modern nationalized industrial production: a high degree of specialization and standardization, bureaucratized and hierarchical administration, long-term planning, increased reliance on science and technology, a drive for maximum productivity, a quantification of

performance and, above all, an alienation of both the producer and consumer. (1982a, p. 41)

The media, with the constant stress on quantification of specialized performance, and the focus on the coaches and managers as being the place where decisions are made, ritually celebrate the most alienating features of the capitalist labor process. This is accomplished by a stress on the sports world as, above all, a *human* realm rather than a technical one. The media transform authority structures that are hierarchical and exploitative into ones that become identified by the personal and the human (see Lipsky, 1981). An abstract alienated authority is personally mediated by very visible owners and coaches who are not an impersonal corporate elite but concerned leaders who *care* along with the ordinary fans.

Gender

All societies differentiate along lines of sex. It is a universal marker of human identity. These biological divisions, however, do not have the same meaning cross-culturally. The social understanding of biological difference is what many writers have termed the domain of *gender*. This refers to the specific cultural and social meanings surrounding what it means to be male or female in any society. This is obviously a huge subject, and I do not want to do more here than give the briefest indication of the role that mediated sports play in the complex processes that produce this meaning. There are, I think, three analytical dimensions to the issues: (a) How do mediated sports define notions of masculinity? (b) How do mediated sports deal with the relation between male and female athletic performance? (c) How do mediated sports define notions of femininity? (For discussions of these issues, see Hargreaves, 1986; Sabo & Runfola, 1980; Willis, 1982.) Much important work remains to be done in this area.

Race

Mediated sports present perhaps the most visible arena for racial minorities. While, in many other cultural forms, minorities have a token role, in contemporary sports they play an absolutely fundamental role. As such, black players act as powerful role models for black youngsters. However, just as for gender, race in sport is defined within a hugely ideological field. In 1987, a major controversy was created by the insensitive (although entirely reflective of the group of which they are a part) remarks by Al Campanis and Jimmy "the Greek" Snyder on blacks not having the intellectual capabilities needed for managerial positions in sports. The absence of blacks from managerial posts and even from playing positions that stress decision making and thinking provides powerful definitions of the kinds of activities that particular groups of people are capable of performing. Again, in the 1987 basketball season, the accurate (although perhaps ill-timed) remarks of Dennis Rodman and Isiah Thomas—that white players (such as Larry Bird) are given credit for working hard to achieve what they have done, while black players (such as Magic Johnson) are credited with natural ability that did not have to be cultivated or worked upon—showed how sensitive minority groups are to media definitions. Again, much work remains to be done in this area.

Sports Culture and the Culture of Consumption

While the stress in this section has been on the meaning of the mediated sports text, we should not forget that one very important part of these texts is that of messages that principally concern commodities, rather than sports—the advertisements. There needs to be a focus on the manner in which the world of consumption articulates with the ideology of sports that we have been discussing (see Jhally, 1987). Especially important in this regard is the manner in which the essentially naturalizing form of sports ideology is attached to other (equally) political domains so as to render them natural as well. Rick Gruneau, writing of the 1984 Olympic Games, notes that

> the combination of the location in Los Angeles, the organization of the Games by a private corporation, the advertising strategies employed by Olympic and other sponsors, the style of the Reagan Presidency, and the frequent speculation on Olympic programs about the future financial careers of victorious athletes, all became elements in a common discourse. Within this discourse, the themes of athletic success, healthy lifestyles, community, and Olympic ideals were continually circuited back to the success of corporate capitalism and the values prominent in American consumer culture. . . . Sport, like art itself, has become drawn into the discourses of modern publicity—a vehicle for expressing the common sense of modern consumer culture. (1988, pp. 22–23, 26)

Readers and Decoding

The study of texts is important, but only to a point. It is very useful to know what a formal analysis can tell us about the structure and content of the message, but we cannot simply infer *audience* readings from *our* readings. As Fred Fejes (1984) has pointed out, however, the field of critical media studies has been very reluctant to take this step toward audience research (for good historical reasons). I think this step is now imperative, especially as regards the cultural understanding of sport. An ethnography of sports viewing and the manner in which media messages are a *part* of the process through which meaning is constituted have to be included in the future of critical cultural studies. If we take seriously Althusser's formulations on ideology as an imaginary lived relation, then we have to investigate the way in which sports discourses fit into the web of social practices of different groups. For instance, Althusser points out that the ruling classes do not propagate their ideology as a false myth but as the way in which they experience their real relations. They have to believe their own myths of freedom before they can convince others of them. Thus, in relation to sports, it is possible that, for example, images of competition are appropriated differently by groups in different social and class locations—the bourgeoisie see it as a reflection of existing relations, whereas others look to it as a realm of escape, where justice actually appears to prevail, unlike real life.

Moreover, there needs to be a recognition that sports is a realm of *popular pleasure*. People like sports. We need to focus on why some cultural forms become popular, become *principles of living*. Furthermore, "what are the *different* ways in which subjective forms are inhabited—playfully or in deep seriousness, in fantasy or by rational agreement, because it is the thing to do or the thing *not* to do" (Johnson, 1986–1987, p. 72)? There are real dangers associated with this move. A focus on the audience has the potential to elevate and to privilege the audience's own understanding of its situation in a way that divorces the analysis from the wider contextual conditions of power. Tania Modleski has warned of this recent trend in which, ostensibly, critical cultural studies come close to winding up as studies of "uses and gratifications" (1986).

To avoid these obvious temptations, we have to keep in mind two important analytical points. The first has to do with the nature of the texts that audiences decode. Although, in abstract theory, the meanings associated with these are open-ended, in concrete practice, social constraints act to close the range of possible meanings. Recognizing that texts are open to more than one interpretation, Stuart Hall warns that

> polysemy must not, however, be confused with pluralism. Connotative codes are *not* equal among themselves. Any society/culture tends, with varying degrees of closure, to impose its classifications of the social and cultural political world. These constitute a *dominant cultural order,* though it is neither univocal nor uncontested. This question of the "structure of discourses in dominance" is a crucial point. (1980, p. 135)

The second analytical point flows from the first: Audience readings take place in particular *conditions,* and the identification of these becomes vital. For instance, sports on television are a certain type of *watching,* where one's time is being sold to advertisers. What effect do the surrounding conditions have on the nature of our watching? Why are we watching rather than doing other activities? How have cultural patterns changed with the introduction of television? These questions (and many others that could be posed here) emphasize that *reading* takes place in certain social conditions that are connected to the way in which people live their everyday lives, and we cannot ask questions about audience decoding divorced from these wider questions. In general, we need to remember Richard Lipsky's (1981) insight that sports can both provide an escape from particular social conditions and be a powerful form of socialization back into those same conditions.

Lived Cultures and Social Relations

> In a "determinate" moment the structure employs a code and yields a "message": at another determinate moment the "message" via its decodings, issues into the structure of social practices. We are now fully aware that this reentry into the practices of audience reception and "use" cannot be understood in simple behavioral terms. The typical processes identified in positivistic research on isolated elements—effects, uses, "gratifications"—are themselves framed by structures of understanding, as well as being produced by social and economic relations, which shape their "realization" at the reception end of the chain and which permit the meanings signified in the discourse to be transposed into practice or consciousness (to acquire social use value or political effectivity). (Hall, 1980, p. 130)

Stuart Hall here has given us the challenge that a critical cultural approach must meet. Ultimately, all the analyses of production, texts, and audiences must be integrated and contextualized within the broader frame of how people live their lives and the constraints and possibilities imposed by wider social, cultural, political, and economic movements. I wish here to mention briefly *some* of the factors that a critical approach to mediated sports must consider in attempting this wider framing (in addition to all the ones previously mentioned).

The first issues are historical ones. Nicholas Garnham (1983) has noted that there is a *class* basis to cultural consumption. These issues need to be analyzed and linked to the distribution of what Pierre Bourdieu has called *cultural capital*. Additionally, we need to analyze the manner in which the arena of cultural consumption has shifted and changed through this century, especially since the introduction of television. Obviously, this will be linked to the process that has been labeled *the industrialization of culture*, in which cultural products are increasingly provided directly by the market, rather than by nonmarket areas of social life. This again is related to the declining importance of cultural institutions, such as the family, religion, and traditional working-class community. In the latter regard, Stanley Aronowitz (1988) has noted that, as the objective basis for working-class cultural life was eroded by economic movements in the 1950s, the locus of the new forms of community shifted to the emerging medium television, and that, although a coherent working-class no longer exists, the residual images of that culture are still present on TV in the guise of cop shows and the camaraderie associated with beer commercials. The relation of sports (especially its mediated, commercial form) to this disappearing cultural realm is a vital axis around which relevant research questions can be posed.

Questions need also to be posed in terms of the relations between the meanings of commercial sports and the shifting field of gender relations. Many writers have suggested that sports have become a refuge for men who are increasingly threatened by the appearance of new gender roles and relations. Whatever the merits of this kind of argument, we need answers to the question of why sports have become defined in the almost exclusively male manner in which they appear in our culture, as well as exploration of the historical shifts in the nature of this identity.

In more general terms, there needs to be an analysis of the relation between the predominant forms of mediated sports (the relative importance of baseball and football within popular culture in different historical periods) and the shifting nature of the surrounding social and economic relations. For instance, some writers, such as McLuhan, have argued that the emergence of football as the most popular sport in the past thirty years is connected to its being much more suited to television (*the medium is the message*) than other sports. Others have suggested that there is a close correlation between cultural forms and the wider economic system and that the emergence of football is strongly related to the shift from a competitive capitalism to its contemporary corporate and administered form. Again, we need to devote more thought to these issues.

There are also other, more contemporary issues. For example, why are sports so important as a form of nationalism, and what are their ideological and cultural links to the military-industrial complex? Also, in addition to the linking of sports discourses to the naturalizing of the commodity-form, the language of sports has also been used in other spheres, especially the political. Why has sports language become an important way to describe the activities of the state (see Balbus, 1975)? Similarly, issues connected to the arms race are often couched in sporting terms. In all these spheres, the key factor to be conceptualized is the nature of *competition* in these realms (which becomes increasingly more obscure) and the ability of sports to provide an illumination to the darkness (see Jhally, 1988). Again, the field awaits a close historical analysis of the changing nature of competition in many domains and the relation of this to the discourse of mediated sports competition.

Conclusion

Richard Johnson (1986–1987) has argued that cultural studies in general need to focus on two sets of questions. The first group has to do with the *use-values* of cultural forms and the issues of pleasure and popularity. The second group concerns the *outcomes* of these cultural forms. Do they lead to repression or freedom? How do they define social ambitions? Do they encourage a questioning of the existing social realm? Do they point to alternatives? Answers to these questions cannot be found by focusing on production or on texts or audiences alone: "They can best be answered once we have traced a social form right through the circuit of its transformations and some attempt to place it within the whole context of relations of hegemony within the society" (Johnson, p. 72). Ultimately, of course, for our purposes here, what is called for is a thorough, nonreductive analysis of the articulation of mediated sports to social, cultural, political, sexual, racial, and economic factors—in short, a totalistic theory of sport and society and sport *in* society. The basic analytical research framework outlined in this chapter should enable us to get started on this important work.

References

Alt, J. (1983). Sport and cultural reification: From ritual to mass consumption. *Theory, Culture and Society, 1*(3).

Altheide. D., & Snow, R. (1978). Sports versus the mass media. *Urban Life, 7*(2).

Althusser, L. (1971). Ideology and ideological state apparatuses. In L. Althusser, *Lenin and philosophy.* London: New Left.

Althusser, L. (1977). *For Marx.* London: New Left.

Aronowitz, S. (1988). Working class culture in the electronic age. In I. Angus & S. Jhally (Eds.), *Cultural politics in contemporary America.* New York: Routledge.

Balbus, I. (1975, March). Politics as sports. *Monthly Review.*

Buscombe, E. (Ed.). (1974). *Football on television.* London: British Film Institute.

Cantelon, H., & Gruneau, R. (1988). The production of sport for television. In J. Harvey & H. Cantelon (Eds.), *Not just a game.* Toronto: University of Toronto Press.

Chandler, J. (1983). Televised sport: Britain and the U.S. *Arena Review, 7*(2).

Clarke, A., & Clarke, J. (1982). "Highlights and action replays": Ideology, sport, and the media. In J. Hargreaves (Ed.), *Sport culture and ideology.* London: Routledge & Keagan Paul.

Clarke. A., Hall, S., Jefferson, T., Roberts, B. (1976). Subcultures, cultures, and class. In S. Hall & T. Jefferson (Eds.), *Resistance through rituals.* London: Hutchinson.

Critcher, C. (1986). Radical theorists of sport: The state of play. *Sociology of Sports Journal, 3*(4).

Fejes, F. (1984). Critical mass communications research and media effects: The problem of the disappearing audience. *Media, Culture and Society, 6*(3).

Garnham, N. (1983). Public service vs. the market. *Screen, 24*(1).

Gitlin, T. (1983). *Inside prime time.* New York: Pantheon.

Gramsci, A. (1971). *Selections from the prison notebooks.* London: Lawrence & Wishart.

Gruneau, R. (1988). Television, the Olympics, and the question of ideology. In R. Jackson & T. McPhail (Eds.), *The Olympic movement and the mass media.* Calgary, Canada: Olympic Organizing Committee and University of Calgary.

Hall, S. (1980). Encoding/decoding. In S. Hall et al. (Eds.), *Culture, media, language.* London: Hutchinson.

Hall, S. (1985). Signification, representation, ideology: Althusser and the post-structuralist debates. *Critical Studies in Mass Communication*, 2(2).

Hargreaves, Jennifer. (1986). Where's the virtue? Where's the grace? A discussion of the social production of gender relations in and through sport. *Theory, Culture and Society*, 3(1).

Hargreaves, John. (1982a). Sport, culture and ideology. In J. Hargreaves (Ed.), *Sport Culture and Ideology*. London: Routledge & Kegan Paul.

Hargreaves, John. (1982b). Sport and hegemony: Some theoretical problems. In H. Cantelon & R. Gruneau (Eds.), *Sport, culture and the modern state*. Toronto: University of Toronto Press.

Hoch, P. (1971). *Rip off the big game*. Garden City, NY: Doubleday.

Horowitz, I. (1978). Market entrenchment and the Sports Broadcasting Act. *American Behavioral Scientist*, 21(3).

Jhally, S. (1984). The spectacle of accumulation: Material and cultural factors in the evolution of the sports/media complex. *Insurgent Sociologist*, 12(3).

Jhally, S. (1987). *The codes of advertising: Fetishism and the political economy of meaning in the consumer society*. New York: St. Martin's.

Jhally, S. (1988, July). *Competition, sports and the commercialized media*. Paper presented at the annual meeting of the International Association for Mass Communication Research, Barcelona, Spain.

Johnson, R. (1986–1987). What is cultural studies anyway? *Social Text*, 16 (Winter).

Lipsky, R. (1981). *How we play the game*. Boston: Beacon.

Modleski, T. (Ed.). (1986). *Studies in entertainment*. Bloomington: Indiana University Press.

Peters, R. (1976). *Television coverage of sport*. Unpublished manuscript, Center for Contemporary Cultural Studies, Birmingham, UK.

Real, M. (1975). Super Bowl: Mythic spectacle. *Journal of Communication*, 25(1).

Sabo, D., & Runfola, R. (Eds.). (1980). *Jocks: Sports and male identity*. Englewood Cliffs, NJ: Prentice-Hall.

Seifart, H. (1984), Sport and economy: The commercialization of Olympic sport by the media. *International Review of Sport Sociology*, 3–4.

Thompson, E. P. (1961). The long revolution. [Book review]. *New Left Review*, 9–10.

Thompson, E. P. (1963). *The making of the English working class*. New York: Vintage.

Whannel, G. (1983). *Blowing the whistle*. London: Pluto.

Whannel, G. (1984). The television spectacular. In A. Tomilson & G. Whannel (Eds.), *Five ring circus: Money, power, politics at the Olympic Games*. London: Pluto.

Williams, B. (1977). The structure of televised football. *Journal of Communication*, 27(3).

Williams, R. (1961). *The long revolution*. New York: Columbia University Press.

Williams, R. (1976). *Keywords*. New York: Oxford University Press.

Williams, R. (1977). *Marxism and literature*. New York: Oxford University Press.

Willis, P. (1977). *Learning to labor*. New York: Columbia University Press.

Willis, P. (1982). Women in sport in ideology. In J. Hargreaves (Ed.), *Sport, culture and ideology*. London: Routledge & Kegan Paul.

Wren-Lewis, J., & Clarke, A. (1983). The World Cup: A political football. *Theory, Culture and Society, 1*(3).

Sports and Cultural Politics: The Attraction of Modern Spectator Sports[*]

with Bill Livant

The socialist tradition is based upon a vision of a society of freely associated producers, a society founded upon cooperative productive relations and the extension of cooperation to the whole of social life. Consequently, the socialist tradition has tended to view negatively competitive productive relations and competition in social life. Progress in social relations (the progress toward socialism) is seen as a movement away from competition and toward cooperation. Socialists evaluate social progress as the elimination, the withering away, of competition from social life. The struggle for socialism is the struggle to remove the competitive fetters to cooperation: first and foremost, the competition of classes.

It is because socialists wish to eliminate competition in practice (i.e., wish that it were not there) that they also tend to erase it in theory and to examine presently existing competition through a biased haze. This makes it difficult to consider competition *dialectically*, to examine the mutual relations, the interdependence of competition and cooperation in any particular sphere of social life. Nowhere is this undialectical consideration of competition clearer than in the critical analysis of *sports*, one of the areas of social life in which competition is most prominent and visible and to which it seems intrinsic under present

[*] This essay first appeared in *Rethinking Marxism* 4, no. 4 (1991): 121–127. Reprinted by permission.

conditions. Sports are an area in which the repugnance of critical socialists to competition is most manifest. Indeed, for a long time, even the very importance of sports was ignored. However, as spectator sports have become one of the most prevalent features of modem societies, radical thinkers have turned their critical attention to it (albeit largely to deplore it). Competition in sports is seen as a mirror reflection of capitalist productive and gender relations. Examined *culturally*, mass-spectator, televised, professional sports are part of the system of legitimation of contemporary capitalism. As British cultural critic Garry Whannel writes in his book *Blowing the Whistle,*

> Sport offers a way of seeing the world. It is part of the system of ideas that supports, sustains and reproduces capitalism. It offers a way of seeing the world that makes our very specific form of social organization seem natural, correct and inevitable. (1983, p. 27)

Spectator sports thus are *part of the problem* of contemporary social life, and, aside from a few derogatory comments, their analysis is not high on the agenda of a progressive cultural politics.

Within the domain of progressive publications, *Zeta* magazine, a Boston-based monthly, is therefore quite unique in that it has a semiregular column that deals with sports in a serious way; in the June 1989 issue, Matthew Goodman poses a fundamental question to those of us on the Left who like/watch/follow/enjoy sports: Are U.S. sports worth supporting? Positing two views of sport, one based on cooperation and camaraderie, the other based on greed, individualism, and competition, Goodman notes with dismay that American sports are being pushed more and more in the latter direction, and, consequently (and sorrowfully), he is having serious doubts about his status as a fan. In raising these important questions, Goodman is raising the paradox that Ike Balbus identified as long ago as 1973 (in his review of Paul Hoch's *Rip-Off the Big Game*) when he pointed to the phenomenon of the *radical as sports fan*—the person who criticizes all institutions of capitalist society but who still loves sports.

While Goodman has raised an important point, he may have posed the wrong question. It is not a matter of whether one should or should not support sports but of what form the struggle over the definition of sports should take. Unless one simply wishes to abandon sport as an area of contestation, the question is really one of *cultural politics:* are sports worth struggling over? We believe they are, because sports may be not simply part of the problem, but also *part of the solution* to the transition to a more just society. Above all, sports are a realm of *popular pleasure* in contemporary life. It is tapping into the nature of the attraction that may give us an answer to the question concerning the role that sports can play in a progressive cultural politics. Indeed, we believe that at the heart of the attraction of modern sports lies a vision of *socialism* and *socialist competition.* The struggle is over how to recover presently existing competitive sports for a positive socialist vision and to show how this vision is itself central to the attraction to sports, to the love of sports in the population. This requires that we examine closely the way in which competition presents itself in sports and daily life as both different and identical.

The Difference between Sports and Life: The Heaven of Sports

There is an intrinsic relation between sports and competition. Sports are fundamentally about competition. Any attempt to clarify the nature of sports and their immense appeal must clarify the nature of competition. To do this, we must first put away our petit bourgeois panic about competition and ask the important question: how does competition appear to the population in sports compared to daily life, such that people identify and seek refuge in sports competition? There are three aspects to the comparison.

First, in daily life, competition is very rarely direct but is experienced in a *mediated* form. We compete for jobs, raises, promotions, security, and status and against a foggy field of competitors whom we do not even know. Most of our behavior in markets is in just this situation. In sports, on the other hand, competition is most often *direct and unmediated*. We can see the competitors; we can see the interdependency of their performances. The competitors and their interdependence seem to us direct, in contrast to the pea soup of mediations that mask our competition in daily life.

Second, in daily life, the *basis* of competition is obscure. We are mostly in the dark about what it takes to succeed at it, to win, or even to survive. The process of capitalism itself constantly mystifies the basis of success and constantly generates new mysteries. People have little secure basis that whatever they are doing will give them a better chance to succeed. The basis of competition is mystified. In sports, the basis of competition seems to be present, to be open to observation. The rules are clear, and there seems to be an objective basis for the judgment of competition. This is rare in competition in daily life.

Third, in daily life, because the competition is mediated, and because the basis of competition is obscure, our emotional involvement is highly *unpleasant*. We have to compete against competitors that are largely unknown, on an unknown basis, with little idea of what we have to do to win. And we *have* to compete. If we fail to compete, or if we do compete and then fail, very unpleasant things happen to us. We lose face, money, position, power . . . even sexual attractiveness (for men). The field of competition is obscure, the penalties severe. Because we cannot see clearly, and because it matters so much, the state of our emotions is both intense and confused. The state of our emotions is unpleasant. But, in sports, this is not so. Our emotional involvement is highly *pleasant*. The competition seems clear to us, and we think we know what it is about. When we, as spectators, enter it and identify with it, our emotions are focused and not muddled. Best of all, we can play and not lose, just because we are spectators.

The secret, then, of the immense attractiveness of sports is that they present a *spectacle of unmystified competition*. It is around this image that people unite. In sport, it seems to us that, unlike life, we can see how society works, we can see who are the competitors, we can see what it takes to win. To see these things has enormous effects on us. It makes us feel smart; it makes us feel sane. In short, it makes us happy. Sports cannot show us how our society *really works*. But they can show us how we *desire* it to work. We desire a society of unmystified competition. The attraction of sports is founded upon its seeming clarification of the alienated relations of competition of modern society.

At the same time, these sports also socialize us into tolerating and enduring competition as we experience it in daily life, by encouraging us to conceive our chaotic, obscure conditions of daily competition along the model of sports competition. But what is this model, and whence does it come? We have argued previously that competition in sports seems to be unmystified and that we can really know how it works. Indeed, where, in our everyday grapplings with competition, are we granted the luxury, the clarity, of an *instant replay*, a replay that gives us a basis to sit in judgment—*informed judgment*—not only on the players, but on the very authorities constituted to judge the game? This constitutes power, the *power of reason*. (The controversy over whether to allow instant replays into the sport itself is very interesting, i.e., how should the contradiction between reason and constituted authority be handled?) And we participate in this power of reason; it empowers *us*. Where, in everyday capitalist life, can we sit in judgment on the invisible powers who sit in judgment on us? The seeming reason of competition in sports empowers us in another way. Because the competition seems clear, *justice can be done*. The outcome is fair, the win was earned, and the winner deserved to win. In sports competition, it seems to us that reason prevails, justice is done, and we can understand it all. And we hunger for this. Sports competition is the *heaven* of competitive reason and justice, as life is its *hell*. Hence, sports are immensely attractive. They provide both an *escape* from hell and a *socialization* into living with it. Hidden in our hunger for this heaven is the hope that the present hell could be remade in the image of heaven. In fact, hidden in our love of sports is the hope of *socialism*.

We can see the great difference between competition in sport and life if we turn the tables. Try to imagine sports competition with the mystified characteristics that we find in real life. We find it impossible to do. Sports would not work in such darkness. But capitalism does, day after day. This is the reason why our rulers propagate the image of competition in sports as indeed the image of competition in life. In every sphere of life (including war), Nixon, Reagan, and Bush Sr. reach for the language of sports to describe the most atrocious deeds. (To explain his intransigence concerning negotiations during the Persian Gulf War, George Bush Sr. reverted to the explanation of "having a game plan and sticking by it" and the jock-culture macho phrase of "kicking ass." Indeed, especially during the early weeks of the war, the language of sports was very visible in media reports.) The *terrible simplifiers* seemingly make life clearer by describing them as sport. There is a good basis for this: Sports competition *is* clearer. Hence, our rulers try to get us to imagine real competition, our real darkness, with the clarified characteristics that we find in sports competition. We are attracted to sports because their competition is different from our present social life. Sports are clear; our social life is dark. But we are forced to live that life whose ruling ideology only makes it darker. We are constantly told that the dark competition of our lives is as clear as sport.

The Identity of Sports and Life: The Private Appropriation of Collective Activity

So far, we have stressed the difference between competition in sports and daily life. Where this life is dark, there will be a limit to the light that sport can shed on the nature of competition. It is important to discover this limit, this boundary of light from darkness, because it is, in fact, a boundary between *resistance* and *submission* to the system of social life in the sphere of sport. To discover this boundary, we need to separate the *division of labor* in sport from its *appropriation*. We noted previously that, in sports, one can see the competition in an unmediated fashion. In fact, examined closely, we can see that competition (any competition) is a *collective* activity, a collective labor in which the contributions of the winner and the loser are interdependent. The collective nature of competition is central to the experience of sports. One-sided contests in which the collective activity is subordinated are uninteresting. We need only ask the television networks about the drop in viewers during an event as one side overwhelms the other. As all professional sports leagues know, it is competitive balance that is vital to the health and profitability of a league. (In the United States, the draft system is the most obvious tool toward this competitive balance.) The great sports events of our culture are those that have balanced competition at their heart.

For example, one of the most historic and memorable tennis matches in recent history was the 1980 Wimbledon final in which Bjorn Borg defeated John McEnroe. What that match indicated was not that Borg was a great player but just how great, in fact, he was. Borg needed McEnroe to push him to new heights of achievement. If Borg had routinely won in four sets, as at one time looked likely, that match would not stand out in our collective sports memory. But because McEnroe won the fourth set tiebreaker 18 to 16, he forced Borg to be even better. Whatever *beauty* we perceive in the realm of sports is dependent on both competitors. In his superb autobiography *The Game*, Ken Dryden, ex-goaltender for the Montreal Canadiens hockey team, writes of how his greatest moments occurred against Boston teams and that, without the tremendous opposition they provided, he could not have performed as he did. He needed their competition for the fulfillment of his own dreams.

What people are attracted to in sports, then, is the beauty of collective activity. They are drawn to the *process* of competition rather than to its results. We see beauty as a property of the personality, of the competitor, *in competition*. Not apart from the competition, but within it. Beauty therefore is a property *of the competition*, which is manifest through the competitors. When we perceive beauty in sports, the beauty of the competitors is the *figure*, and the beauty of the competition is the *ground*.

In a capitalist society, however, it is the private appropriation of social labor that is the determining feature, and, hence, in capitalized sports, it is the winners who appropriate the results of the process of competition. The winners go on to something better. They will appear again next week. They can convert their winning notoriety into sponsorship of commodities and so reap greater benefits and even more visibility for their appropriation of the results of collective activity. The losers disappear from view, their fate too desperate to be contemplated. As George Allen once remarked famously in reflecting the ethos of U.S. culture, "Losing is worse than death. You have to live with losing." The more this private appropriation occurs, the more the very existence of this ground, not to speak of its collective character, is suppressed, and the more the beauty is presented to us *only* as the property *of the competitors*. It is the private nature of appropriation that suppresses the collective character of beauty. It suppresses the beautiful character of the competitive *process* and reproduces beauty as an attribute of the competing *subjects*.

The rejection of competitive sports by critical socialists is based upon a failure to distinguish the process from the appropriation of its results. When we cannot distinguish between the process and the competitors, it will appear to us that properties that belong to the labor process as such belong only to the competitors. The labor process, the cooperative-competitive process, then appears only as a scene in which these *preexisting* properties of the competitors simply display themselves. Hence, what is really *social* labor appears decomposed into merely *individual* labor. Because the winner takes all, it appears that he or she does all, a process that we can label as the *personalization of competition*.

Personalization might almost be called a U.S. trademark, a concept at the core of all its major cultural conceptions. It is inevitable in a society that virtually denies that classes exist. This is the point of identity between our sports and our social life. Sports may be clear and open to everyone in specifying their competitors, in framing their rules, in recording and measuring their process and their outcomes. In all of this, sports make competition light. But sports share the mystification,; they reproduce the darkness of competition in the personalization of competition.

The North American sports-media complex embodies a highly *capitalized* system of sport. The more capitalized is sport, the greater the contradiction between the cooperative labor of the competitive process in sport and the private appropriation of its result. The greater this contradiction, the more the image of competition is personalized. This process of personalization is important; it forms the major basis on which the audience identifies with the sport. A particularly horrendous example is the behavior of many parents, contrasted with their children, in Little League. The kids, as often as not, focus on the competition. They want to play the game. But the parents do not. Wedded to the personification of competition is parental attachment to the child; perhaps through the child is attached the parent's own ego. The kids wish to be left alone to play and to enjoy the game. The innocent want the process while their parents want the result.

To summarize, the image of competition in sport, unlike its image almost everywhere else, is an image of *fair* competition. This is not merely an image; to an important degree, sport *embodies* this. But this is a limited fairness. Sports reproduce the social mystification of competition by personalizing a process of social cooperation. In fact, we may argue that, in this fundamental respect, sports are darker than competition in everyday life. Precisely because sports competition is fair, it personalizes competition *more* than does everyday competition, in all its darkness. Thus, sports are an area of capitalist social life with contradictory possibilities for changing that life. And we can only begin to grasp the outlines of the nature of socialist sport and socialist competition. Socialist competition in sport is *uncapitalized* competition. As such, it makes manifest, makes visible, what now must be extracted from the present structure of competition by analytical labor—the actual basis of competition as cooperative social labor. Such *unalienated, unmystified competition* is, in fact, compatible with the fact that competition continues under socialism: from each according to their ability, to each according to their work.

The Battle for Definitions of Sports

In this paper, we have stressed the progressive possibilities that exist in sports. The visions that we see in sports, the visions that attract us to it (and there are others that we have not listed, such as the cooperation involved in team sports), are visions of what a progressive socialist society would look like. Socialists should take advantage of these possibilities, for at the very heart of the mass spectacles that are designed to narcotize the population from open rebellion are images of what a transformed capitalism could look like. Sports provide images of what competition and cooperation would look like in another social setting. Role models with these potentialities should not be ignored. The definitions of what sports are about are definitions that should be fought and struggled over. As Gramsci noted, the *superstructures* are the *site* of class struggle, and we should not ignore an institution that shows, in spectacular fashion, the nature of a progressive society that might follow the present one. We should especially not ignore this possibility when people identify themselves so strongly with that world. If only the nature of the attraction could be made clear and a course outlined where life would imitate in a true fashion the utopian dream of sports. That is the political struggle over sports. It is one of the crucial sites of a progressive cultural politics.

References

Balbus, I. (1973, May 7). The American game of life. *The Nation*.
Dryden, K. (1983). *The game*. Toronto: Totem.
Whannel, G. (1983). *Blowing the whistle*. London: Pluto.

Gender

Advertising, Gender, and Sex

What's Wrong with a Little Objectification?*

I start this paper with an assumption: Advertising is a very powerful form of social communication in modern society. It offers the most sustained and most concentrated set of images anywhere in the media system. The question that I wish to pose and attempt to give an answer to from this assumption is what lies behind the considerable *power* that advertising seems to have over its audience. Particularly, I wish to do this without reverting back to one-dimensional explanations of manipulation and the use of sophisticated techniques by advertisers. I do not want to deny this element (there is, of course, a huge amount of accumulated knowledge in the advertising industry concerning persuasion), but I wish to probe *culturally* rather than technically.

   Erving Goffman, in his book *Gender Advertisements* (1979), was concerned with similar types of questions, although he did not phrase them in the same way. He instead asked another question: Why do most ads not look *strange* to us? Goffman believes that, when we look at ads carefully, they are, in fact, very strange

* This essay first appeared in *Working Papers and Proceedings of the Center for Psychological Studies*, vol. 29, ed. R. Parmentier and G. Urban (1989). Reprinted by permission.

creations, particularly in regards to their portrayals of gender relations. He shows us that, in advertising, the best way to understand the male–female relation is to compare it to the parent–child relation in which men take on the roles of parents, whereas women behave as children normally would be expected to. In advertising, *women are treated largely as children.*

Goffman supports his argument by pointing to a number of aspects of gender relations in advertising. For instance, in examining the portrayal of hands, he finds that women's hands are usually shown just caressing an object or just barely touching it, as though they were not in full control of it, whereas men's hands are shown strongly grasping and manipulating objects. Goffman is concerned with what such social portrayals say about the relative social positions of men and women. Beds and floors, for example, are associated with the less clean parts of a room; also, persons using them will be positioned lower than anyone who is sitting or standing. A recumbent position also leaves people in a poor position to defend themselves and thus puts them at the mercy of others. These positions are of course also a "conventionalized expression of sexual availability" (1979, p. 41). Goffman's sample of ads shows that women and children are pictured on beds and floors much more than are men. In addition, women are constantly shown drifting away mentally while under the physical protection of a male, as if his strength and alertness were enough. Women are also shown in the finger-to-mouth pose, directly reminiscent of children's behavior. Furthermore, when men and women are shown in physical contact, invariably, the woman is snuggling into the man in the same way that children solicit protection and comfort from their mothers.

If grown women are largely treated as children in ads, why does this not look strange to us? Goffman comments that, indeed, the most negative statement that we could make of advertisements is that, *as pictures of reality,* they do not look strange to us. To answer this question, he reverts back to the vocabulary of social anthropology, particularly the concepts of ceremony, display, and ritual. These are actions or events that seek to give structure and stability to a shared social life, to communicate the system of meaning within which individuals are located and within which they must be viewed. It is the use of this cultural resource that makes ads resonate with meaning for the audience. Ad maker Tony Schwartz has given the most eloquent expression of this *resonance theory* of communication, whereby "the critical task is to design our package of stimuli [ads] so that it resonates with information already stored within an individual and thereby induces the desired learning or behavioral effect" (1974, p. 25) Schwartz's concern is not with the message itself as a communicator of meaning, but rather with the use-value of the message for the audience:

> The meaning of our communication is what a listener or viewer *gets out* of his experience with the communicator's stimuli. The listener's or viewer's brain is an indispensable component of the total communication system. His life

experiences, as well as his expectations of the stimuli he is receiving, interact with the communicator's output in determining the meaning of the communication. (p. 25)

The job of the advertiser is to understand the world of the segmented audience, so that the stimuli that is created can evoke the stored information: It has to resonate with information that the listener possesses. However, we should not confuse this *resonance* with *reflection*. As adman Jerry Goodis says, "Advertising doesn't always mirror how people are acting, but how they're dreaming. . . . In a sense, what we're doing is wrapping up your emotions and selling them back to you" (Nelson, 1983, p. C2).

Thus, advertising draws its materials from the experiences of the audience, but it reformulates them in a unique way. It does not reflect meaning but rather constitutes it. Advertisers, according to Schwartz, should be in the business of "structured recall." The purpose is to design commercials that create pleasurable emotions that will be triggered when the product is viewed in the marketplace. As Schwartz says, "I do not care what number of people remember or get the message. I am concerned with how people are affected by the stimuli" (1974, p. 69).

Goffman is particularly interested in how advertisers use the cultural resource of gender and how they reconstitute what gender means in social terms. While *sex* refers to the biological distinction between males and females, *gender* is the culture specific arrangement of this universal relationship. Specific relations between men and women are very different around the world and can be given many different definitions depending upon the specific cultural pattern that exists in any society. Of course, there is nothing *natural* about gender relations—they are socially defined and constructed. As such, any culture must constantly work to maintain existing gender relations. This is achieved during the course of social life by *gender displays*—conventionalized portrayals of the culturally established correlates of sex. In our daily interactions, we are constantly defining for ourselves and other people what it means to be male and female in this society. From the way we dress, the way we behave, and the structure of our interactions to things such as body postures and ceremonial activities (opening doors, giving up chairs, etc.), we are communicating ideas about gender by using culturally conventionalized routines of behavior. These displays, or *rituals of gender behavior*, help the interpretation of social reality; they are guides to perception. It is from these conventionalized portrayals of gender that advertising borrows so heavily, and that is the reason why, according to Goffman, most ads do not look strange to us, for they are an extremely concentrated reflection of one aspect of our social lives—they are a reflection of the realm of gender displays. Advertisers largely do not *create* the images they depict out of nothing. Advertisers draw upon the same corpus of displays that we all use to make sense of social life. "If anything, advertisers conventionalize our conventions, stylize what is already a stylization, make frivolous use of what is already something considerably cut off from contextual controls. Their hype is hyper-ritualization" (1979, p. 84).

This, however, is not merely a simple reflection of reality—ads are neither false nor true. As *representations*, they are necessarily abstractions from what they reflect. Indeed, all communication is an abstraction at some level. For too long, the debate on gender has been focused on the extent to which advertising images are true or false. Ad images are neither false nor true reflections of social reality, because they are in fact *a part of social reality*. Just as gender displays are not true or false representations of real gender relations, neither are ads true or false representation of real gender relations or of ritualized gender displays—they are *hyperritualizations* that emphasize some aspects of gender displays and deemphasize others. As such, advertisements are part of the whole context within which we attempt to understand and define our own gender relations. They are part of the process by which we learn about gender.

In as far as our society defines sex as gender through culture (and not through biology or nature), we are not fundamentally different from any other past or present society. All cultures have to define gender for their own purposes, and they all have conventionalized forms to accomplish this socialization. Gender relations are social and not natural creations in any setting.

However, I believe that our culture is different in one very important sense. Gender is only one aspect of human individuality; political, occupational, educational, creative, artistic, religious, and spiritual aspects, among others, are also very important elements of individuals' lives. Human existence is potentially very wide and very varied in the experiences it offers. In our culture, though, advertising makes the balance between these things very different—indeed, everything else becomes defined through gender. In modern advertising, gender is probably the social resource that is used most by advertisers. Thousands of images surround us every day of our lives and address us along gender lines. Advertising seems to be *obsessed* with gender.

There are two reasons for this obsession. First, gender is one of our deepest and most important traits as human beings. Our understanding of ourselves as either male or female is the most important aspect of our definition of ourselves as individuals. It reaches deep into the innermost recesses of individual identity. Second, gender can be communicated at a glance (almost instantly) because of our intimate knowledge and use of the conventionalized codes of gender display. Advertisers are trying to present the world in ways that could be real (Goffman calls ads "commercial realism"), and so they are forced to draw upon the repertoires of everyday life and experience. What better place to draw upon than an area of social behavior that can be communicated almost instantly and that reaches into the very core of our definition of ourselves? As Goffman writes,

> one of the most deeply seated traits of man, it is felt, is gender; femininity and masculinity are in a sense the prototypes of essential expression—something

that can be conveyed fleetingly in any social situation and yet something that strikes at the most basic characteristics of the individual. (1979, p.7)

While every culture has to work to define for its members what gender relations should be, no other culture in history, I believe, has been this obsessed with explicit portrayals of gender relations. Gender and (because of the way in which gender has been narrowly defined) sex have never been as important as they are in our culture. Never in history has the *iconography* of a culture been so obsessed or possessed by questions of sexuality and gender. Through advertising, questions of sex and gender have been elevated to a *privileged* position in our cultural discourse.

The reasons why this should be the case are not mysterious. First, the discourse through and about objects that is a part of the cultural discourse of any society comes to be defined largely through marketplace information in the consumer society. That is, it fills the void that is left when the traditional institutions that provided this meaning decline in influence (see Jhally, 1987). Within the domain of advertising, imagistic modes of communication historically have become more important, as has the need for concentrated or instant forms of communication (see Leiss, Kline, & Jhally, 1986). Gender communication meets the needs of advertising very nicely here.

This may also offer an answer as to the source of the power of advertising. The representations of advertising are part of the context within which we define our understanding of gender. Advertising draws us into *our* reality. As Judith Williamson writes on this point,

> Advertising seems to have a life of its own; it exists in and out of other media, and speaks to us in a language we can recognize but a voice we can never identify. This is because advertising has no "subject." Obviously people invent and produce adverts, but apart from the fact that they are unknown and faceless, the ad in any case does not claim to speak from them, it is not their speech. Thus there is a space, a gap left where the speaker should be; and one of the peculiar features of advertising is that we are drawn in to fill that gap, so that we become both listener and speaker, subject and object. (1978, pp. 13–14)

We do not *receive* meaning from above, we constantly recreate it. It works through us, not at us. We have to do the work that is not done by the ad, "but which is only made possible by its form." We are drawn "into the transformational space between the units of the ad. Its meaning only exists in this space; the field of transaction; and it is here that we operate—*we are this space*" (Williamson, 1978, p. 44). This crucial mediation by the audience is the basis of what Schwartz calls *partipulation,* whereby the ad does not manipulate the audience but invites their participation in the construction of meaning. It is also behind Marshall McLuhan's notion that the audience works in the consumption of the television image. These systems of meaning from which we draw the tools to complete the transfer are referred to by Williamson as *referent systems*. They constitute the body of knowledge from which *both* advertisers and audiences draw their materials. As such, mass media advertising literally plays the role of a mediator. For the audience to properly *decode* the message (transfer meaning), advertisers have to draw their materials from the social knowledge of the audience and then transform this material into messages (*encode*), developing appropriate formats and shaping the content in order that the process of communication from *audience to audience* be completed (Hall, 1980).

The question is what gets changed in this process? For clearly advertising does not and cannot *reflect* social reality. As hyperritualistic images, commercials offer an extremely concentrated form of communication about sex and gender. The *essence* of gender is represented in ads. That is the reason why advertising is relatively immune from criticism about its portrayals of gender. The existing feminist critiques, those based on the content analysis of occupational roles in ads and those that focus on the forms of the objectification of women, are pitched at an intellectual level that does not recognize the emotional attraction of the images. We cannot deny the messages of advertising; we cannot say that they are false, because they bear some resemblance to ritualized gender relations. Furthermore, we cannot deny them, because we define ourselves at our deepest level *through the reality of advertising*. We *have* to reach a socially accepted understanding of gender identity in some way. It is not an option one can refuse. If we do not cope at this level, then the evidence suggests that it is very difficult to cope at any level. Gender confusions cloud the entire domain of social identity for individuals. To completely deny the messages of advertising is to deny our definition of ourselves in gender and sexual terms—it is to deny ourselves as socially recognizable individuals in this culture. As Wendy Chapkis writes in her book *Beauty Secrets*, "The most important function of gendered appearance is to unambiguously distinguish men from women" (1986, p. 129). If the dominant definitions of gender are not accepted, deviant individuals are relegated to the perverted section of our culture (e.g., transsexuals and transvestites). I believe that is the reason why the feminist critiques concerning regressive representations in advertising have not been very successful; they have not recognized the basis of its *attraction*. The attraction for both men and women is important to recognize, although it is, of course, varied in its specific focus: In terms of the representation of women, men want possession of what they see, whereas women identify with it.

If the critique does not recognize this attraction, then the attack on advertising becomes an attack on *people*. People thus feel guilty about being attracted to the images of advertising while being told that they should not find them attractive. Much of the best feminist writing on sexual imagery has, of course, been directed at pornography rather than advertising (or the two have simply been equated as the same). Ellen Willis writes of this for pornography:

Over the years I've enjoyed various pieces of pornography—some of the sleazy Forty-second Street paperback sort—and so have most women I know. Fantasy, after all, is more flexible than reality, and women have learned, as a matter of survival, to be adept at shaping male fantasies to their own purposes. If feminists define pornography, per se, as the enemy, the result will be to make a lot of women ashamed of their sexual feelings and afraid to be honest about them. And the last thing women need is more sexual shame, guilt and hypocrisy—this time served up as feminism. (1983, p. 462)

Similarly, film theorist Annette Kuhn in her book *The Power of the Image* comments on the pleasures of reading the film text:

Politics is often thought of as one of life's more serious undertakings, allowing little room for pleasure. At the same time, feminists may feel secretly guilty about their enjoyment of images they are convinced ought to be rejected as politically unsound. In analyzing such images, though, it is possible, indeed necessary, to acknowledge their pleasurable qualities, precisely because pleasure is an area of analysis in its own right. "Naive" pleasure then, becomes admissible. And the acts of analysis, of deconstruction and of reading "against the grain" offer an additional pleasure—the pleasure of resistance, of saying "no": not to "unsophisticated" enjoyment, by ourselves and others, of culturally dominant images, but to the structures of power which ask us to consume them uncritically and in highly circumscribed ways. (1985, p. 8)

A critique of advertising has to start by giving people permission to recognize the pleasure, the strength, of the images of advertising and of where that power rests. From that, we can start to unfold the exact role that advertising plays in our culture from a critical perspective. There is, of course, a great danger involved in this move, for the recognition of pleasure becomes a distorted conception if it is not simultaneously contextualized within the context of power relations (in this case, patriarchal). Pleasure can be used against people under the guise of freedom.

Now, defining gender and sexual identity is a difficult activity at the best of times; in modern consumer society, this difficulty is compounded by individuals being bombarded by extremely concentrated images of what gender is about. Advertising, it seems, has a privileged place in the discourse on gender in consumer societies due to its prominence in our daily lives. As a result, *what* advertising says about gender is a very important issue to understand. Gender could be defined in many ways (achievement, control of our lives, independence, family, creativity, etc.). It is a multidimensional aspect of human individuality. In advertising, however, gender is equated almost exclusively with sexuality. Women especially are defined primarily in sexual terms: What is important about women is their sexual behavior. As the debate on pornography has indicated, viewing women from this narrow and restricted perspective can result in treating women as less than truly human. The concentration on one aspect of behavior detracts from seeing people as people. Rather, they are seen as standing for something or being associated with one thing. As Judith Williamson notes on this point,

> If meaning is abstracted from something, from what "means" it, this is nearly always a danger signal because it is only in material circumstances that it is possible to "know" anything, and looking away from people or social phenomenon to their supposed abstract "significance" can be at worst an excuse for human and social atrocities, at best, a turning of reality into apparent unreality, almost unlivable while social dreams and myths seem so real. (1978, p. 169)

This is the basis of the feminist critique of objectification, of course. When subjectivity is denied, then one need not worry about people as people but only about how they may further your ends. Objects have no interest, no feelings, and no desires other than the way they affect yours. Women become defined as an object for the other. Within advertising, this is reflected in four basic ways in terms of the representations of women: (a) as *symbols* for an object and, thus, as exchangeable with it; (b) as a *fragmented* object made up of separate component parts that are not bound together in any coherent way to create a personality; (c) as an object to be *viewed*; and (d) as an object to be *used*.

I want to stress that gender identity is constructed in part through social representations of which the most pervasive and powerful forms in the consumer society are those associated with advertising (for women especially, representations in advertising are much more powerful than those of pornography). The social construction of gender identity is not an option, it is a necessity. Judith Williamson writes more broadly on this:

> Advertising may appropriate, not only real areas of time and space, and give them a false content, but real needs and desires in people, which are given a false fulfillment. We need a way of looking at ourselves: which ads give us falsely . . . we need to make sense of the world: which ads make us feel we are doing in making sense of *them*. (1978, p. 169)

The radical feminist literature has drawn a conclusion from this analysis of contemporary patriarchy and its representations. Feminism requires the articulation of new types of gender relations and new types of sexuality. In rejecting standard notions of beauty and sexuality (vital in a patriarchal culture for the construction of female identity), others have to be provided. Within the debate on pornography, this has led to calls for *erotica* versus pornography or a sexuality that focuses on relationships. Again, Ellen Willis has commented insightfully on these issues in relation to pornography and the women's movement:

In the movement's rhetoric pornography is a code word for vicious male lust. To the objection that some women get off on porn the standard reply is that this shows how thoroughly women have been brain-washed by male values. . . . And the view of sex that most often emerges from talk about "erotica" is as sentimental and euphemistic as the word itself: lovemaking should be beautiful, romantic, soft, nice, and devoid of messiness, vulgarity, impulses to power, or indeed aggression of any sort. Above all, the emphasis should be on *relationships*, not (yuck) *organs*. This goody-goody concept of eroticism is not feminist but feminine. (1983, p. 464)

That is, in the political battle with the standard forms of patriarchal sexuality (and of course representations) there has to be an *alternate*, a different option, defined. This cannot be left to talking about the future and not basing our present actions on utopian possibilities. In the battle over gender, we have to have that alternative vision *now*. The problem for feminists who reject the standard notions is to build a positive one that will *attract* people (both men and women). It is to recognize that culture is a battlefield, a site of contestation of visions and definitions of social relations (both real and imagined). I think that, up to now, that alternative has simply not been one around which to rally people. The cultural battle has been lost. Even a radical feminist such as Susan Brownmiller can recognize the problem. She says,

On bad days, I mourn my old dresses, I miss the graceful flow of fabric . . . and pretty colors. Sensible shoes announce an unfeminine sensibility. . . . Sensible shoes aren't fun. . . . Sensible shoes aren't sexy. . . . They are crisply efficient. As a matter of principle I stopped shaving my legs and underarms several years ago, but I have yet to accept the unaesthetic results. . . . I look at my legs and know they are no longer attractive, not even to me. They are simply legs, upright and honest and that ought to be good enough, but it isn't. (Chapkis, 1986, p. 131)

Wendy Chapkis also asks how women's liberation ended up on the sensible side over the sexual, the "efficient, upright and honest" over the colorful and fun: ultimately, of how the choice came down to one *between* principle and pleasure.

What a grim post-revolutionary world is envisioned. Artifice-free functional clothing is genderless and often comfortable. It is also unquestionably sensible attire for many activities. But what would functional clothing look like if our intended activity is sex. Mightn't a lacy bra or sheer stocking have erotic appeal less because they are symbols of female *powerlessness* and more because they are familiar symbols of female sexuality. (1986, p. 133)

If gender symbols have a legitimate erotic role, then the challenge seems to be to find a way to allow for gender play without gender privilege. As Wendy Chapkis's eight-year-old sister says about this in relation to her future life, "Wendy is a feminist. When I grow up, I am going to be just like her except I'll dress better" (1986, p. 7). As mentioned previously, Judith Williamson refers to advertising as providing a false way of looking at ourselves, a false fulfillment of real needs and desires. I also want to argue that ads give us a false way to look at ourselves, but I wish to establish *where* precisely falsity lies. It does *not* lie in the individual advertisement. There is nothing necessarily false about the consumption of individual messages. That is what draws us in. Individually, each message communicates a certain meaning. Each individual ad is produced for a certain strategic purpose in terms of communication. Conventionalized sexual imagery (e.g., high heels, slit skirts, and nudity) draws us in and makes an ad attractive for us. It is very difficult to criticize a single ad in isolation, unless it is blatantly sexist or violent. Even the ones that explicitly objectify women become attractive or draw us in, because objectification is a *pleasurable part* of sexuality. More and more of the feminist literature is starting to recognize this quite fundamental point that we all objectify men and women in some way at some time, that it can fulfill a socially positive function. As Ann Snitow notes in commenting upon objectification and pornography,

> The danger of objectification and fragmentation depend on context. Not even in my most utopian dreams can I imagine a state in which one recognizes all others as fully as one recognizes oneself. . . . The antipornography campaign introduces misleading goals into our struggle when it intimates that in a feminist world we will never objectify anyone, never take the part for the whole, never abandon ourselves to the mindlessness or the intensities of feeling that link sex with childhood, death, the terrors and pleasures of the oceanic. Using people as extensions of one's own hungry will is hardly an activity restrained within the boundaries of pornography. (1985, p. 116)

Wendy Chapkis recognizes that

> there is something impossibly earnest about the demand that we feel sexual attraction only in a non-objectified, ungendered fashion. It may be impossible not to objectify an attractive stranger. Until one learns enough to fill in the blanks, the attraction can't help but be built on the image s/he chooses to project and the fantasy which the observer then creates. (1986, p. 134)

Recognizing that gender play and variation is difficult in a mainstream heterosexual world, Chapkis gives some pertinent examples from her lesbian experiences of how objectification may be used in creative and pleasurable ways (for both, not just one side), where power is not so rigidly exercised:

> I slowly press myself against the fading pretense of butch restraint and then withdraw. She wants feminine, I'll give her feminine: promising but deliberately

delaying her release. Now I lead this subtle dance. My painted nails flash a message that has nothing to do with passivity. Those fingers dipped in blood and red lacquer can penetrate her depths. . . . These are symbols of control and surrender. But they are fluid; mouth and fingers, sheer underwear and leather ties, teasing out a woman's desire. (p. 136)

Similarly, Cynthia Peters and Karen Struening write in *Zeta* magazine,

Although there are important insights in the work of those theorists who challenge and repudiate men's objectification of women, there is a moment in the objectification process that must be saved. We are all sexual objects, and it is a good thing that we are. Sexual interactions require that we be able to see the other as a source of pleasure and sexual gratification. . . . We must ask ourselves, do we want a world where the gaze is always evaded, in which words are never used to tease and flirt, in which the body is never seen as an object of sensual desire? Must sexuality be barred from the theater of public spaces? (1988, p. 79)

Parts of daily life do have to do with sexuality, and, thus, there is nothing wrong with individual messages that focus on sex and gender. (That is, unless one took a moralistic stance on advertising in which some messages are inherently unacceptable for public or private viewing. Groups on the political right criticize advertising from this perspective. Similarly, some radical feminist theorists would argue against these images on the basis that all representations of heterosexual sex are representations of patriarchal domination.) Some parts of sexuality have to do with objectification, so that individual ads in that sense are not false. The falsity arises from the *system of images,* from the ads as a totality and from their cumulative effect. All (or at least many) messages are about gender and sexuality. It seems that, for women, it is the *only* thing that is important about them. The falsity then arises from the message *system,* rather than individual ads. It arises from the institutional context within which ads are produced and suggests that attempts to modify its regressive features should be concentrated at this level.

The argument I have made depends wholly on an understanding of the context of social phenomenon. While there is nothing wrong with a *little* objectification, there is a great deal wrong and dangerous with a *lot* of objectification—that is when one is viewed as *nothing other than an object.* Peters and Struening again write the following:

Many women walk through public spaces fearing the gazes, gestures and words directed at them. Although many women bring sexuality into the streets with fashion and body language, they do not think of the street as an entirely safe place for sexual play. They can (and do) seek the gaze of the other, but most women are aware of the attendant dangers. They know they cannot be objects of sexual attention with impunity. Many women have ambivalent responses to being addressed as sexual objects. While some women experience the gratification and pleasure . . . many others recount feelings of humiliation, anger, outrage, and diminished self-esteem. (1987, p. 79)

Commentating from a lesbian perspective, Wendy Chapkis recognizes not only the pleasure, but also the danger of sexual play in a world of male violence, "where sexually provocative means asking to be attacked" (1986, p. 138). It is little wonder that many women simply withdraw from the standard conceptions of beauty, especially in public spaces.

Escapes from this situation are difficult to imagine, but imagined they must be, because, despite all I have said about pleasure and objectification, we cannot forget that the advertising system offers us the most negative and dangerous set of images of sexuality and gender anywhere in our culture. Battles can take place on all kinds of individual levels over definitions concerned with the meanings of gender and the body. But they will be relatively meaningless unless one can affect the overall context of their interpretation. The discourse through and about objects (of which advertising sexuality is a part) is, at the present time, a profoundly *undemocratic* discourse. It is controlled only by advertisers and media. What is needed is not monitoring of individual images but a restructuring of the total system of images, so that sexuality can be separated from objectification, and objectification can be separated from patriarchal power. We need to take *back* the erotic, not construct a new eroticism using none of the symbols of the past: to redefine, for example, silk stockings as symbols of female sexuality rather than to expel them from the lexicon of a new female sexuality. Wendy Chapkis writes,

Sex, like its sister appearance, should be made more fun not more of a burden. Playing with the way we look, creating a personally or sexually provocative image has pleasures of its own. Denying ourselves those pleasures because they have been used against us in the past is understandable but hardly the final word in liberation. (1986, p. 146)

Within Marxist social theory, it has been recognized that whatever comes after capitalism will depend on the development of productive forces under capitalism, that there are progressive tendencies and movements within the belly of the beast. Could a similar case be made with regard to the cultural realm? Can the progressive elements of contemporary culture be rescued and recontextualized in the transition to a more egalitarian society? Can we base a cultural politics on some of the products and outcomes of the contemporary cultural marketplace? Or will a future society involve a total overthrowing of capitalist social and cultural relations?

Some objects, phrases, and images have a deep connotative meaning that makes them incredibly powerful symbols of identification. We cannot simply give them away to the forces of reaction. One way to accomplish this would be to force new voices of liberation, new erotic images of the diversity of female beauty, into the present totalitarian discourse, to intervene at the level of the system of images, "to dissolve the commercial monopoly on sex appeal" (Chapkis, 1986, p. 146).

References

Chapkis, W. (1986). *Beauty secrets*. Boston: South End Press.

Goffman, E. (1979). *Gender advertisements*. New York: Harper and Row.

Hall, S. (1980). Encoding/decoding. In S. Hall, D. Hobson, A. Lowe, & P. Willis (Eds.), *Culture, media, language*. London: Hutchinson.

Jhally, S. (1987). *The codes of advertising: Fetishism and the political economy of meaning in the consumer society*. New York: St. Martin's Press.

Kuhn, A. (1985). *The power of the image*. London: Routledge & Kegan Paul.

Leiss, W., Kline, S., & Jhally, S. (Eds.). (1986). *Social communication in advertising*. London: Methuen.

Nelson, J. (1983). As the brain tunes out, the TV ad-men tune in. *Globe and Mail*.

Peters, C., & Struening, K. (1987, February). Out on the street. *Zeta*.

Schwartz, T. (1974). *The responsive chord*. New York: Anchor.

Snitow, A. (1985). Retrenchment versus transformation: The politics of the antipornography movement. In V. Burstyn (Ed.), *Women against censorship*. Vancouver: Douglas & McIntyre.

Williamson, J. (1978). *Decoding advertisements: Ideology and meaning in advertising*. London: Boyars.

Willis, E. (1983). Feminism, moralism, and pornography. In A. Snitow, C. Stansell, & S. Thompson (Eds.), *Powers of desire: The politics of sexuality*. New York: Monthly Review Press.

Intersections of Discourse

MTV, Sexual Politics, and *Dreamworlds*[*]

In my activities as both a researcher and teacher of popular culture, I have been influenced and guided, for good or bad, by a couple of insightful observations. The first comes from Erving Goffman in his still brilliant book *Gender Advertisements*, when he says, perhaps the most negative thing that we can say about commercials is that "as pictures they are not perceived as peculiar and unnatural" (1979, p. 25). That is, as something that purports to represent reality, advertising, for the most part, is perceived as a natural and unproblematic aspect of the landscape of contemporary social life.

The second comment is from an unknown source, concerning the way in which the everyday environment in which we live becomes so taken for granted that it disappears from the frame of our active consciousness: "We're not too sure who discovered water, but we're pretty sure it wasn't the fish." It was with these ideas in mind that I started a project that could help people (initially my own students) obtain some cognitive and emotional distance from the world of images in which we are now immersed—to make the commercial culture in which we live strange and to pay attention to the sea of images that constitute an important part of our contemporary environment—as well as provide a frame of reference

[*] This essay first appeared in *Reconceptualizing Audiences*, ed. J. Cruz and J. Lewis (Boulder, CO: Westview Press, 1994), pp. 151–168. Reprinted by permission.

for understanding that world. The resulting videotape, *Dreamworlds: Desire/Sex/Power in Rock Video*, acts as a very illuminating case study of decoding behavior. This paper tells the story of what essentially became a very widespread audience study concerning the interpretation of popular culture and, equally importantly, the struggle over intervening in that popular culture.

The text around which the interpretations are organized is the *Dreamworlds* video. The different audience groups include American high-school and college students, academics, feminist scholars, journalists, right-wing religious groups, university bureaucrats, lawyers, and members of the so-called ordinary American public. The issues involved in the interpretations include questions of both content (gender images and sexual politics) and form (the use of video and visual imagery as tools of academic inquiry and cultural politics).

Background: Failure, Failure, Failure . . . Success?

I have been teaching large-lecture introductory courses on mass media and advertising in American universities since 1985. From the beginning, discussions of the cable channel MTV have formed an important part of my teaching for a number of reasons. First, MTV represents (or did in its formative years) the ultimate dream of network executives—a channel that featured nothing but advertising—and demonstrates the playing out of the logic of a commercial television system. It acts therefore as a condensed version of the system in total, representing both concretely and abstractly the essential, core meaning of the broader system of institutions of which it is a part.

Second, by becoming the main marketing mechanism for popular music (and changing the way in which what we hear is chosen, as well as the meaning that we give to the products of the recording industry), it demonstrates in a very concrete way the indissoluble link between the material and the symbolic. It highlights the way in which issues of image and style are constitutive of broader cultural domains (such as music, movies, and fashion).

Third, and most relevant to the discussion here, it draws renewed attention to other concerns—most visibly, the issue of the representation of women in popular culture. From its inception, MTV has drawn widespread feminist criticism for its narrow and demeaning depictions of women. While this has not been the subject of much sustained academic work, the discussion of sexism and MTV was, and is, prevalent within many journalistic commentaries.

It was within this context that I was starting to develop video material to use in my teaching, especially as regards highlighting the issue of sexism in the media—using MTV as a case study. Initially, this took the form of bringing in different tapes with relevant videos recorded on them and playing them in class. My students were glad to have the chance to watch and to listen to videos but looked at me blankly when I attempted to suggest that there was some systematic pattern to female representation, especially on those videos aimed at young male consumers. I concluded that the space between the videos, necessitated by physically changing the tapes, was too distracting.

When editing equipment became available for my use, I solved this problem by editing clips (of between one and three minutes) onto a single tape. When I presented this to my students, a strange thing (at least from my perspective) transpired—they sang along with their favorite songs!

The next step was a vital one. Familiar images needed to be taken out of their normal context. Stripping the original music away seemed an obvious move at this stage, as it seemed to be acting as a block to critical distance. Furthermore, I replaced the music with a very somber and slow soundtrack featuring the music of groups such as the German synthesizer band Tangerine Dream. The response of my students (for whom the images on display were very familiar and pleasurable) was not the enthusiastic identification of the previous attempt but neither was it the spark that they needed to really think about the images in new analytical ways. While I had developed a little bit of structure to the sequence in which the images were presented, it was obviously not enough on its own to provide new frameworks of understanding. The second time that I used it in a class I talked over it as it played and attempted to provide additional structure.

Also, at this stage, I was still including quite long segments from the videos, so that there was a fair bit of extraneous material from the viewpoint of looking at female representation. From a strategic marketing perspective, the use of female bodies within the videos is usually brief and fragmentary—short, sharp shots of intense visual pleasure are presented at periodic points—and is designed to ensure the most intense type of watching and to discourage casual viewing; rapt attention is required to ensure that the fleeting glimpses of concentrated sexuality are not missed. By reproducing this strategy, I was, I believe, making it harder to pay analytic attention to those images as they still appeared as short bursts of pleasure.

By now, I was moving to the idea of producing a much more stand-alone piece and started systematically to collect and research music videos from the viewpoint of gender representation. I also was thinking of a video piece that would present, structured with commentary, wall-to-wall images without any extraneous material. To this end, I produced my first complete piece of educational video around this material. Looking back on it, I now realize that it was much too descriptive. I outlined the main ways in which women and sex are used in videos; the roles, behaviors and activities in which the women engage; the camera techniques used, and focused on examples of explicit violence toward women and the way in which these women sent out signals that really meant "yes," even when they said "no." I ended with an implicit argument that images of this kind might cultivate attitudes that could legitimize rape.

Student reaction to this version was lukewarm. Even though I had decontextualized the images a great deal and provided a narrative that could aid the development of analytic frameworks of understanding, there was still something missing. It was interesting without being earth shattering. Again, looking back on it, I now realize what was happening. Commercial images are directed at parts of the body other than the brain—their aim is to provide emotional and sexual pleasure (or as close as you can get to that using visual imagery). I had produced a video exclusively for the head. People could thus get both messages without contradiction. The challenge was now to create an educational message that incorporated both emotional and intellectual strategies and to make the argument as explicit as possible. In the meantime, I saw the movie *The Accused*, starring Jodie Foster and Kelly McGillis, which dealt with the real-life case of a gang rape that had taken place in a New Bedford (U.MAS.) bar.

The next version was close to the final version. My narration had moved from description to greater analysis, and I tried to include humor and some sarcasm into my commentary to make it as entertaining as possible. The images were as concentrated as they could be—the wall-to-wall effect had almost been perfected (using examples from more than two hundred different music videos). The video was divided into seven parts and not only looked at videos of male bands, but also included segments dealing with female artists, as well as the commercials that appeared between the music videos.

The vital new addition, however, was at the end of the video. After the discussion of women in videos saying "no" (but actually really meaning "yes") to male sexual advances in music videos, I asked what would happen if these assumptions regarding behavior were applied to the real world. The next fifteen minutes of the video were spent cutting back and forth between the depiction of the gang rape scene from *The Accused* and two rock videos: Sam Kinison's "Wild Thing," featuring Jessica Hahn being thrown about a mudless mud wrestling ring, as various rock stars—including Billy Idol and Steven Tyler—stand around and cheer the activities, and Motley Crew's "Girls, Girls, Girls," which featured many real-life Florida strip clubs and strippers. The audio portion from the rape scene was left on over the top of the music video images to try and demonstrate that, recontextualized within a brutal and violent sexual assault, the images and the soundtrack fitted perfectly. The rape soundtrack was a fitting accompaniment to the music video images, the two blending into one. It concluded with about one unedited minute of both the actual soundtrack and visuals from the Mötley Crüe video. Thus, it ended with the actual material under consideration (music videos) presented as a whole, but now within a context totally different from MTV.

The last ten minutes of the video sought to ground the emotional wrenching just experienced within a more analytical frame. The relation between individual images and their place within a system of messages was addressed, as well as the effect of commercial images on the cultivation of attitudes toward rape. The tape ended by presenting statistics to do with date rape and attitudes toward date rape on American college campuses; it suggested that the violence and misunderstandings are not outside but inside our intimate relations and that images are related to the way in which we think about these issues (and ultimately, although not simply or directly, to our behavior).

Student reaction to this version was very strong. The video had the desired effect of disrupting the viewing of pleasurable (although largely unnoticed) images of popular culture. I will assess the reactions below. The version just described was about seventy minutes long. I subsequently edited it down to its present length of fifty-five minutes, utilizing examples from 165 different videos.

The tape in its fifty-five–minute version was completed in the fall of 1990. Seeking to get it into the hands of other teachers of popular culture, I invested a few thousand dollars of my own funds and produced three thousand brochures describing the tape, and, utilizing some professional association mailing lists, I mailed it out to faculty in departments of women's studies and communication (broadly defined). The cost of the tape was set at $100 (U.S.) for institutional purchase and $50 (U.S.) for individual purchases. The Department of Communication at the University of Massachusetts handled the money that came in. I was reimbursed when there were sufficient funds. There was some interest in the tape from fellow academics, and, by the spring semester (March 1991), about 100 to 125 tapes had been distributed in one form or another (either purchase or complimentary).

It was at this point that MTV Networks (a division of Viacom International, Inc.) entered the picture and, through their actions, precipitated some quite widespread national (and international) media coverage of the tape. The end result was to increase dramatically the reach of the tape, and, by May, 1992, some one thousand tapes had been distributed around the country for use in educational settings. Consequently, there has been a wide range of responses to the tape.

A Feminist Critique

The public controversy meant that the tape got into the hands of a number of feminist scholars, teachers, and activists, who recognized its value as a first-stage consciousness-raising effort and who have used it effectively in that way. The great majority of responses from persons describing themselves or their work as feminist have been highly positive (including endorsements from Ms. *Magazine* editor Robin Morgan and lecturer/critic Jean Kilbourne).

However, I was also coming under criticism from some feminists. The complaint was that *Dreamworlds* did not go far enough and that all young women got from it was a sense of victimization, which they knew about already. The same feminist response that denied the need to highlight victimization (for both males and females) also argued that *Dreamworlds* glossed over and misunderstood other very significant developments in popular culture—alternative, powerful images of autonomous women. In this regard, Madonna is a key icon, and she was regarded as providing a different and alternative image. Popular culture is seen as a battle-ground on which important victories have already been won. This was a reaction to a brief comment I make in the tape to Madonna as fitting into the dreamworld without serious problems. In response to my reading, some feminist critics saw Madonna as an artist refusing to speak from a position of victimhood, and, even though she appeared in the formal role of a stripper, hers was a different, more powerful presentation. One response even went so far as to suggest that my rejection of Madonna as a positive cultural development was part of a finger-pointing frenzy in which women who express any form of sexuality are merely a figment of men's sexist imaginations. It was not just sexism I was against, it was sex itself, and the tape was accused of bearing an eerie resemblance to right-wing calls for censorship based on puritanical standards (although the tape does not say one word about censorship or morality).

On questions of strategy, I was called to task for reproducing the power and strategy of the original images in such a way that undermined the critique I was making. It was suggested that I examine more avant-garde and feminist filmmaking practices to ensure distanciation, critique, and viewer displeasure. I was also encouraged to include a female narrator, as men (or, rather, boys) must learn to take a woman's voice seriously.

What this critique indicated to me was that the meaning of the tape was not as clear cut as some people may think, and that wider discourses were coming into play in how different audiences understood the tape. I will take this up in detail in a later section.

An Academic, Liberal Critique

Dreamworlds was presented at the opening plenary session of the Rhetoric and Ideology Conference held at Temple University in April of 1991. The tape came under heavy attack (as well as some lively defense) from commentators and the audience. (What was interesting was that the pop music critic of the *New York Times*, Jon Pareles, reproduced a critique in his review of the tape which indicates that there may be some convergence in liberal, academic analyses of popular culture.) There were five main issues raised.

First, there was the accusation of selectivity or nonrepresentation. One commentator argued that, after viewing the tape, she had gone and watched MTV for a few hours and that my tape did not accurately represent the videos that she saw—that the images that I had reproduced were a small part of the videos on display during her watching. Jon Pareles conducted the same experiment and came up with a figure of one in six videos that used blatant sexist imagery. That is, the images that I had used were not significant.

Second, the tape was accused of being extremely puritanical in its critique of commercial sexuality.

Third, it was argued that linking up the images to issues of sexual violence and date rape was misleading. The rape statistics had been overblown, and, anyway, young people were able to distinguish between fantasy (the videos) and other more real domains of socialization. MTV videos are an innocent world that people knew and recognized as fantasy. It did not affect the way in which they lived the rest of their lives.

Fourth, by decontextualizing and recontextualizing, it was claimed that I had distorted the original meaning of the images. The meaning of the images for which I argued, as part of a male adolescent dreamworld, was not the meaning the images actually had for their consumers.

Fifth, *Dreamworlds* was a long way from reasoned and balanced discussion of the issues. It sought to push viewers toward a particular interpretation, especially through its visual strategies. Jon Pareles described it as using smear tactics.

Measuring and Recognizing Significance

The question of significance is, of course, a vital question for researchers of many subjects, but especially so for communication scholars. We seek, after all, to discover the social significance of symbolic and cultural forms. How we go about measuring that significance is at the heart of many theoretical and methodological debates. One way to do it is by content analysis in which the number of appearances equates with significance. That is obviously the method suggested in the critique advanced in the previous discussion. However, there are assumptions built into such a methodology, the most important of which is that frequency of occurrence equals significance, and that all single occurrences of different phenomena have the same significance. From such assumptions, a theory of culture can be constructed by statistics.

I do not want to belittle what we can learn from such an approach (it must form part of any adequate analysis), but such a view has little to say about the semiotic difference between cultural phenomena and even less to say about the interaction between cultural phenomena and the audience. It has little to say of use on the process of the construction of cultural meaning. It is illuminating in this regard that Jon Pareles and my academic critics thought that the best way to test my thesis was to go and watch MTV for a few hours. This indicates that they were unfamiliar with the world of MTV—they had to go and find out about it. It was a view from outside the sphere of significance of the target audience. (An alternative methodology may have involved speaking to young people about what they thought of the subject of sex and videos.) I find it important that this criticism comes very rarely from the student viewers of the tape. When they see the images of *Dreamworlds*, they instantly recognize them as an important part of their world and their culture. Even when the images are on the screen for mere seconds, they register. This suggests that the images to which the tape refers are an important and deep part of the discursive space in which young people live. They play a part in the construction and maintenance of gender identity. That discourse is certainly not the only important thing there, but it has significance. It means something. (As a matter of interest, as a response to this criticism, I actually conducted my own informal content analysis of three different time periods on MTV, and, based on a sample of eighty-nine videos, I counted six out of ten that, in some way, use the type of images that appear in *Dreamworlds*.) There is not space here to discuss this fully, but the question of effect is essentially the same as the question of significance. Significant stories of how the world works help us understand the world in which we live. That understanding is one basis of behavior.

To the charge of distortion and decontextualization, I plead guilty with no mitigating circumstances. Operating and struggling on the terrain of commercial images requires new tools and new modes of address. The tape is an attempt to create an alternative voice, to raise new issues to the level of cultural debate. Balance, reason, and objectivity become possible when a debate already exists. *Dreamworlds* is part of an attempt to create that debate and therefore must articulate as powerfully as possible an alternative position. This means recognizing the rhetorical structure of modern image-based communication and using it to say something about that world itself. If the tape distorts the meaning of the original material, then the audience to whom it is directed will be aware, as they are intimately familiar with that world. And they will reject *Dreamworlds* as a work of false propaganda. If the tape, by decontextualization, brings the meaning of familiar images to the surface level of consciousness, then new discussion can take place. That decision, whether or not this is unfair distortion, will be made by the young viewers to whom *Dreamworlds* hopes to speak. I will be happy to live by their responses.

Audience Reactions: Students

When I first showed the tape in its near finished form to my classes, I was mostly worried about one thing—what if they found it long and boring and it could not hold their attention. This could have been an especially acute problem, as the tape was shown originally in large darkened lecture halls (three hundred seats) with video projection. What was to stop them from treating this like a trip to the movies and talking to their classmates about their images?

I need not have worried. My strategy of creating a quite seamless flow of intense images of sexuality meant that the tape could not be watched casually. The intensity and the force of the original images could now be used back against the images themselves. My editing (of already highly edited material) was very tight and left no space for drifting off. The use of different music directed even more attention to the visuals. When the audience was hooked visually, the narration could not be ignored or tuned out.

In the reactions to the tape, some commentators have worried that I had essentially created the "best of MTV sexist images" and that it could simply reinforce (rather than disrupt) the effect of the images. (There is a similar debate about pornography and whether showing the pornography even for critical analysis might, in some audiences, simply produce an additional opportunity to enjoy the original material.) That is, some men might find this arousing. This is a potential danger in that the original music video images are indeed pleasurable (if they were not, they would not be used). I was very aware of this, but I saw this more as an opportunity than a threat. Young people would watch the images. I could get their attention. Could that attention then be directed against the images that were the focus of the watching? My strategy was twofold: (a) to decontextualize by changing the music, reediting, and adding narration and (b), by relentlessly presenting one image after the other, by piling them on, to change initial pleasure into something different—overconsumption, a feeling of being full. The original images do their work in very specific contexts, and, as already pointed out previously, they are fleeting. Could too many of these images lead to a different effect?

The tape has been shown at many colleges and universities across the United States, and many colleagues have sent back to me the written reactions of their students. I have the reactions of literally hundreds of students. I also have written reactions from my own students, as well as the reactions of audiences of students for whom I have screened the tape at other colleges. The following comments are drawn from these reactions.

The positive reactions to the tape can be separated into two groups. The first is that of students who saw the video as giving them a way of looking at a familiar aspect of popular culture in a new way. Although differing in intensity, it was the majority reaction. Informal responses from colleagues who have used it in courses suggest that the "I never thought about it before, but I will now" response is the dominant reading. From my perspective this is also the preferred reading:

"An interesting and effective way to present the material. We see these videos everyday, but we don't realize how exploited women in the videos really are. It gave me more insight and allowed me to view the exploitation of women in media from a different perspective (observer?) instead of viewer, and as a serious problem."

"Sometimes the obvious is not as obvious as it seems until someone points it out to you directly. I've watched MTV for years, and I guess I've never really noticed how much women are exploited as sex objects and helpless children. The video *Dreamworlds* really opens my eyes to this. It angers me to be portrayed like that."

"The video is quite an eye-opener. Many of us have seen the videos used as examples but never really understood the impact that they have. There is a strong argument that the constant bombardment of the images of women as objects or just looking for and needing a man really affects many people's view of what is real and what isn't."

"I was really disturbed by this film. Not in the sense of the material presented. In the sense that I really wasn't aware of such a major problem. I watch MTV all of the time, and I enjoy seeing beautiful women in sexy outfits. Now that I am aware of such a problem, I feel like a jerk for admiring these women. I thought the movie overall was an excellent presentation. After I see presentations of this kind, I wonder what the hell is going on in our society."

"This video was really powerful. It made me aware of the implications of images I was completely familiar with and had never seen as abnormal. It made me look at MTV from a different perspective."

"Shocked. Amazed. Confused. Disgusted. Enlightened. Any one of these terms could describe how I felt after I witnessed the video *Dreamworlds*. At first, I was not sure where the subject was heading, but, after about five minutes, I was hooked. Like most people my age, I watch MTV. But, I never realized exactly what the music videos were saying. The way women were portrayed is nothing short of sexist. I had seen almost all of the videos shown but I never gave them a second thought. But, I will never look at a music video the same again."

A second set of reactions was also largely positive but much more broken down along gender lines and featured female viewers becoming angry at the images of popular culture:

"The film was intense and had a great impact on me. I felt that the points discussed were very informative and aroused my interest. I was very angry at the images of women, especially ones that I had never realized before due to advertising's internalization of the social system."

"Being female, I felt like a victim, and the reality became very clear as I viewed the many clips. It was rather frightening and numbing to watch the shots, and I became aware how programmed or accustomed I was to seeing this not only on MTV but in ads on TV, magazines, and newspapers."

Far from female viewers seeing the tape as only confirming their victimhood, and, thus, as not having anything new to say to them (as some feminist critics claimed), some responses revealed the manner in which the images of femininity had been internalized and were quite central to the way in which identity was constructed.

"This was a very provocative, disturbing film. I am glad such a documentary exists and is being shown—such critique is necessary in a world where far too much goes unquestioned. On a personal note, it made me rethink about my own life, and how I look at things and deal with others. As I am a woman, the film greatly disturbed me and made me question not only how I am presented but how I present myself. It clarified many of my own mixed emotions. So much of the time I feel completely torn: torn between the way I want to act (for myself in an intelligent, introspective way) and the way I feel I should want to act . . .

The film made me think about how much time I spend on my exterior, how much advertising and videos really do affect one. When I went home that day, I cried for a bit and then proceeded to throw out every bit of cosmetic I owned, which, sadly, was quite a lot. While this gesture may seem a bit silly, I feel so much better for it—as I feel that I have made somewhat of a conscious choice not to involve myself in that world any longer."

"I walked out of class on Thursday stunned. I have always watched MTV (until recently) and, in a way, had viewed the women in the videos as a type of role model, as far as looks and appearance is concerned. Now I see how the 'ideal' MTV woman shapes, twists, and corrupts the minds of developing children."

Feminist scholars who believe that young women do not need to be alerted about victimization are making a very dangerous political assumption. It results from overestimating the influence of feminist criticism beyond the narrow and often isolated domain of academia. As Naomi Wolf has demonstrated recently in her book *The Beauty Myth* (1991), the culture responded forcefully to the real successes of the second wave of feminism by putting concerns about the body and sexuality at the heart of how women are encouraged to construct identity. An impossible standard of beauty (now only achievable for the vast majority through cosmetic surgery) keeps women in a constant state of anxiety and ill health. The power of the beauty myth comes from its internalization by women. To suggest that such a key ideological component of modern patriarchal culture is transparent and obvious (and hence does not need discussion) is folly of the most dangerous kind.

What is clear from these comments is that the power of images is much more apparent to those whom they affect the most. The argument for the effect of the images was much easier to make to females who felt themselves to be the intended victims.

There were also reactions that I did not expect and had not foreseen. Some women felt not only angry, but also vulnerable and frightened of the social world in which they have to live.

"At the end of the film, I must say I felt vulnerable. It was frightening to see the direct similarities of the rock videos with the clip from *The Accused*."

"This film really hit home with me. I don't know if it made me mad, as it scared me. . . . I know I sound pretty harsh on this subject, but it also hits home with me in that I fall into one of the statistics mentioned at the end of the film, and I know first hand how destructive sex can be when displayed continuously like this."

For many viewers, the video had the effect of highlighting not simply the issue of images, but also that of sexual violence and date rape. Frequent comments concerned a previous lack of awareness of the extent of the problems.

However, there were a number of negative reactions also. I did not expect to escape strong criticism on a message directed to young people that argues that their popular culture is concerned not only with pleasure, but also with power and violence. I especially thought that male viewers would be defensive about their images. The main negative comments were divided into two types.

First, there was the accusation of going overboard with the not-so-subtle techniques of flooding and intercutting. Sometimes, these comments were made in the context of an otherwise positive evaluation of the tape.

"I found most of the points in your film thought provoking and your statistics on rape shocking. But your presentation seemed more concerned *with scaring me instead of teaching me. The end spoilt the rest of the film.*"

A very small number of responses accused me of selectivity:

"I think it looks a lot worse than it is when you string a bunch of videos together and bombard the audience with them. They don't have that impact when seen on MTV as they usually are. Also the same maybe thirty or so videos are sampled over and over. There are hundreds of videos, and they don't all show sex in the way others do or sex at all."

(One instructor has made a virtue of responses of this type by showing it to students in TV production classes, who criticize it for its manipulative techniques. The response is used to draw students' attention to the political nature of all production and all communication.)

All in all, I would settle for this range of responses. In general, the tape has made commercial images strange for their consumers and has made them pay attention to the sea of images in which they navigate their daily lives. The tape has helped provide a certain critical distance from popular culture. Whether the responses were positive or negative, consumers of popular culture reacted (normally in a quite strong way) to the tape and had to think about the world in which they lived and the effect of images on that world.

However, there were two other kinds of responses that I found to be very interesting and that do not belong under the category of either positive or negative responses, but more properly could be labeled *aberrant decodings*. The first one read the tape as arguing that rock video images cause rape, even though I had been very careful in explicitly establishing that this was not what I was saying. I did not want to deny the connection but wanted to link the two through the discussion of the cultivation of attitudes—rather than a simple direct causal link. My strategy of visual juxtaposition (especially in the use of the material from *The Accused*) was based on eliciting an emotional reaction to the material. For some viewers, this visual argument overwhelmed the accompanying audio narrative argument—they did not hear it or could not understand it within an appropriate frame.

In this regard, the issue of context is crucial. In the instructions that accompany the tape, I am very clear that the tape should not be shown cold and that there has to be appropriate discussion of the relevant issues under consideration before the tape is screened. It is significant that these types of responses occurred in situations in which there was not this opportunity to ground the issues and the meaning of the tape.

The second aberrant response was quite prevalent (across a range of other reactions also). Here, the focus became the actual actresses, models, and dancers who appeared in the videos. My references in the tape to the women of the dreamworld were read not as references to the fictional world that videos create, but as referring to the real-life women who participate in their production. The issue became their willingness and their freedom to participate in the construction of the dreamworld. Consequently, the responsibility of the effects of the dreamworld was shifted to their shoulders. This response reflects a failure to abstract in any meaningful way from the representations on the screen. They are not representations—they are the real thing.

Public Responses: Sexual Politics in an Age of Right-Wing Moralism

Immediately upon publication of the first story concerning the tape in the general press (in *Newsweek*), I started to receive mail from members of the general public offering statements of support. A large amount of it came from people (mostly female) who were grateful for the raising of the issue of sexism, especially coming from a man.

However, the tape, as described in the press reports, was also playing into some other discourses that were very disturbing. Here is one letter that I received from South Carolina:

> "I read the article about you in Newsweek and am pleased beyond words by any criticism of MTV. I believe you may be the head of a million plus army who is outraged and appalled by the obscenity, profanity, and pornography for the sole purpose of indoctrinating young minds . . .

What a shame that the foundation this country is built on is represented by NEA [National Endowment for the Arts], MTV, Department of Welfare, filthy books and movies, etc.

I noticed by the paper the other day that the Negroes are making up some new laws as they go along with the college administration fraudulently putting blacks above whites which is to "pay them back" for 300 some odd years ago being sold into slavery by one of their kind.

If the liberals feel sorry for the blacks, they are more than welcome to pay my share of the highly inflated, coerced taxes for DSS [Department of Social Services], AFDC [Aid for Families with Dependent Children], abortions, federal housing, food stamps, etc. I can hardly pay my bills but I am supposed to support these individuals."

Obviously, the writer of this letter thought that a critique of MTV must automatically put me on the same political side as her. For her, MTV is a codeword for liberalism or secular humanism. I also received letters of support from a group called Morality in Media, a right-wing watch-dog group. Interestingly, other groups read my critique of rock video images as an attack on rock music, and I received yet more letters from anti–rock music groups. This came to a head when I learned from the producers of *Inside Edition*, a tabloid news show, that the PMRC (Parent's Music Resource Center)—a group started by the wives of influential congressional leaders to lobby for labeling on record albums—had recommended my name to them as someone who could present the opposing view in a story on "the rock video girls." It has to be stressed that all this reactionary positive support came not from viewing the tape but from the media stories on the tape.

Intersections of Discourse: Closed and Open Texts

What the literature on audiences from the perspective of cultural studies suggests is that media messages do not have any one meaning, that not all people make the same sense of a message. The interpretation of a message depends upon what resources of interpretation we bring to its understanding. Social subjects are the point of intersection of a number of different discourses (or stories) about the world and ways to understand it.

Through our lives, we are exposed to many different stories about how the world works. Depending upon our background and experience, we have been influenced by many different things, by many factors. For example, our experience as males and females give us different stories through which to make sense of the world. Similarly, our racial experience gives us different ways in which we understand the world—not because of any essential factor, but because we are born into a world that positions, in general, blacks and whites at different places and provides them with different experiences. For both gender and race, natural distinctions are translated via cultural into symbolic distinctions. Similarly, our social class experience gives us different ways in which we understand the world—stemming from differences of biology, culture, and education.

If we want to understand what effect the media have, in terms of what meaning people give to a media message, we have to see how the media message interacts with the other stories that people have been told—they will make sense of the media story in terms of their background, on what they bring to the message, and how the message interacts with the other stories to which they have access.

However, this is not a simple process. It is not simply a matter of saying that we make sense of messages in terms of what we bring to the message. The message also has power to influence how we make sense of it—because all messages, especially media messages, are saying "make sense of me this way—this is what I mean." The way a message is structured, put together, and so on, orients us toward an understanding of it. So, the outcome is a result of an interaction between the message and the audience.

Again, it is not so simple as saying that there are messages, and there are people, and it depends upon who is more powerful, because the stories that we use to make sense of the world, the stories that come from our experience, from our life history, from the factors that have influenced us, are in constant process. The stories are always in flux—so the media can influence those stories. The media, especially the modern media because of their sheer presence in our daily lives, are always telling stories about race, gender, and class, etc. Their stories interact with our experience and the other stories in which we live to produce the meaning around those things. Because our understanding of ourselves is always a process that never stops—it happens every single minute we are alive—we have to pay attention to the discursive environment in which we live to understand that process. To understand the effect of a media message, then, we have to understand the intersections of these different discourses, how the different stories fit together.

Looking at the media from this perspective requires us to make important distinctions about the nature of media messages and their interaction with other discourses. An open message is one in which the intersections of discourse are so loose, in which there are so many competing discourses, that it is open to many different interpretations. The message is polysemic—it has many different meanings for the audience. A closed message is where the intersections of discourse are fairly tightly woven together—most people locate themselves at the same intersecting spot and thus produce shared meanings.

The process in which we are all engaged, as actors in the social world, is to try to produce closed communication messages. We do not want to be misinterpreted or misunderstood. We want to communicate because we want to affect the world, and we produce what we hope are appropriate texts. Now, whether a text is closed or open is not a property of the text by itself. It depends upon the other discourses available to people to make sense of it. It is thus a property of the context, of the other discourses that intersect with it.

What does the story that I have been telling in this article, the story of the production and interpretation of *Dreamworlds*, tell us about this process? A great deal, I believe.

First, from my perspective as the producer of an interventionist text designed to get young people who are the consumers of commercial images to look at them and understand them in new ways, the question of intersecting discourses was vital. The decision to use videotape as the medium of intervention was of paramount importance in this regard. Video allows a mode of address with which young people are familiar and engaged. Writing a book would not have had the same effect. (I have been approached numerous times at the University of Massachusetts by students who tell me that they have seen *Dreamworlds* in some other context than my class and that they liked it. I have never had students approach me and say that they have read one of my books and that they really enjoyed it. When I have screened the tape at other colleges, the rooms are normally crowded to overflowing. I am convinced that a lecture by me on the same topic would not be attended to the same degree.)

Additionally, the decision to use nothing but the images of popular culture as the language of the tape involved both potential and risk. The positive aspect was that it would be easier to get attention beyond a surface level. The risk was that the pleasure involved in the identification would overwhelm any attempt at decontextualization and distanciation. The language of camera movement and fast editing may not be able to provide a way of understanding the images themselves—this is the fear behind the calls of some people for me to explore more avant-garde and nonconventional techniques. I deliberately chose the language and strategy I used because I wanted to be sure of actually making contact and speaking with the audience. MTV is the language of a modern, image-based culture, and any attempt to have a voice in that culture will have to adopt that language, at least initially. For those engaged in cultural politics, this is not a choice. This is the language of the modern age. Such a strategy involves risk, to be sure, but there are no guarantees in politics. Texts may become open, and meaning may not be able to be pinned down as producers intended, but the guarantee of closed texts would mean confining the audience to those on the margins who already know the message—a politics of preaching to the converted.

The decision to use a male narrator also stemmed from this concern. Although I hoped that many types of audiences would see the tape, I must admit that the person I had in mind as the prime target was a young male. I wanted to say something significant to him about his pleasure and its relationship with power. Using a female narrator would have risked losing him ("not another woman moaning about fun images") before the analysis even began.

I wish to remind the reader here of the process of making the final version of *Dreamworlds*. For the first few attempts, all of the potential problems actually occurred. The text was open long before it became closed. I believe that the present text is pretty closed—its dominant reading is one that I would accept. But it was the end result of a long period of failure—and it is still read in ways that disturb me.

The intersection of *Dreamworlds*, discourse with that of sexual politics was certainly the most interesting aspect of the reaction. It highlighted for me both the potential and the danger of articulating a critique of commercial sexual imagery. It became clear to me that it is very difficult to distinguish between critiques of sexuality in contemporary culture. The dominant critique of sexuality is a fundamentalist one—either the moralistic based one from the right or the politically motivated critique (although ultimately based on essential/natural notions) of radical feminists, such as Andrea Dworkin. In such a view, it is sexuality that is bad. If one believes that strongly, then a critique of commercial sex becomes a critique of sex. The right-wing therefore saw the tape, as least as it was represented in press reports, as an ally in the fight against secular humanism. In the letter that I quoted at length previously in this discussion, it was clear that the writer existed at the intersection of discourses connected with racism and sexuality and that the critique of MTV was sort of like a code that conjured forth other things as well.

Similarly, a student at a Southern university, for whom the Bible is a very significant discursive context within which meaning is constructed, concluded a review of the tape in the following way:

"It is a sad state of affairs when, by using a few commercial techniques and precise camera angles, promoters can make God's second greatest creation to look like trash and turn God's first creation into a trash collector."

In this regard, I have continued to view *Dreamworlds* as an open text and have struggled to close it in my preferred direction. In my subsequent discussions around it, I have tried very hard to pull it back to my meaning and not that of the fundamentalist right. For instance, as the news story broke, I appeared (via telephone) on quite a few radio talk shows on which I was obviously expected to be the moralistic and (by virtue of my university affiliation) expert protector of public virtue. As radio talk can only happen in short bursts of two or three sentences at a time, I quickly developed a line that stated that my problem with MTV and commercial images in general was not that there was too much discussion of sex but that there was not enough! After a stunned response from the host, I would continue that the problem was not sexuality, but the narrow definition given it by an advertiser-dominated media system whose function it was to sell us things. What we needed was more discussion by different and varied voices—more access and more democracy to break the authoritarian control of public space and media by corporate interests. As soon as I started to talk about the specific nature of the critique and the issues of democracy and access it raises, as well as those of the repression of other sexualities (primarily homosexual), I became for the fundamentalists, thankfully, the enemy again.

Conclusion: Texts, Audiences, and Madonna

The response of some feminists to the tape can be located similarly within the intersection of discourses surrounding sexual politics. For these feminists, there was a main area of concern—the right-wing attack on women's reproductive rights. Reflecting their marginal status as regards mainstream politics, some feminists saw the tape not as a tool in the struggle for a progressive sexual politics, but only as a potential threat that the right could use to further their attack. It might be well intentioned, but it could ultimately do more harm than good.

It is this same context, I believe, that leads to the appropriation of Madonna as an almost sacred feminist icon. The attack on abortion rights is a fundamental attack on women's control of their own bodies. From this perspective, Madonna is a powerful symbol of a woman in charge, controlling her body for her own sexual pleasure. My reading of Madonna's broader cultural meaning as being not that different from the other women that appear on MTV becomes an attack on an autonomous female sexuality.

So who is right? Is Madonna a feminist or a bimbo?

From the viewpoint of purely textual criticism, I think you could argue it both ways. If armed with feminist theory and different views of other sexualities, then, certainly, Madonna could be read in a progressive way. If not, then Madonna's meaning is not so clear. Again, the point is one of intertextuality—of the intersection of discourses. Madonna's genius lies in never being pinned down to a position, in negotiating brilliantly the line between the taboo and the accepted. She both challenges conventions and uses dominant sexual codes. (When she crosses the line and insists on explicit lesbian sexuality and uninhibited female pleasure and power, as in the video for "Justify My Love," she is banished from MTV.) The question, then, is not what academics make of her, but how the culture makes sense of her. How do males make sense of her? How do females make sense of her?

The answer is ultimately to be found in empirical analyses of both texts and audiences and the interaction between them. In the absence of this, I would be willing to argue for that reading of the tape as a dominant cultural reading—although certainly not the only one. Some of the initial empirical work on audiences and Madonna would support the interpretation of *Dreamworlds* (see Brown & Schulze, 1990).

At one level, these questions could be seen as only of arcane interest to academics. However, for those of us who regard the academy as being inherently involved in cultural production, these are issues of high political importance. Our analysis of the relationship between texts and audiences will guide, in part, our discussions of cultural and social policy. If we believe that we can understand a good deal of how the society works by sitting in our offices and conducting sophisticated analyses of texts, we will be more and more cut off from the "dirty" semiotic world of cultural life where knowledge and power intersect. Alternatively, if we only deal with what audiences say about their interaction with that world, we are in danger of floating off into the voluntaristic world of uses and gratifications. It is only by examining the whole terrain of the semiotic world that we inhabit, by subjecting both texts and audiences and the cultural process in general to the greatest analytic scrutiny possible, that we can start to offer strategies of democratic resistance.

References

Brown, J., & Schulze, L. (1990). The effects of race, gender, and fandom on audience interpretations of Madonna's music videos. *Journal of Communication, 40*(2), 88–102.

Goffman, E. (1979). *Gender advertisements.* New York: Harper and Row.

Wolf, N. (1991). *The beauty myth.* New York: William Morrow.

Missing the Mark: School Shootings and Male Violence[*]

with Jackson Katz

The events at Columbine High School twelve days ago have plunged us into a national conversation about *youth violence* and how to stop it. Proposals came last week from all corners—the Oval Office, Congress, living rooms across America. That we are talking about the problem is good, but the way we are talking about it is misdirected.

It is tempting to look at the murderous attack in Littleton as a manifestation of individual pathologies, an isolated incident involving deeply disturbed teenagers who watched one too many video games. That explanation ignores larger social and historical forces and is dangerously shortsighted. Littleton is an extreme case, but, if we examine critically the cultural environment in which boys are being socialized and trained to become men, such events might not appear so surprising.

Political debate and media coverage keep repeating the muddled thinking of the past. Headlines and stories focus on youth violence, "kids killing kids," or, as in the title of a CBS *48 Hours* special, "Young Guns." This is entirely the wrong framework to use in trying to understand what happened in Littleton—or in Jonesboro, AR, Paducah, KY, Pearl, MS, or Springfield, OR.

* The essay first appeared in *The Boston Globe*, May 9, 1999. Reprinted with permission.

This is not a case of kids killing kids. This is boys killing boys and boys killing girls.

What these school shootings reveal is not a crisis in youth culture but a crisis in masculinity. The shootings—all by white adolescent males—are telling us something about how we are doing as a society, much like the canaries in coal mines whose deaths were a warning to miners that caves were unsafe.

Consider what the reaction would have been if the perpetrators in Littleton had been girls. The first thing everyone would have wanted to talk about would have been: Why are girls—not kids—acting out violently? What is going on in the lives of girls that would lead them to commit such atrocities? All of the explanations would follow from the basic premise that being female was the dominant variable.

But when the perpetrators are boys, we talk in a gender-neutral way about kids or children, and few (with the exception of some feminist scholars) delve into the forces—be they cultural, historical, or institutional—that produce hundreds of thousands of physically abusive and violent boys every year. Instead, we call upon the same tired specialists who harp about the easy accessibility of guns, the lack of parental supervision, the culture of peer-group exclusion and teasing, or the prevalence of media violence.

All of these factors are of course relevant but, if they were the primary answers, then why are girls, who live in the same environment, not responding in the same way? The fact that violence—whether of the spectacular kind represented in the school shootings or the more routine murder, assault, and rape—is an overwhelmingly male phenomenon should indicate to us that gender is a vital factor, perhaps the vital factor.

Looking at violence as gender neutral has the effect of blinding us as we desperately search for clues about how to respond.

The issue is not just violence in the media but the construction of violent masculinity as a cultural norm. From rock and rap music and videos, Hollywood action films, and professional and college sports, the culture produces a stream of images of violent, abusive men and promotes characteristics such as dominance, power, and control as means of establishing or maintaining manhood.

Consider professional wrestling, with its mixing of sports and entertainment and its glamorization of the culture of dominance. It represents, in a microcosm, the broader cultural environment in which boys mature. Some of the core values of the wrestling subculture—dominant displays of power and control, ridicule of lesser opponents, and respect equated with physical fear and deference—are factors in the social system of Columbine High School, where the shooters were ridiculed, marginalized, harassed, and bullied.

These same values infuse the Hollywood action-adventure genre that is so popular with boys and young men. In numerous films starring iconic hypermasculine figures, such as Arnold Schwarzenegger, Sylvester Stallone, Wesley Snipes,

Bruce Willis, and Mel Gibson, the cartoonish story lines convey the message that masculine power is embodied in muscle, firepower, and physical authority.

Numerous other media targeting boys convey similar themes. Thrash metal and gangsta rap, both popular among suburban white males, often express boys' angst and anger at personal problems and social injustice, with a call to violence to redress the grievances. The male sports culture features regular displays of dominance and one-upsmanship, as when a basketball player dunks "in your face" or when a defensive end sacks a quarterback, lingers over his fallen adversary, and then, in a scene reminiscent of ancient Rome, struts around to a stadium full of cheering fans.

How do you respond if you are being victimized by this dominant system of masculinity? The lessons from Columbine High—a typical suburban *jockocracy,* where the dominant male athletes did not hide their disdain for those who did not fit in—are pretty clear. The seventeen- and eighteen-year-old shooters, tired of being ridiculed or marginalized, weren't big and strong, and so they used the great equalizer: weapons. Any discussion about guns in our society needs to include a discussion of their function as equalizers. In Littleton, the availability of weapons gave the shooters the opportunity to exact a twisted and tragic revenge: fifteen dead, including themselves, and twenty-three wounded.

What this case reinforces is our crying need for a national conversation about what it means to be a man, since cultural definitions of manhood and masculinity are ever shifting and are particularly volatile in the contemporary era.

Such a discussion must examine the mass media in which boys (and girls) are immersed, including violent, interactive video games, but also mass media as part of a larger cultural environment that helps to shape the masculine identities of young boys in ways that equate strength in males with power and the ability to instill fear—fear in other males, as well as in females.

But the way in which we neuter these discussions makes it hard to frame such questions, for there is a wrong way and a right way of asking them. The wrong way: "Did the media (e.g., video games, Marilyn Manson, and *The Basketball Diaries*) make them do it?" One of the few things that we know for certain after fifty years of sustained research on these issues is that behavior is too complex a phenomenon to pin down to exposure to individual and isolated media messages. The evidence strongly supports that behavior is linked to attitudes, and attitudes are formed in a much more complex cultural environment.

The right way to ask the question is, "How does the cultural environment, including media images, contribute to definitions of manhood that are picked up by adolescents?" Or, "How does repeated exposure to violent masculinity normalize and naturalize this violence?"

There may, indeed, be no simple explanation as to why certain boys in particular circumstances act out in violent, sometimes lethal, ways. But leaving aside the specifics of this latest case, the fact that the overwhelming majority of such violence is perpetrated by males suggests that part of the answer lies in how we define such intertwined concepts as *respect, power,* and *manhood.* When you add on the easy accessibility of guns and other weapons, you have all the ingredients for the next deadly attack.

Media and Race

Affirming Inaction: Television and the Politics of Racial Representation*

with Justin Lewis

Introduction

One of the abiding concerns in contemporary North American culture has been the many attempts to deal with race and racial inequality. Since racism is often understood as a perception dependent upon negative or stereotypical images, debates about race have often centered around the issue of representation, with analytical glances increasingly cast toward television as the main image maker in our culture.

In order to make sense of the many competing claims about the way in which black people are represented on TV, we carried out an extensive study based upon a content analysis of primetime television together with a series of fifty-two focus group interviews (made up of twenty-six white, twenty-three black, and three Latino groups) from a range of class backgrounds. The interviews were designed to probe attitudes to race and the media representation thereof. To facilitate these discussions, each interview began with the viewing of an episode of *The Cosby Show*.

* This essay first appeared in *Marxism in the Postmodern Age: Confronting the New World Order*, ed. A. Callari, S. Cullenberg, & C. Biewener (New York: Guildford Press, 1995), pp. 133–141. Reprinted by permission.

The Cosby Show was chosen because it has, in many ways, changed the way in which television thinks about the portrayal of African Americans. During the time that it took for *The Cosby Show* to go from being innovative to institutional, African Americans became a fairly common sight on network television in the United States. And not just any African Americans: our content analysis confirmed that we now see a plethora of middle- and upper-middle-class black characters populating our screens. Major black characters—from *ER* to *Sportsnight*—are now much more likely to be well-heeled professionals than blue collar workers. In this sense, Bill Cosby can be credited with spurring a move toward racial equality on television. Fictional characters on U.S. television have always inclined to be middle or upper-middle class—since the late 1980s, black people have become an equal and everyday part of this upwardly mobile world.

The Cosby Show was, in this sense, more than just another sitcom. It represents a turning point in television culture, to a new era in which black actors have possibilities beyond the indignities of playing a crude and limited array of black stereotypes, an era in which white audiences can accept TV programs with more than just an occasional token black character. There is, it seems, much to thank Bill Cosby for. He has quite literally changed the face of network television.

At first reading, our study suggested that the upward mobility of black representation precipitated by *The Cosby Show* was an unambiguously positive phenomenon. It appeared, from our focus groups, to promote an attitude of racial tolerance among white viewers, for whom black television characters have become ordinary and routine, and to generate a feeling of pride and relief among black viewers. But *The Cosby Show* and the new generation of black professionals on U.S. television are caught up in a set of cultural assumptions about race and class that complicate the political ramifications of such a trend.

It is true that, in recent decades, the size of the black middle class in the United States has grown. This much said, the social success of black TV characters in the wake of *The Cosby Show* do not reflect any overall trend toward black prosperity in the world *beyond* television. On the contrary, the period in which *The Cosby Show* dominated television ratings—1984 to 1990—witnessed a comparative decline in the fortunes of most African Americans in the United States. The racial inequalities that scarred the United States before the civil rights movement could only be rectified by instituting major structural changes in the nation's social, political, and economic life—an idea informing Great Society interventions in the 1960s and 1970s. Since the election of Ronald Reagan in 1980, both Republican and Democratic administrations have generally withdrawn from any notion of large-scale public intervention in an iniquitous system, committing themselves instead to promoting a global, free enterprise economy. This laissez-faire approach has resulted in the stagnation or gradual erosion of advances made by black people during the 1960s. For all the gains made in the fictional world of TV, by almost all demographic measures (such as education, health, levels of incarceration, income, and wealth), the United States remains a racially divided society.

As William Julius Wilson has documented, maintaining these divisions is a set of socioeconomic conditions that keep most people in their place (1987). The so-called American dream of significant upward mobility is an aspiration that few can or will ever realize. It is an idea sustained by fictions and by anecdotes that focus on the exceptions rather the rules of class division. If we are to begin any kind of serious analysis of racial inequality in the United States, we must acknowledge the existence of the systematic disadvantages that exclude most people on low incomes in poor neighborhoods—a condition in which black people in the United States have disproportionately been placed—from serious economic advancement.

Left unchecked, it is the laws of free market capitalism—rather than more overt, individual forms of racial discrimination—that reproduce a racially skewed class structure. Most major institutions in the United States have officially declared themselves nonracist and have invited black citizens to compete alongside everyone else. This is important but insufficient. If three white people begin a game of monopoly, a black player who is invited to join the game halfway through enters at a serious disadvantage. Unless blessed by a disproportionate degree of good luck, the black player will be unable to overcome these economic disadvantages and compete on equal terms. This is, in effect if not in intention, how the United States has treated most of its black citizens: It offers the promise of equal opportunity without providing the means—good housing, good education, and good local job opportunities—to fulfill it.

There is a wealth of evidence about the operation of these structural inequalities (see, for example, Wilson, 1987; Hacker, 1992). What is remarkable about our culture is that it refuses to acknowledge the existence of class structures, let alone understand how they influence racial inequalities. And yet, at certain moments, we *do* accept these things as obvious. We expect rich white children to do better than poor black children. We expect it, because we know that they will go to better schools, be brought up in more comfortable surroundings, and be offered more opportunities to succeed. And our expectations would, most often, be proved quite right. The child who succeeds in spite of these odds is a glamorous figure in our culture, precisely because they have defied these expectations. Unfortunately, our culture teaches us to ignore these social structures and offers us instead a naive obsession with individual endeavor. Instead of a *collective* war on poverty, we have welfare reforms that increase poverty and homelessness in the name of *individual* responsibility.

We would argue that U.S. television—and popular culture generally—are directly culpable for providing an endless slew of apocryphal stories that sustain a cultural refusal to deal with class inequalities and the racial character of those inequalities.

The Upscale World of Television Fiction

Television in the United States is notable in creating a world that shifts the class boundaries upward. If the path to heaven is more arduous for the rich than the poor, the opposite can be said of entry to the ersatz world of television. Data from the University of Pennsylvania's Cultural Indicators project suggests that, in recent decades, television gives the overwhelming majority of its main parts to characters from middle-class and professional class backgrounds, while significant working-class roles are few and far between (Jhally & Lewis, 1992). This is in notable contrast to the norms of other English-speaking television programs from countries like Britain and Australia, where working-class characters are much more commonplace. In the United States, the TV world is skewed to such an extent that the definition of what looks normal on television no longer includes the working class. This bias is neither obvious nor clearly stated: On the contrary, television's professionals are generally universalized, so that the class barriers that divide working-class viewers from upper-middle-class TV characters melt away. As some of our working class viewers said of Cliff Huxtable, "he may be a doctor, but he's not as aloof as some of the real doctors they encounter in the non-TV world." As these two respondents put it,

> "I guess he doesn't really seem professional, you know, not the way a doctor would be. The ones I meet are very uppity, and they really look down on the lower class."

> "They don't play the status they are in the show. You expect them to be living a much higher class, flashing the money, but they're very down to earth."

Television's characters are thus well off but accessible. These are pictures of the American dream, and they are paraded in front of us in sitcoms and drama series night after night. On television, most people, or most people with an ounce of merit, are making it.

But, surely, it's only television, isn't it? Most people realize that the real world is different, don't they? Well, yes and no. Our study suggests that the line between the TV world and the world beyond the screen has, for most people, become exceedingly hazy. Many of the respondents in our study would shift from immersion in television's world to critical distance in the same interview, praising *The Cosby Show* at one moment for its realism and criticizing it at another for its lack of realism. Thus, for example, one respondent began with an endorsement of the show's realism:

> "I think that Cosby is much more true to life; you can put yourself right into the picture. Just about everything they do has happened to you, or you've seen it happen."

At a later point in the interview, the same respondent argued that

> "It's totally a fantasy to me, a fairy tale . . . I think if you bring in the real hum-
> drum of what really life is all about, it would be a total bore. I would much prefer
> to see a little bit of fairy tale and make-believe."

We watch, it seems, at one moment with credulity and at another moment with disbelief. We mix skepticism with an extraordinary faith in the television's capacity to tell us the truth. We know that the succession of doctors, lawyers, and other professionals that dominate television's stories are not real, yet we continually think about them as if they were. We have thereby learned to live in the dreams of network executives.

Exceptions to this—perhaps the most notable in recent television history being *Roseanne*—become conspicuous because (at least until the last series when the family wins the lottery) they defy this norm. Simply by being sympathetic and assertively working class, the characters in *Roseanne* stood out from the sea of upscale images that surrounded them. In the United States, there are nearly twice as many janitors as all the lawyers and doctors put together, and, yet, on television, the legal or medical professions are run of the mill, whereas to portray a major character as a janitor seems *ostentatiously* class conscious. The negative response to *thirtysomething* in the 1980s was, in this context, extremely revealing. Here was a show that dealt fairly intimately with the lives of a group of middle- and upper-middle-class people. In demographic terms, these characters were the standard fare offered by network television, where most characters of any importance are middle or upper-middle class. Why, then, was this show in particular invariably described, often pejoratively, as a yuppie drama?

The answer tells us a great deal about the way in which class is represented on television. The show *thirtysomething* was unusual *not* because it was about young professionals, but because it was *self-consciously* about young professionals. It was difficult to watch an episode without being aware that this was a group of people that were, in class terms, fairly privileged. Here was a show that was conspicuously and unapologetically class conscious. When most TV characters display a liberal concern for the poor or the homeless, we are invited to applaud their altruism. When characters on *thirtysomething* did so, we were more likely to cringe with embarrassment at the class contradictions thrown up by such philanthropic gestures. Thus, *thirtysomething*'s principal sin was not that it showed us yuppies, but that it made them appear part of an exclusive world that many people will never inhabit. With its coy realism, *thirtysomething* was killjoy television, puncturing the myth of the American dream.

Although we see echoes of this class consciousness on shows like *Frasier*, they are represented in ways that tend to elide rather than confirm class distinctions. It is not just that Frasier and Niles Crane's high-cultural, upper-middle-class affectations are often parodied, but that the constant presence of their working-class father reminds us that class background is unimportant.

The prosperous, comfortable world in which most television characters live is generally *welcoming*, and it is into this world that upscale black characters—from the Huxtables onward—fit like the proverbial glove. It is, we would argue, hard to underestimate the significance of this in the politics of representation. Thus, we can say that in order to be normal on television—the prerequisite for a positive image—black characters are *necessarily* presented as middle or upper-middle class. Indeed, *The Cosby Show* itself used two of television's favorite professions—what, after all, could be more routine than a household headed by a lawyer and a doctor? But, unlike *thirtysomething*, it also had to *look* normal, to portray these wealthy professionals as a regular, everyday family. The respondents in our study suggested that the show was particularly skillful and adroit in absorbing this contradiction; indeed, its popularity depends upon this combination of accessibility and affluence. Professionals and blue-collar workers can both watch the show and see themselves reflected in it. Social barriers, like class or race, are absent from this world. They have to be. To acknowledge the presence of such things would make too many viewers uncomfortable. Television has thereby imposed a set of cultural rules upon us that give us certain expectations about the way the TV world should be.

The bombardment from this image world makes it very difficult for people schooled in the evasive language of North American television to seriously comprehend the world around them. If a serious analysis of class structures is generally absent from our popular vocabulary, then that absence is confirmed by a television environment that makes upward mobility desirable but class barriers irrelevant. As a consequence, when our respondents tried to make sense of class issues thrown up by a discussion of *The Cosby Show*, many were forced to displace the idea of class onto a set of racial categories. This was often the case for our black respondents, who often became enmeshed in the debate about whether the show was "too white" (an idea that, incidentally, the great majority repudiated). And yet, we would argue, the very terms of such a debate involve a misleading syllogism: one that declares that since black people are disproportionately less *likely* to be upper-middle class, if they become so they have not entered a class category (upper-middle class) but a *racial* one (white). One of our black middle-class respondents revealed the confusion involved in this way of thinking when he said, "What's wrong with showing a black family who has those kind of values? I almost said *white* values, but *that's not the word I want*" (our emphasis). The context of portrayal like *The Cosby Show* is not so much white culture (whatever that may be), but *upper-middle-class culture*. It is partly by echoing the stilted discourse of U.S. television that many of our respondents found it difficult to make such a distinction.

In creating *The Cosby Show*, Bill Cosby can hardly be blamed for playing by the rules of network television. Indeed, what our study makes clear is that it was *only* by conforming to these cultural limitations that he was able to make a black family so widely acceptable to white TV viewers. The discomfort or distance that most of the white viewers in our study expressed about black television characters was articulated *not only* in racial terms, but also—albeit indirectly—in class terms. What many white viewers found off-putting about other black sitcoms was not blackness per se, but *working-class blackness*.

> "I mean it's not a jive show, like *Good Times*. I think those others shows are more jive, more soul shows, say as far as the way the characters are with making you aware that they are more separate. Where Cosby is one of American down the line thing, which makes everybody feel accepted."

> "I remember that it [The Jeffersons] was a little bit more slapstick, a little bit more stereotypical. They were concerned with racial issues. And it was much more interested in class, and the difference between class, middle class versus working class."

> "They talk with the slick black accent, and they work on the mannerisms, and I think they make a conscious effort to act that way like they are catering to the black race in that show. Whereas Cosby, you know, definitely doesn't do that. He's upper middle class, and he's not black stereotypical. There's a difference in the tone of those shows, completely."

The Price of Admission and Its Political Consequences

While there may be dimensions to this race/class inflection that go beyond television, the difficulty some white viewers have in inviting black working-class characters into their living rooms is partly a function of television's class premise, in which normalcy is middle and upper-middle class and working-class characters are, to some extent, outsiders. In terms of the politics of representation, our study raises a difficult question: if black characters must be upscale to be accepted into this image world, is such an acceptance worth the price of admission? In order to answer this question, we must consider the broader consequences of this representational move.

Among white people, the repeated appearance of black characters in TV's upwardly mobile world gives credence to the idea that racial divisions, whether perpetuated by class barriers or by racism, do not exist. Most white people are extremely receptive to such a message. It allows them to feel good about themselves and about the society of which they are part. The many black professionals who easily inhabit the TV world suggest to people that, as one of our respondents put it, "there really is room in the United States for minorities to get ahead, without affirmative action."

If affirmative action has become a hot issue in contemporary politics, it is because the tide has turned against it, with states and universities (including our own) buckling under pressure to abandon the policy. As Gray suggests in his analysis of the Reagan years, conservatives are able to use their opposition to such policies as a way of mobilizing white votes (Gray, 1996). Indeed, our study reveals that the opposition to affirmative action among white people is overwhelming. What was particularly notable was that, while most white people are prepared to acknowledge that such a policy was *once* necessary, the prevailing feeling is that this is no longer so.

"I think I've become less enamored of it. I think that when the whole idea was first discussed, it was a very good idea . . . In recent years, I don't think it's necessarily getting anybody anywhere."

"I think in a lot of respects it's carried too far and that it results in reverse discrimination because you have quotas to meet for different job positions and that kind of stuff, it's like, a white person no longer has equal opportunity towards a job because you have to fill a quota."

"Well, I think it has gone too far, where the white people don't have the opportunities. I think it has come to a point where people should be hired now, not because of their color or their race, but because of what they're able to do. I mean there are people who are much better qualified but can't get hired because they are white, and I don't think that's right. Maybe in the beginning, they needed this . . . but it has gone too far."

There are, of course, circumstances in which a qualified black person will receive a warm reception from employers concerned to promote an equal opportunity image. Any cursory glance at social statistics, however, demonstrates that this is because employers are sheepish or embarrassed by current levels of inequality in the workplace. Almost any social index suggests that we live in a society in which black and white people are not equal, whether in terms of education, health, housing, employment, or wealth. So why is affirmative action suddenly no longer necessary? Partly, we would suggest, because our popular culture tells us so.

During our content analysis of the three main networks, we came across only one program that offered a glimpse of these racial divisions. What was significant about this program, however, was that it did not take place in the present, but in the past, during the early days of the civil rights movement. TV was only able to show us racial divisions in the United States by traveling back in time to the bad old days. Most of the black characters in TV's here and now seemed blissfully free of such things. Attempts by Hollywood to deal with racial inequality adopt the same strategy. Racism, whether on *Driving Miss Daisy*, *The Long Walk Home*, or *Amistad*, is confined to the safe distance of history. There are some notable exceptions—such as Spike Lee's work—but the general impression is clear: the social causes of racial inequality are behind us.

Television, despite—and in some ways because of—the liberal intentions of many who write its stories, has pushed our culture backwards. White people are not prepared to deal with the problem of racial inequality, because they are no longer sure if or why there is a problem. In their survey of contemporary American belief systems, James Patterson and Peter Kim found that

> In the 1990s, white Americans hold blacks, and blacks alone, to blame for their current position in American society. "We tried to help," whites say over and over, "but blacks wouldn't help themselves." This is the basis for what we've called the new racism. Everything flows from it. It is a change from the hardcore racism that existed in our country's earlier years. It is also a dramatic contrast to the attitudes of the 1960s, when many whites, from the President on down, publicly stated that black people were owed compensation for centuries of oppression. (1992, p. 183)

The use of upscale black television characters, as our study made increasingly clear, is an intrinsic part of this process. Television becomes Dr. Feelgood, indulging its white audience so that their response to racial inequality becomes a guilt-free, self-righteous inactivity.

This has saddled us, as Patterson and Kim suggest, with a new, repressed form of racism. For, while television now portrays a world of equal opportunity, most white people know enough about the world to see that black people achieve less, on the whole, than white people—a discourse emphasized by television news (Entman, 1990). They know that black people are disproportionately likely to live in poor neighborhoods, to drop out of school, or to be involved in crime. Indeed, overall, television's representation of black people is bifurcated—a Jekyll-and-Hyde portrayal in which the bulk of ordinary working-class black Americans have few images of themselves outside of those connected with crime, violence, and drugs.

Media Images: Accentuating the Positive and the Negative

The most striking aspect of the interviews with black Americans in our study was the ubiquity of comments about the role that media images play in how white America looks at them—of how stereotypical images of blacks as criminals impacted upon their own everyday interaction with white society and institutions. As one person put it,

> "Nobody can believe that you can actually have the intelligence, the fortitude, the dedication and determination to go out and earn a decent living to afford

you some nice things. The mentality today is that if you're black and you get something, you either got it through drugs or through prostitution."

The role that the media played in the cultivation of this perception was clearly understood. As another of our respondents stated,

"We seem to be the only people in the world that TV tries to pick out the negative to portray as characteristic of us. What television is doing to us, I think, is working a hell of a job on us."

For minority groups, then, living in the kind of residential and social apartheid that characterizes much of contemporary America, media images are vital, as they are the primary way that the broader society views them. Black America, after all, is well aware of what white perception of black males, in particular, can lead to. In the Rodney King case, an all-white suburban jury acquitted four Los Angeles Police Department officers for a brutal beating on the basis that the person receiving the beating was, in the words of one of the jurors, "controlling the action." When your image of black people is as subhuman criminals, muggers, drug addicts, gang members, and welfare cheats, then even when a black man is lying hog-tied on the ground, he is still dangerous, and any action to subdue him becomes justified.

It is not surprising, in this framework, that Bill Cosby's self-conscious attempt to promote a series of very different black images was so well-received by the black respondents in our study. But if it is a kind of representational rescue mission, it is one with an almost fairy-tale script. Thus, we can move from news images of black criminals to fictional images of black lawyers and judges in a matter of network minutes.

In this way, media images turn real and complex human beings into crude one-dimensional caricatures, which then come to define minority populations for the majority. Perhaps the apotheosis of this bifurcated imagery was the figure of O. J. Simpson. If many white Americans were bemused by the degree to which black Americans felt they had a stake in the innocence of a rich TV celebrity, it was because they did not understand the representational issues at stake. The rush to a judgment of innocence was a mechanism of self-defense against a popular culture that offers a limited and bifurcated view of black life, one that can be symbolized by two characters in the recent history of black representation: Bill Cosby and Willie Horton.

The Cosby Show epitomized and inspired a move in network television toward the routine presentation of black professionals in drama and situation comedy. The flip side to this is the world of the news or so-called reality programming (such as *Cops*), where it is blacks as violent criminals, drug-dealers, crackheads, and welfare mothers that dominate the screen. Perhaps the embodiment of this side of the story is Willie Horton, the image used by the George Bush Sr.

presidential campaign in 1988 to scare white America away from voting for Mike Dukakis. (In a now-infamous TV campaign ad that is credited with turning the election around, Horton was represented as a crazed murderer, whom the Dukakis prison furlough program, in a moment of foolish liberal do-gooding, allowed out of prison.)

These are the two predominant images of black Americans with which the majority of white people are familiar. The O. J. case was pivotal, as Simpson came to be located precisely at the conjuncture between the two. He *was* Bill Cosby (affluent, friendly, smiling, and cultured). If he was guilty of a brutal double murder, he would *become* Willie Horton. The representational identity of black America as a whole, given the incredible visibility of the case, was the prize at stake. As writer Anthony Walton comments on what is at stake in these battles over representation,

> I am recognizing my veil of double consciousness, my American self and my black self. I must battle, like all humans, to see myself. I must also battle, because I am black, to see myself as others see me; increasingly my life, literally, depends upon it. I might meet Bernard Goetz in the subway . . . the armed security guard might mistake me for a burglar in the lobby of my building. And they won't see a mild-mannered English major trying to get home. They will see Willie Horton. (1989, p. 53)

In this context, it is little wonder that black Americans took the Simpson case so *personally*. His innocence would, in some ways, maintain the representational progress forged by Bill Cosby, while his guilt would tilt it back to Willie Horton. He *had* to be innocent because African Americans, like all people, want the world to recognize their humanity and their dignity. In a context in which their identity is at stake, the evidence had little relevance. Any story—however implausible—of conspiracy and racism would eradicate the forensics and the DNA tests, etc. That is precisely what Johnny Cochran offered the jury and black America, and it was accepted with thanks.

But, for white viewers, how can sense be made of this bifurcated world? How can black failure in reality programming be reconciled with television's fictions, so replete with images of black success? How can one explain racial inequalities in the context of the racial equality of television's upscale world? Without some acknowledgment that the roots of racial inequality are embedded in our society's class structure, there is only one way to reconcile this paradoxical state of affairs. If black people are disproportionately unsuccessful, then they must be disproportionately less deserving. While few of our respondents were prepared to be this explicit (although a number came very close), their failure to acknowledge class or racial barriers means that this is the only explanation available. The consequence, in the apparently enlightened welcome that white viewers extend to television's black professionals, is a new, sophisticated form of racism. Their success casts a shadow of failure across the majority of black people who have, by these standards, failed. Television, which tells us very little about the structures behind success or failure (Iyengar, 1991), leaves white viewers to assume that the black people who do not match up to their television counterparts have only themselves to blame.

In a rather different way, the effect of *The Cosby Show* on its black audience is also one of flattering to deceive. The dominant reaction of our black viewers to the show was "for this relief, much thanks." After suffering years of negative media stereotyping, most black viewers were delighted by a show that portrayed African Americans as intelligent, sensitive, and successful:

> "I admire him. I like his show because it depicts black people in a positive way. It's good to see that black people can be professionals."

> "Thank you, Dr. Cosby, for giving us back ourselves."

The problem with this response is that it embraces the assumption that, on television, a positive image is a prosperous image. This dubious equation means that African Americans are trapped into a position in which any reflection of more typical black experience—which is certainly not upper-middle class—is stereotypical. As one of our black respondents said, even though he was painfully aware that *The Cosby Show* presented a misleading picture of what life was like for most black Americans, "There's part of me that says, in a way, I don't want white America to see us, you know, struggling or whatever." On TV, there is no dignity in struggling unless you win.

This analysis of stereotyping dominates contemporary thought. It is the consequence of a television world that has told us that to be working class is to be marginal. Thus it is that viewers in our study were able to see the Huxtable family on *The Cosby Show* as both regular and everyday *and* as successful, well-heeled professionals.

For black viewers, this deceit amounts to a form of cultural blackmail. It leaves two choices: either to be complicit partners in an image system that masks the deep racial divisions in the United States or else be forced to buy into the fiction that, as one respondent put it, "there are black millionaires all over the place," thereby justifying *The Cosby Show* as a legitimate portrayal of average African-American life.

The Structural Confines of Network Television

If our study tells us anything, it is that we need to be more attentive to the attitudes cultivated by so-called normal, everyday television. In the case of representations of race, these attitudes can affect the way in which we think about issues such as race and class, and, in so doing, can even influence the results of elections.

As we have suggested, it doesn't have to be this way. There is no reason why TV characters cannot be working class and dignified and admirable—or even just plain normal. Bill Cosby's more recent sitcom—*Cosby*—is one attempt to do this, although his enormous popularity as a performer gives him a license that other shows, such as the short-lived *Frank's Place*, do not have. Other television cultures have managed to avoid distorting and suppressing the class structure of their societies; why can't we manage it in the United States?

The American dream is much more than a gentle fantasy; it is the dominant discourse in the United States for understanding (or misunderstanding) class. It is a cultural doctrine that encompasses vast tracts of American life. No politician would dare to question our belief in it—any more than they would publicly question the existence of God. Even though politicians of many different persuasions pay lip service to the dream (it is, in conventional wisdom, what's great about America), it is not a politically neutral idea. It favors those on the political right that say that anyone, regardless of circumstance, can make it if they try. In such an egalitarian world, the free market delivers a kind of equity, making public intervention and regulation an unnecessary encumbrance. For government to act to eradicate the enormous social problems in the United States is to defy the logic of the dream. Intervention implies, after all, that the system is not naturally fair and that opportunity is not universal.

The American dream is, in this context, insidious rather than innocent. It is part of a belief system that allows people in the United States to disregard the inequalities that generate its appalling record on poverty, crime, health, homelessness, and education. It is not surprising that the more fortunate cling to the self-justifying individualism that the dream promotes. One of the saddest things about the United States is that, sometimes, the less fortunate do too.

The ideological dominance of the American dream is sustained by its massive presence in popular culture. The television and film industries churn out fable after fable, thereby reducing us to a state of spellbound passivity in which decades of stagnating incomes for many Americans have been accepted with little protest. The success for which we are encouraged to strive is always linked to the acquisition of goods, a notion fueled by the ubiquitous language of advertising, in which consumers do not usually see themselves in commercials; instead, they see a vision of a glamorous and affluent world to which they aspire. Underlying the preponderance of middle- and upper-middle-class characters on display is the relentless message that this is what the world of happiness and contentment looks like. In this context, ordinary settings seem humdrum or even depressing. Not only do we expect television to be more dramatic than everyday life, but, in the United States, we also expect it to be *more affluent*. We don't just want a good story, we want a classy setting.

"I liked the background. I like to look at the background on a TV program; I enjoy that. The setting, the clothes, that type of thing. I don't enjoy dismal backgrounds."

"This is nice; it looks good, and it's kind of, you accept it; they have a beautiful home, and everything is okay."

This is the language of advertising. It is also, now, the discourse of the American dream. This language is now so much a part of our culture that these attitudes seem perfectly natural. It is only when we look at other television cultures that we can see that they are not.

Few other industrial nations leave their cultural industries to be as dependent upon advertising revenue as they are in the United States. In the United States, very little happens in our popular culture without a commercial sponsor. This takes place in a lightly regulated free-market economy in which cultural industries are not accountable to a notion of public service, but rather to the bottom line of profitability.

Apart from tiny grants to public broadcasting, the survival of radio and television stations depends almost entirely on their ability to sell consumers (viewers or listeners) to advertisers. Moreover, broadcasters in the United States are required to do little in the way of public service. There are no regulations that encourage quality, diversity, innovation, or educational value in programming. This means that the influence of advertising is twofold. Not only does it create a cultural climate that influences the form and style of programs that fill the spaces between commercials, but it also commits television to the production of formulaic programming. Once cultural patterns are established, it is difficult to deviate from them without losing the ratings that bring in the station's revenue.

This is not merely a tyranny of the majority and the logic of the lowest common denominator. A ratings system driven by advertising does not so much favor popularity as the quest for the largest pockets of disposable income. The 1999 season of *Dr. Quinn, Medicine Women* was cancelled by CBS *even though* it was regularly the most popular show on television during its Saturday night time-slot. The problem was simply that its viewers were generally not wealthy enough to be of interest to advertisers. The ad-driven chase for well-heeled demographics thereby gives network television an in-built class bias, creating a climate in which portrayals of working-class black characters may make good television but are an unlikely way to attract television's most sought-after demographic group.

This brings us back to the many representational offshoots of *The Cosby Show*. In order to be successful and to stay on the air, *The Cosby Show* had to meet certain viewers' expectations. This, as we have seen, meant seducing viewers with the vision of comfortable affluence that the Huxtables epitomize. Once television has succumbed to the discourse of the American dream, where a positive image is a prosperous one, it cannot afford the drop in ratings that will accompany a redefinition of viewers' expectations. TV programs that do so are necessarily short lived. Programs such as *Frank's Place, Cop Rock,* or *Twin Peaks* all deviated from a norm, and, while still watched by millions of viewers, did not attain the mass audience required to keep them on the air. This puts us on a treadmill of cultural stagnation. It is a system in which the bland repetition of fantasies tailored to the interests of wealthier viewers makes sound business sense.

In such a system, *The Cosby Show's* survival depended upon meeting the demands of a formula that pleases as many people as possible, *especially* its more upscale audience. And our study suggests that it did so with consummate success, pleasing black and white people, blue-collar workers and professionals, all in slightly different ways. The more blue-collar *Cosby* has been less universally embraced, and, in this context, we should applaud Bill Cosby's attempt to use his popularity to offer audiences a less upscale image.

When our book, *Enlightened Racism: The Cosby Show, Audiences, and the Myth of the American Dream,* was first published in 1992, we were widely credited with holding *The Cosby Show* responsible for promoting the routine fiction of effortless black success. But this was not the thrust of our argument. *The Cosby Show* and the many black professionals portrayed in its wake are genuine attempts to make television's upscale world more racially diverse. The problem is not with *individual* instances of black success, but with a television environment whose structural conditions make a wider array of images less profitable.

References

Entman, R. (1990). Modern racism and the images of blacks in local television news. *Critical Studies in Mass Communications, 7*(4).

Gray, H. (1996). *Watching race: Television and the struggle for blackness.* Minneapolis: University of Minnesota Press.

Hacker, A. (1992). *Two nations: Black and white, separate, hostile, unequal.* New York: Scribner's.

Iyengar, S. (1991). *Is anyone responsible?* Chicago: University of Chicago Press.

Jhally, S., & Lewis, J. (1992). *Enlightened racism: The Cosby Show, audiences, and the myth of the American dream.* Boulder, CO: Westview.

Patterson, J., & Kim, P. (1992). *The day America told the truth.* New York: Dutton.

Walton, A. (1989, August 20). Willie Horton and me. *The New York Times Magazine.*

Wilson, W. J. (1987). *The truly disadvantaged.* Chicago: University of Chicago Press.

The Politics of Cultural Studies: Racism, Hegemony, and Resistance[*]

with Justin Lewis

In response to Herman Gray's recent review of our book, *Enlightened Racism: The Cosby Show, Audiences, and the Myth of the American Dream*, we would like to make a general comment regarding the purpose of the book and the current debate on audience research in cultural studies. In general, we found Gray's comments thoughtful and fair-minded (apart from a few minor quibbles, with which we have no intention of boring you). He does, however, raise an important general issue, which we feel calls for some clarification on our part.

Gray expresses a concern that our analysis is too ideologically driven, that we focus on those aspects of our interview data that indicate television's culpability in the cultivation of certain reactionary attitudes toward race and class. One of our main arguments, in brief, is that the assimilation of fictional black characters into the upper-middle-class world of the United States sustains myths of class-lessness and the American dream in such a way that viewers (particularly white viewers) assume that social inequalities between black and white people must be the result of the failure or refusal of most African Americans to take advantage of the opportunities repeatedly displayed on television. This analysis, Gray suggests, ignores the more complex, discursive interplay between television and television

[*] This essay first appeared in *American Quarterly* 46, no. 1 (March 1994): 114–117. Reprinted with permission.

viewers, which produces a range of contradictory and multidimensional ideological positions.

While we do spend some time discussing the complexity and range of responses in our focus groups, we would acknowledge that the polemical thrust of our concluding chapters might justify this criticism. Yet, our focus on television's ideological power was quite deliberate, for three reasons.

First, we feel that there is an increasing tendency in recent audience research (particularly within cultural studies) to emphasize the ideological *weakness* of television or other cultural industries in the face of audiences who resist or evade dominant ideological meanings. In this sense, the absence of audience studies that look at those moments where television does contribute toward the construction of reactionary ideologies is remarkable. We would argue that television's role is hegemonic. In that sense, it is always about contestation and negotiation (as well as complicity), and we agree with Gray that readings are always contingent (the result of a complex interplay of discourses) and that the effects of texts come from their articulation or disarticulation with other prevailing stories circulating in the semiotic-cultural environment—that they are always, in Gray's terms, *situated*.

In other words, there is semiotic space for the resistance and evasion of dominant messages, but, we would argue, that space is limited and, in political terms, largely (though not wholly) unsuccessful. This argument within cultural studies is uncontroversial, and, yet, it is a view that tends to be assumed or neglected in audience research (particularly in the United States, where, ironically, television's hegemonic power is less ambiguous than in most other developed countries). Our desire was simply to redress that balance, to point out that, although there is ambiguity, there is also widespread compliance.

Certainly, this process is not smooth and manifests all kinds of contradictions, but such a conclusion on our part is an attempt to move beyond individual readings and to address the question of *determination* on a social-cultural level. Our conclusions were not arrived at a priori by our theoretical framework. They are supported, we believe, by our data. They are contingent and situated.

Our second point is more complex. It is invariably assumed that the presence of ambiguity and fragmentation in audience readings is part of the struggle *against* hegemony, that polysemy dents television's semiotic power. Our argument in *Enlightened Racism* is that it ain't necessarily so. We try to show that television's ambiguity can be the fibrous tissue of its ideological muscle. So, for example, the ability of *The Cosby Show* to appeal to different groups in different ways is part of its ideological strength, since our data suggest that it leads a variety of contradictory subject positions in much the same direction. Black and white viewers clearly celebrated the appearance of the affluent black television characters for very different reasons and interpreted what they saw in different ways, but they were both pushed into an ideological framework in which the role of class structures (and, dare we say it, capitalism) in perpetuating racial inequality is entirely absent.

Gray argues that we are too committed to a structuralist and materialist approach, to a too top-down reading of ideology in which television serves the interests of the powerful. Actually, we find this top-down–bottom-up notion of power an inadequate way of capturing the complexity of cultural processes. (As we have indicated, we prefer to work with the full Gramscian concept of hegemony.) In this context, one could read our analysis of *The Cosby Show* as a *failure* of top-down power. Its creator, Bill Cosby, is, in many ways, an innovative cultural warrior who was attempting to reverse what he felt to be years of demeaning images of African Americans on television—images with *real* determining effects *on* minority populations (see Chapter 7 of our book *Enlightened Racism*). The creation of the Huxtables was an attempt to make black Americans human (and a point of identification) for white Americans. "They are just like us." Such a connection in the type of race-stratified society within which we live should surely be hailed as a progressive step forward. And our data show that, in many ways, Cosby succeeded.

But this success took place in a semiotic environment that had the effect of channeling it in a reactionary direction. The other discourses it articulated with and fed into (such as classlessness and the American dream) changed the meaning of the new images and created what we call a new *enlightened racism* in which white Americans love the Huxtables and are happy to invite them into their living rooms but still look at the vast number of black Americans as mired in a set of problems of their own making. This overall effect of the show (and, importantly, of the many other images of affluent African Americans that it unleashed and legitimated) is no longer under Cosby's control. It is now a function of the *field of representation* that it partly constitutes. (The case of Cosby is, in this respect, similar to that of Bruce Springsteen in the mid-1980s, when his angry and highly cynical anthem "Born in the USA" was widely read and appropriated as a celebration of Reagan's America.)

Our third point concerns the general tendency in American cultural studies toward depoliticization. It is significant, in this regard, that our quite specific conclusions are read by Gray as a general commitment to a structural position. It seems that merely to address the *question* of structural determination is to be located (negatively) within a set of carefully defined disciplinary positions (ideology/resistance, domination/contestation, structuralist/culturalist, and society/individual). In our opinion, a critical cultural studies that does not address this question is not worthy of the name, and *Enlightened Racism* is an attempt to contextualize the recent turn toward audience resistance by placing the question of determination back on the agenda. In broad terms, it is to offer a counterperspective to the depoliticization of American cultural studies presently under way—to refuse the binary opposites presented to us and to insist on a framework that remembers both sides of Marx's famous aphorism: people make history (meaning) but not in conditions of their own choosing. It seems to us that a lot of recent analyses have focused on the making of history as isolated from the conditions—hence, the turn toward polysemy and pluralism divorced from questions of power in American cultural studies.

We chose not to state these arguments explicitly in the book, because we hoped to address an audience outside the academy to whom they might have seemed esoteric. These points are, however, germane to very contemporary academic debate within and outside cultural studies, and we welcome the opportunity to make them.

Media Literacy

The Struggle for Media Literacy *

with Justin Lewis

The argument we wish to make is, in essence, a simple one: media literacy should be about helping people to become sophisticated citizens rather than sophisticated consumers. The mass media, in other words, should be understood as more than a collection of texts to be deconstructed and analyzed so that we can distinguish—or choose—between them. They should, we will argue, be analyzed as a set of institutions with particular social and economic structures—structures that are neither inevitable nor irreversible. Media education should certainly teach students to engage with media texts, but it should also, in our view, teach them to engage—and challenge—media institutions.

While we see textual analysis as an integral part of media education, we would suggest that, in any media system, the fact that we see some messages and not others raises the question of power and the active construction of the social world. In this light, our arguments here are prompted by comments made by an important and influential pioneer in the American media literacy movement, Renee Hobbs, following the National Media Literacy conference in Los Angeles in October, 1996. Hobbs was concerned that "for some participants, media literacy has been either deliberately or accidentally conflated with activism around

* This essay first appeared in the *Journal of Communication* 48, no. 1 (1998): 109–120. Reprinted with permission.

media reform issues." In her view "it is inappropriate to lump media activism together with media literacy." Instead, she argues that "at the heart of the media literacy movement is the open, questioning, reflective, critical stance towards messages" and defines media literacy as "the process of accessing, critically analyzing media messages and creating messages using media tools. The goal of media literacy is to promote autonomy through the development of analysis, reasoning, communication and self-expression skills" (Hobbs, 1996).

We will argue that such avoidance of thorny political territory is to sidestep widespread citizen concerns and to miss an opportunity to demonstrate the valence and necessity of not merely understanding the world but of changing it. In making this argument, we take our lead from the work of Len Masterman in Britain, for whom

> the democratization of institutions, and the long march toward a truly participatory democracy, will be highly dependent upon the ability of majorities of citizens to take control, become effective change agents, make rational decisions (often on the basis of media evidence) and to communicate effectively perhaps through an active involvement with the media. (1997, p. 60)

This is, we would argue, particularly important in a media system in which most messages are either explicitly or implicitly commercial (either straightforward advertisements or content designed to deliver audiences to advertisers in the most efficient and profitable way—see Barnouw, 1978; Jhally, 1987). The mass media may be producing art, but they are also producing commerce (as well as reproducing power), and we feel that it is impossible to fully understand one without comprehending the other. Unlike some of the more public service–oriented broadcasting systems in Europe and elsewhere, the goals of a loosely regulated, commercial media have no educational, cultural, or informational imperatives. As much of the literature on the political economy of the media indicates, they are there to maximize profits and to serve a set of corporate interests, and these imperatives provide a framework that helps to shape both the form and content of media texts (Bagdikian, 1997; Herman & Chomsky, 1988; Garnham, 1990; Schiller, 1984, 1989, 1996).

We would therefore argue for a contextual approach to media education, one in which the media text is a stage in a process of ideological production. As Richard Johnson suggests in his classic introduction to British cultural studies, while we may be able to distinguish between a series of analytical moments—production of text, the text itself, and reception of text—we need to be able to understand the determinations and connections between them (Johnson, 1986–87). Along with Johnson, we would urge those involved in media education to think of the circuit of cultural production of commodities.

In what follows, we will argue, as briefly as we can, for a contextual, rather than a text-centered, approach. Such a perspective, we will suggest, allows students to imagine ways of changing media systems and thus creates the possibility of a more democratic media. We will propose, in so doing, an emphasis on political economy in the face of the current trend toward text-centered approaches. Having stressed the importance of the production end of the circuit, we will then consider the role in media education of teaching production skills. We will conclude with a more practical consideration of the politics of media literacy, arguing against the pragmatism of text-centered approaches.

Textual versus Contextual Approaches

The notion of *literacy*, particularly in relation to forms like television, is a complex one. The call for media education exists not in response to a functionally illiterate media public, but to a public who are already voracious readers, viewers, and listeners. Media literacy is more than a matter of basic comprehension. Few people, after all, need to be taught how to make sense of television or, in most cases, to appreciate its "preferred meanings" (Hall, 1980; Morley, 1980, 1986). On the contrary, the fact that so many have the ability to make sense of a barrage of disconnected, split-second images amidst a sophisticated range of realist conventions implies that—in one restricted sense at least—a high degree of literacy already exists.

Media literacy is, therefore, more than a matter of comprehension—it is concerned with the form and scope of that comprehension. We would, however, go further to assert that media literacy is not a simple matter of reading media well, whether in the traditional Leavisite sense (of distinguishing between "good" and "bad" texts, see Leavis, 1950) or in the more deconstructive sense of understanding textual strategies, possibilities, or pleasures (Barthes, 1974, 1975, 1988). There is, we would argue, more to media education than a framework for appreciating the finer nuances of the *Seinfeld* narrative, the montage of the opening credits of *ER*, or the ways in which the extreme close-up shot in *60 Minutes* situates the spectator.

The distinction that we would like to make is between a text-focused form of media literacy and a contextual approach in which the unraveling of media texts takes place in the context of their production and reception. This is not to downplay the importance of textual analysis: it is at the level of the text, after all, that vital issues of representation are played out, and a sophisticated textual analysis can tell us something about both encoding and decoding (Hall, 1994). But, we would argue, a textual analysis that takes place without an examination of the institutional, cultural, and economic conditions in which texts are produced and understood is necessarily limited.

Media literacy, in short, is about more than the analysis of messages; it is about an awareness of why those messages are there. It is not enough to know that they are produced—or even how, in a technical sense, they are produced. To appreciate the significance of contemporary media, we need to know why they are produced, under what constraints and conditions they are produced, and by whom they are produced.

Raymond Williams has documented the way in which early struggles over literacy were bound up with questions of power and control (1977). In the early years of industry, workers were trained to read but not to write. This allowed them to follow orders or to read the Bible for moral instruction but not to express their own needs or interests. Although contemporary television audiences are not so consciously deprived, their situation is in many ways analogous. They are expected to consume rather than to produce—to pick from the display offered by commercial television rather than to debate the terms and conditions in which broadcasting takes place.

We therefore need to differentiate between a text-centered approach that restricts itself to proficiency in reading and Raymond Williams' more general form of cultural criticism in which both the reading and the production of texts are understood within sets of social relations (Williams, 1974, 1980). Similarly, Janice Radway's work on romances and the Book of the Month Club engages with determinations at every stage in the circuit of production and reception (Radway, 1994).

As both Williams' and Radway's work suggests, an analysis of political economy should not be restricted to a narrow set of economic relations. The media are determined by a set of social and economic conditions that involve the key dividing lines of our culture, whether they be race, class, gender, sexuality, age, or mobility. This may be a complex point, but we are concerned that media education in the United States will flounder if it cannot locate media texts in a broad set of social realities.

Roland Barthes' well-known announcement of the death of the author is illustrative here (Barthes, 1977). His argument is, in many way, a celebration of textual analysis in which a focus on production or reception becomes a constraint on the practice of reading. Barthes' argument works because he is engaged with a particular site—traditional literary criticism—in which the politics of production are less central. He is concerned with how literary texts—many of which have been around for some time—are read and understood, not with the production, marketing, and distribution of contemporary fiction.

Media studies, on the other hand, is forced to deal with limits and constraints, to explain absences—like, for example, the existence of a black working class on U.S. television (Jhally & Lewis, 1992)—and the consequences of those absences. And, to do so, it is required to go beyond the text.

If this contextual approach makes media literacy less *safe*, it also, we would argue, makes it more enticing. So, for example, asking high school students to critique an advertisement by the Campaign for a Drug Free America may or may not encourage a vague cynicism about how those in authority view (or attempt to situate) American youth. This kind of cynicism is, on its own, unhelpful to both the high school student and their teachers. If the teacher is able to go beyond the text, to point out that the Campaign for a Drug Free America is a consortium funded by America's leading alcohol, tobacco, and pharmaceutical companies (Cotts, 1992), the students are confronted with a more concrete political reality. The conclusions they draw may still be cynical, but it is likely to be a more directed cynicism, one born of analysis rather than attitude. Students can do more than play textual games; they can question the rules.

Similarly, an analysis of the news should not only be concerned with the way in which stories are constructed but also who is and who is not allowed to speak (Herman & Chomsky, 1988). A purely textual critique of television news is more speculative. For students to seriously evaluate a news story, they need to be able to go beyond the text to consider the various stories that surround it and thereby to place it within a context that enables them to see the choices ABC or CNN have made.

Political Economy and Citizenship

If the political economy of the media seems a rather dry subject for students to consider, it need not be so. In our experience, students often find this level of analysis rather easier to grasp than a text-focused analysis. There is, in this respect, a healthy literature on political economy from which to draw (Schiller, 1984, 1989, 1996; Herman & McChesney, 1997; Bagdikian, 1997), much of which is, in our experience, extremely useful in allowing students to appreciate issues raised by a textual analysis. Pedagogically, this is less complex or arduous than it sounds. When automobile ads almost invariably show cars driving along empty roads, often across pristine landscapes with cloudless skies, we might ask students not only what is being left out of these images—traffic, pollution, smog, etc.—but also, why? In whose interest is it to see the automobile as a symbol of freedom, exploring rather than despoiling the American landscape, and what role do these interests have in media production? And what are the consequences of seeing the automobile only in these terms?

Our experience indicates that students find it difficult to make sense of media messages as part of a vast, complex and contradictory panorama made up of authorless ideologies. The politics of media texts become more tangible if they are seen as produced by real people for specific purposes. If this seems a perilously political approach, it is no less so than allowing students to see the media only on its own terms. It is a little like teaching a literary canon without allowing students to question the limits or foci of that canon—all the more troubling, perhaps, when the media canon is a product of a purely commercial rationale.

This approach undoubtedly has political consequences: just as political education allows citizens to think more critically and constructively about politics, media literacy can provide people with the wherewithal for thinking about the limits and possibilities of media systems. This is, needless to say, no small task—particularly in the United States, where exposure to foreign media is as limited as it is anywhere in the world.

American broadcasting, in particular, is highly distinctive. Unlike the public service models that influence broadcasting in most other industrialized countries, the history of radio and television in America is one of rampant commercialism (McAllister, 1996). In the United States, media corporations have, since the 1930s, been unusually successful in promoting an idea of broadcasting in economic, rather than cultural, terms—as a business rather than a public service (McChesney, 1993). Media regulation in the United States—particularly since the Reagan era—is conspicuous by its absence, and yet most Americans find it difficult to imagine how it could be any other way.

This conceptual limitation has little to do with preference—surveys do not suggest that Americans are especially happy or uncritical about television (Times Mirror, 1993). It is more a matter of education than imagination. It is difficult to propose changes to a system that is regarded as both inevitable and ubiquitous, and when the only alternative ever presented is the dull, propagandist fare of totalitarian regimes. Indeed, it could be argued that one of the successes of commercial broadcasting in the United States has been in persuading Americans that there is no alternative—that the American system, far from being distinctive, is the only conceivable model in a society that values free speech and free expression. The European concept of *public service broadcasting,* with its possibilities of public funding, cross-subsidy of less commercial channels, and regulations to promote education and diversity, remains a well-kept secret. If the British system is capable of offering a wide range of quality programs with a comparatively small number of channels, one can only imagine the breadth and range of a public service system in a country with a media market as large and bountiful as the United States.

As we have suggested, this implicates the notions of citizenship and cultural democracy. When the British government sanctioned a fourth network (Channel Four) at the beginning of the 1980s, it was at the center of a public debate about the funding, remit, regulation, and purpose of a new television network. While some were critical of the scope of that debate (Blanchard & Morley, 1982; Lambert, 1982), most recent changes in the North American broadcasting landscape have occurred with little or no public input. The lack of public debate surrounding the passage of the Telecommunications Act of 1996 is a graphic example of how a major restructuring of the media environment disappeared from public view. For us, what is most worrying about this absence is less the lack of consultation and discussion than an ideological climate in which the public is so accustomed to being interpolated as mere consumers in a corporate world that any notion of democratic input seems difficult to grasp.

A brief anecdote told to us by our colleague, Michael Morgan, indicates the extent of the problem. During an exam, students were asked to identify which type of media system was most common in countries worldwide: (a) a government-run or public service model or (b) a commercial model. Before the exam, students were told that, when they came to this question, they should not even bother to read it, since the correct answer was choice "a." Despite this apparently unambiguous advice, half his students proceeded to get the answer wrong. This is not a question of dullness—the students performed well enough overall. But the correct answer ran so counter to their own preconceptions that many disregarded not only what they had learned, but also an answer that they had just been told was correct. They were simply unable to imagine of a world in which the American model was atypical.

The blinkered, ideological assumptions behind this premise are fairly deeply rooted, and it will undoubtedly take more than a few media literacy classes to open American minds to other possibilities. Nevertheless, a media literacy curriculum in which issues of representation and content are taught alongside questions of political economy presents a challenge to regulators who have, in recent years, offered little more than the further deregulation of an already lightly regulated system. Debates about the regulation and subsidy of broadcasting can become public debates, rather than esoteric, lopsided discussions between media corporations, legislators, and a few poorly funded pressure groups.

Those currently campaigning for media reform—whether to regulate children's programming so that it is not simply a marketing vehicle for the toy industry or for a viable public television service or for restrictions to monopoly ownership—are stymied not because their ideas are unpopular but because, at a fundamental level, their relevance is not appreciated. Americans have become used to a system of top-down control, where a citizen's input is restricted to being a blip in the Nielsen ratings and where commercial considerations are inexorably paramount. Media literacy is, therefore, a way of extending democracy to the very place where democracy is increasingly scripted and defined.

The Use and Abuse of Technology

If we have focused on political economy, it is because we see a danger at this moment of the circuit of cultural production and reception becoming excluded from the discussion. Our argument, nevertheless, is not about teaching one thing rather than another, but about the integration of these levels of analysis. A focus on media production that excluded textual analysis would, in our view, be as problematic and fragmented as a purely text-centered approach.

In our experience, the way in which high school teachers may, without guidance, interpret the idea of media literacy suggests that this is a particular danger when teachers are fortunate enough to have the technology for practical classes in media production. In this instance, there are instances when the seductive—and pseudo-empowering—nature of the technology works to exclude both a broad political economy and a critical textual analysis (Frechette, 1997).

For teachers with access to cameras and editing facilities, this technology can be an indispensable component of an educational practice that highlights the question of representation. As Stuart Ewen puts it,

> Media literacy cannot simply be seen as a vaccination against PR or other familiar strains of institutionalized guile. It must be understood as an education in techniques that can democratize the realm of public expression and will magnify the possibility of meaningful public interactions. (1996, p. 414)

In this ideal form, teaching production skills can be a vibrant part of a media literacy project. But we would caution against an unthinking embrace: although media production offers a number of pedagogical opportunities, it may close down as many analytical paths as it opens.

It is sometimes assumed, for example, that a practical knowledge of video production on its own will help demystify the world of television, necessarily promoting a more analytical, critical perspective. There is, however, little evidence to support such an assumption. On the contrary, we have found that students are apt to be seduced by the form, to try to imitate commercial television and, when their efforts fall short, to regard the work of professionals purely in terms of their aesthetic or technical prowess. At best, teaching production as a purely technical set of skills leads to an analytical immersion rather than a critical distance.

Unless the educational limits of teaching production are stressed, it is easy to see how well-resourced schools might answer the call for media literacy simply by offering classes in media production. This would, in our view, not only blunt the critical edge of media literacy, but also allow it to be co-opted into a system of existing educational inequities. If media education is seen as dependent upon the purchase of video cameras and editing equipment, only those schools with sufficient means will be able to participate. Once media literacy is tied to the size of a school's capital budget, it risks becoming yet another symbol of cultural capital.

This is not to say that teaching production cannot or should not be a component of a media literacy project. It is certainly possible—even desirable—to incorporate production classes into a media literacy context, particularly with groups who already feel marginalized by mainstream media. The Educational Video Center (EVC) in New York is a good example of such an initiative: students/participants are encouraged to use video technology to tell stories that are rarely heard on commercial television. This both enhances and develops their sense of critical reflection—they are not so much copying the medium as exploring its potential. This is possible because at the EVC production has been integrated into an overall theoretical approach that highlights the question of power.

The Politics of Media Literacy

As we have suggested, this approach to media education inevitably raises challenging political questions that, in some respects, would be safer to avoid. And yet, we would argue, the feelings of frustration and dissatisfaction that many parents, teachers, and citizens feel is an explicitly political form of discontent—one that gives media literacy its sense of urgency and relevance.

Educators—whether parents or teachers—are tired of competing with television. They are tired of dismissing it as a mere distraction or else resenting it as the evil twin of universal education—the proverbial devil with little substance and all the best tunes. They are also tired of being offered the rather smug retort to their complaints that, if parents or citizens are unhappy with what's offered, they can always turn it off. Most of us, after all, like watching what we consider to be worthwhile, informative, or entertaining. We don't want it to go away—most educators are aware that the bumper sticker invocation to "kill your television" has an ostrich-like impracticality—we want to improve it.

In the current political climate, the political options generally presented to deal with television have been, at best, fairly limited reactions to television's perceived excesses. Calls for censorship, boycotts, or parental control of television viewing—via new technologies, such as the V-chip—all take a fairly negative stance, one in which the basic political economy of loosely regulated commercial television remains intact. If we are to have a television system whose goals are more to do with public service than commerce—whether that means a greater diversity of images and representations, less commercial interruption, more documentary programming, or more educational children's programs—we need to develop a citizenry that appreciates the politics of regulation and funding, to imagine thereby what television might be and how the system might be changed to make it so. The challenge for media literacy, we would argue, is to make this possibility seem less remote.

Whatever this desire for change involves, it will never be fully addressed by a text-centered approach to media education. The demands that give the campaign for media literacy a certain urgency require an approach that addresses questions about social context and social impact. Parents concerned about violence or gender stereotyping in children's programs are unlikely to be mollified by the thought that the *Power Rangers* can be read on a number of different levels or even that their children may eventually come to understand the limits of such stereotypes. They want to know what influence such programming may have and how media producers might be persuaded to offer something less pernicious. They are, in short, concerned not just with the nature of the visual environment, but with the forces that shape it. A contextual approach to media literacy allows students to see the media within a framework of interests and power relations. If some will see a danger here of making media literacy an overtly political project, we take the opposite view. A text-centered approach that fails to address current concerns and dissatisfaction with the media risks losing the political impetus that gives it its current purchase.

For the last four years, we have been involved with the Five-College Media Literacy Institute that introduces teachers to the field of media literacy from the contextual, cultural studies perspective that we have briefly outlined. As many in the field are aware, when teachers return to their schools, there is little support, financial, pedagogical, or structural, for the integration of critical questions around media into the existing curriculum. Creating these supportive environments will be a political task, one that, as Wally Bowen argues with unapologetic vigor, needs to

> connect to the interests and concerns of a broad range of scholars, teachers, health educators, parents and citizens who are seeking ways to critically challenge a media system that exploits children, reduces citizens to consumers, rewards those who poison public discourse, and perpetuates a high-consumption lifestyle that is slowly strangling the planet's life-support systems. (1994)

The implementation of media literacy as a component of the K–12 curriculum will require enthusiastic community support. If a text-centered approach seems a politically safer option, it is also one, in our view, that is less likely to enthuse teachers and parents.

We would acknowledge, however, that a contextual approach with an emphasis on political economy is likely to be less acceptable to some elements within the media literacy coalition than a text-centered approach. Indeed, there is no doubt that advocates for a certain form of text-centered media literacy have been successful in broadening support for media education, and there is certainly an argument that such pragmatism may be more likely to lead to the widespread implementation of media literacy.

As we have stated, this risks diluting the enthusiasm created by the desire for a public voice in decisions about media programming. The rush to embrace media literacy may also lead to its suffocating under the weight of its own incoherence. Even the commercial media industry—perhaps sensing that, in a period of minimal political interference or regulation, the only real danger to its unrestricted growth and profit maximization is a critically informed public—is moving to initiate its own version. Thus, in the inaugural issue of *Better Viewing* magazine, Continental Cablevision (now MediaOne) invokes media literacy and the general empowerment of its viewers. In this self-serving appropriation, informed citizenship means little more than a weekly perusal of *TV Guide*, and it is safe to assume that Continental Cablevision's notion of empowerment does not extend to the regulation of media monopolies or subversive notions of public service broadcasting (Cowie, 1996).

If this attempted colonization is breathtaking in its audacity, it is possible because the phrase itself, with its irresistible invocation of the most basic of skills, is noncommittal in how it applies to the comprehension of mass media. Norman Cowie describes how in

> the United States there is an uneasy consensus among media literacy proponents around a definition that was formulated in Canada in 1989, as "the ability to access, analyze, communicate and produce media in a variety of forms." While this definition appears to serve as a rallying point for coalition building, there is a decided lack of consensus around its terms and practices. (1996, p. 1)

In the face of attempts to build up a critical mass for reform, it is not surprising that the media literacy movement has avoided hard questions and debate around its core concerns. But this avoidance of principle comes at a price: it risks sapping the movement's vitality and replacing it with a vapid ambiguity.

Our advocacy of a contextual approach to media education is influenced by our experience of teaching these issues at the college level, where media analysis thrives in a variety of disciplines in the humanities and liberal arts. The bureaucratic and political contexts of the K–12 situation are very different, and it is easy to see why a more limited, text-based visual literacy worked so well in the confines of this environment. As Wally Bowen puts it,

> The inherent conservatism of U.S. public school bureaucracies discourages the broader examination of media culture inherent in a cultural studies approach, with its emphasis on questions of political economy, power relations, hegemonic influence. . . . The conventional wisdom said that entry into the politically charged minefield of the public school curriculum is achieved by slipping media literacy into the language arts "critical skills" curriculum. (1994)

This defensive posture is perfectly understandable in those places where there is little existing institutional support to create an entirely new field. It has also led to the uneasy consensus that Cowie describes among a disparate group of interests. When your numbers are small, why separate over internal doctrinaire disputes? The sheer scale of the U.S. educational system has meant that the focus on diversity of approaches, which Renee Hobbs argues is the strength of media literacy (Hobbs, 1996), is also our greatest weakness. We would argue with Cowie that "the pluralism that underwrites this diversity has had a depoliticising effect on the very issues that media literacy seeks to address" and that "when one surveys the work that has been accomplished on the basis of a meaningful consensus in countries such as Canada, Western Europe and Australia, it is difficult to feel that our enduring lack of a consensus is viable" (1996, p. 1).

For us, the risk lies in depriving students of a political education that is essential if they are to be capable of making rational decisions amidst a deluge of media messages. To evaluate those messages, students must learn to see them not simply as true or false, realistic or misleading, or stereotypical or positive, but as authored voices with certain interests or assumptions about the world, voices that could be influenced or replaced. As Noam Chomsky (1989) notes, "Citizens of the democratic societies should undertake a course of intellectual self-defense to protect themselves from manipulation and control, and to lay the basis for meaningful democracy" (p. viii). It is important to note that that we are not advocating propagandizing in schools for a particular political perspective, but for a view that recognizes that the world is always made by someone and that a decision to tolerate the status quo is as political as a more overtly radical act.

References

Bagdikian, B. (1997). *The media monopoly*. Boston: Beacon Press.

Barnouw, E. (1978). *The sponsor: Notes on a modern potentate*. New York: Oxford University Press.

Barthes, R. (1974). *S/Z*. New York: Hill and Wang.

Barthes, R. (1975). *The pleasure of the text*. London: Jonathan Cape.

Barthes, R. (1977). *Image-music-text*. Glasgow: Fontana.

Barthes, R. (1988). *Mythologies*. New York: Noonday Press.

Blanchard, S., & Morley, D. (1982). *What's this channel four?* London: Comedia.

Bowen, W. (1994). Can U.S. media literacy movement open door to more points of view? *The New Citizen, 2*(1). Retrieved from http://www.main.nc.us/cml/new_citizen/v2n1/win94c.html

Chomsky, N. (1989). *Necessary illusions: Thought control in democratic societies*. Boston: South End Press.

Cotts, C. (1992). Hard sell in the drug war. *The Nation*, 300–303.

Cowie, N. (1995, Summer/Fall). The future of media literacy in the age of corporate sponsorship. *Video & Learning*, 5–6.

Cowie, N. (1996, May 9). *Media literacy: From the creation of 'critical consumers' to the formation of (radical) political subjects*. Paper presented at conference of the Alliance for Community Media, Burlington, VT.

Ewen, S. (1996). *PR: A social history of spin*. New York: Basic Books.

Frechette, J. (1997). *The politics of implementing media literacy into the United States: A look at the objectives and obstacles facing the Massachusetts public school teacher*. Unpublished master's thesis, University of Massachusetts at Amherst, Amherst, MA.

Garnham, N. (1990). *Capitalism and communication*. London: Sage.

Hall, S. (1980). Encoding/decoding. In S. Hall, D. Hobson, A. Lowe, & P. Willis (Eds.), *Culture, media, language*. London: Hutchinson.

Hall, S. (1994). Reflections upon the encoding/decoding model: An interview with Stuart Hall. In J. Cruz & J. Lewis (Eds.), *Viewing, reading, listening: Audiences and cultural reception*. Boulder, CO: Westview.

Herman, E. S., & Chomsky, N. (1988). *Manufacturing consent: The political economy of the mass media*. New York: Pantheon.

Herman, E. S., & McChesney, R. (1997). *The global media: The new missionaries of corporate capitalism*. London: Cassell.

Hobbs, R. (1996). Media literacy and the big tent. www.medialit.org/readingroom/article394.html.

Jhally, S. (1987). *The codes of advertising : Fetishism and the political economy of meaning in the consumer society*. New York: St. Martin's Press.

Jhally, S., & Lewis, J. (1992). *Enlightened racism: The Cosby Show, audiences, and the myth of the American dream*. Boulder, CO: Westview.

Johnson, R. (1986–1987). What is cultural studies anyway? *Social Text*, 16(Winter).

Lambert, S. (1982). *Channel 4: Television with a difference?* London: BFI.

Leavis, R. (1950). *The great tradition: George Eliot, Henry James, Joseph Conrad*. London: Chatto and Windus.

Masterman, L. (1997). A rationale for media education. In R. Kubey (Ed.), *Media literacy in the information age*. New York: Oxford University Press.

McAllister, M. (1996). *The commercialization of American culture: New advertising, control and democracy*. Thousand Oaks, CA: Sage.

McChesney, R. (1993). *Telecommunications, mass media and democracy: The battle for the control of U.S. broadcasting 1928–1935*. New York: Oxford University Press.

Morley, D. (1980). *The nationwide audience*. London: BFI.

Morley, D. (1986). *Family television*. London: Comedia.

Radway, J. (1994). Romance and the work of fantasy: Struggles over feminine sexuality and subjectivity at century's end. In J. Cruz & J. Lewis (Eds.), *Viewing, reading, listening: Audiences and cultural reception*. Boulder, CO: Westview.

Schiller, H. (1984). *Information and the crisis economy*. Norwood, NJ: Ablex.

Schiller, H. (1989). *Culture, inc.: The corporate takeover of public expression*. New York: Oxford University Press.

Schiller, H. (1996). *Information inequality: The deepening social crisis in America*. New York: Routledge.

Times Mirror Center for the People and the Press. (1993, March 24). *Poll*. Washington, DC.

Williams, R. (1974). *Television, technology and cultural form*. London: Fontana.

Williams, R. (1977). *Marxism and literature*. New York: Oxford University Press.

Williams, R. (1980). *Problems in materialism and culture*. London: New Left Books.

Empowering Literacy: Media Education as a Democratic Imperative[*]

with Jeremy Earp

Introduction

There is almost universal consensus that the cultural environment within which we think about our identities and our places in the world has been radically transformed by the widespread diffusion of new media technologies based primarily on visual modes of representation. Cultural theorist Stuart Hall remarks of this shift, "The image, whether moving or still, has become the predominant sign of late-modern culture," (Media Education Foundation, 1997). Consequently, there is now widespread discussion among a broad variety of groups about the impact of the media. From classrooms to corporate boardrooms, from media arts centers to the halls of Congress, and from the American Medical Association to living rooms across the country, the subject of media influence (particularly on young people) has assumed great urgency in the public mind.

The explosion of the image is simultaneously a moment of great challenge and opportunity. As Italian novelist and semiotician Umberto Eco notes in an oft-cited passage, "A democratic civilization will save itself only if it makes the language of the image into a stimulus for critical reflection—not an invitation for

[*] This essay is adapted from a report commissioned by the Ford Foundation in 2003. Reprinted by permission.

hypnosis." (1979, p. 15) And, indeed, it is around the notion of critical reflection, *"the ability to access, analyze, interpret and produce media in a variety of forms,"*[1] that the field of media literacy has largely defined itself. British media scholar Len Masterman adds that the goal of such efforts within a democratic society should be to enable young people (and citizens) to achieve a level of critical autonomy in relation to any media text that they may encounter.

Young people who have grown up in homes where television is turned on an average of seven hours per day vary between fascination and dismissal in their view of the media onslaught of which they are the prime targets. They are eager, even desperate at times, for new and intellectually rigorous ways to think about and interact with the media environment that has shaped their lives. They are cynical about much of the mass media, but, like most citizens, have no language and no analytical frameworks to deploy to turn their anger into a reasoned and effective understanding of the media's impact on American society. When they acquire these tools, through education, they feel not only more sophisticated, but also more empowered and better defended.

These new media conditions have thrust a concern with *media literacy* onto the forefront of discussion and debate in a variety of venues. The aim of this current report is to enter this discussion, to assess the state of the field of media literacy efforts in the United States, and to offer guidelines and recommendations to grant-making agencies as they think about how best to respond to the changing media environment from their own particular perspectives and interest areas.

From Consumers to Citizens

Given the sheer speed, spread, and influence of contemporary mass media forms and their undeniable power within the public and political spheres, one might logically assume that media education has already made its way into the mainstream of American education. But such an assumption would be wrong. While media-oriented curricula have, indeed, been implemented in schools and community organizations around the country, there remains little consensus about the underlying meaning and purpose of media literacy and education. What one school or organization considers media education and literacy often differs in fundamental ways from the conceptions of others. The result is that media literacy in this country remains a fragmented field, a series of splinter groups united by a common belief that media are a worthy subject of analysis but divided by fundamental differences at the level of basic definition. The history of media literacy in the United States is, in many ways, a history of competing ideas and assumptions about the very nature, value, and purpose of media, education, and literacy itself.

Too often, surveys and evaluations of the field that are designed to define the field by defining its inherent historical and political tensions end up offering solutions that require and reproduce caricatures of competing views and approaches.

Such efforts have, in many ways, done more to obscure the vital issues at stake and simplify the nuances inherent in specific movements than to clarify *how media literacy and education might help people inside and outside of our schools become better citizens, rather than simply better consumers or technicians.*

Recurring and ongoing debates and divisions within media literacy circles have typically obscured—often by simply failing to emphasize in the midst of the sheer complexity of these debates—what, in many respects, is a very simple argument: *the need, at every turn, to link media education to the commercial mediation of information, and to link the commercial mediation of information to the core democratic principles of informed public deliberation and participation.* Our hope is to move beyond academic debates altogether to consider the more fundamental issues at stake here: specifically, the relationships between media and democracy, democracy and public education, and public education and media. Such consideration demands that we think about media education *outside* of traditional educational settings.

Our own assumptions, in the simplest terms, are these: that media education and literacy are, above all, democratic imperatives and necessities; that trends in media policy and ownership—especially their relation to how, why, and what kind of content gets produced—have become increasingly alienated from basic democratic ideas and ideals; and that the abiding goal of media education should be to link explicitly critical viewing and thinking skills, aesthetic considerations, and production skills to a democratic understanding, critique, and transformation of media institutions, information, educational institutions, and the very notion of literacy.

The *commercial interests* and motives that inform both the content and institutional structure of mass media forms are by no means synonymous with *democratic interests* and motives: The commercialization of media represents, by definition, the commercialization of public space, public discourse, public deliberation, and, increasingly, public education—the very life forces of a functioning democracy. This means that media education, if it is to attempt to educate people about media, must emphasize the commercial nature of mass media, specifically the commercial imperatives that shape both the form and content of media texts (see Bagdikian, 1983; Garnham, 1990; Schiller, 1996).

Within this frame, a number of distinctive working definitions of media literacy begin to emerge, definitions that move outside the potentially limited and limiting meanings traditionally associated with *literacy* to take fuller account of the goals of democratic education more generally conceived. In this way, as Robert McChesney notes, media literacy "would be education in not only what the content of media is, and how you can interpret it, but how and why it was produced, how and why the institutions that produce it produce it" (personal communication, August 2, 2002). The explicit goal of media education becomes "not simply to be a better consumer of pre-existing choices and a critic of choices that are given you, but rather a citizen who understands why those are the choices you're given, how those choices came to be, and what you can do to change them" (personal communication, August 2, 2002). Henry Giroux argues similarly against reductive definitions of media literacy that fail to place at the forefront the meanings and demands of democratic citizenship:

> I'm very concerned about not reducing literacy to questions of competency and understanding, but also in a sense to link literacy and media education, per se, to the possibility of interpretation as intervention in the world. In other words, what might it mean to link questions of literacy not just to understanding, but to questions of agency? So that when we talk about media education and literacy being fundamental to [agency], we talk about understanding, we talk about modes of engagement, and we talk about strategies for actual intervention. That's a very different way to theorize the relationship between theory and practice around any notion of media education. And it's certainly at odds with those forms of media education that would be defined in a much more literal way, i.e., by [educational theorist] Diane Ravitch and that group that sees it as simply studying high culture and learning how to dismiss anything that might be considered popular culture while at the same time removing any activist element from the notion of pedagogy. (Personal communication, August 2, 2002)

Conceptualizing media education as crucial to democratic citizenship in no way assumes that all media are bad, or that young people and the public more generally must be protected from the so-called evil influences of media images and messages. It does not assume that media fail to offer pleasure and substance. Neither does it suggest that media education should work as a sophisticated form of censorship. In our view, it is grossly inadequate and beside the point to label the style of critical media education that McChesney and Giroux have in mind as media bashing, protectionist, antithetical to pleasure, or advocating censorship. In fact, we would argue that such characterizations have had the pernicious effect, whether by design or not, of deflecting attention away from the most fundamental and important issue at stake here: *that the hold of commercial media on public space and information limits access to the diversity and flow of ideas and images necessary to a functional, free, and open democratic society.*

Reframing Media Education

We believe that moving outside the frame of traditional academic debates around these issues can help put needed and renewed focus where it belongs: on the relationship between mass media and democracy and the role that education might play in making sense of this relationship.

It is essential to clarify up front that we are *not* arguing for media education as a form of paternalistic inoculation or protection from the so-called immoralities of mass media content, nor for media education as a means to push for censorship of existing content. These arguments, while sometimes interesting, operate within the very media frame that we feel media education needs to question. They remain fixated on media content and its reception to the exclusion of any real consideration of how and why content does and does not get produced in the first place. What we recommend, instead, is that we find better and more effective ways to help develop media literacy and education approaches that move beyond the safe limitations of what is considered pragmatically possible—approaches that shift our focus beyond the pragmatic limitations of what given educational institutions are thought capable of handling, and beyond what is presently given in media.

For media education to be meaningful, for it to meet the needs of the public, we must do the following:

- Conceptualize the educational needs of the public outside the institutional parameters of what we traditionally define as *public education;*

- Pay close attention to what is not given in media, to information, perspectives, and ideas that get excluded;

- Pay particular attention to how and why this narrowing of the information flow occurs, and its implications, given that our media are supposed to be a function of democracy, not the other way around.

John Dewey, who in the early twentieth century initiated an educational reform movement to democratize what he saw as undemocratic trends in American education, pointed to this latter distinction. Dewey's overall approach to educational reform derived from this basic idea: that differences in the very ways schools go about educating young people emanate from a fundamental distinction between the idea of *"education as a function of society"* and *"society as a function of education"* (Lentricchia, 1983, p. 1). This distinction is particularly relevant today. It signals a crucial difference between a philosophy that sees education as a way of helping people adapt to things as they are and a philosophy that sees education as a means of inspiring and equipping students to identify threats to democracy. As McChesney puts it,

> The fundamental point that has to be raised is understanding that the media system that is being discussed in media literacy and education is nothing natural. It's not even the result of the so-called free market. It's the direct result of a series of explosive policies that have been made in the public's name, but usually without the public's informed consent. And these are policies that are being drafted all the time—they weren't made 180 years ago. So the core of media literacy or education has to be to bathe these policies, and the debates

that generate them, in public participation—the core democratic value—on the assumption that the more democratic the understanding of the system and the participation in the policy making is, the better the results will be. (Personal communication, August 2, 2002)

Given that mass media now shape virtually every sphere of public and political life, we would do well to understand Dewey's fundamental distinction—between democracy as a function of education and education as a function of democracy—as the distinction between media education as a function of democratic society and democratic society as a function of media education. In other words, do we believe that media are adequately democratic institutions, and that media education should therefore help students become literate in media discourse, help them navigate and understand the information given them, help them develop and refine their ability to consume what is given? Or do we believe, instead, that it is necessary to question the easy assumption that mass media are democratic institutions given their commercial constitution and their basic need to buy and to sell audiences and to appeal to the public as consumers?

The point is this: If the former view stresses competency within existing media culture as a way of helping individuals function within a democracy, the latter view stresses the need to examine the potentially undemocratic or antidemocratic dynamics at work in media culture itself. The stress of the latter in turn informs a view of media education as an essential means of understanding what is given in media as a specific kind of information and entertainment, with a specific purpose, and leads always to a sustained focus on the relationship between the exclusiveness of what our current media system gives us and the needs of citizens in a democracy. As Mark Crispin Miller puts it,

> It's a given that media literacy is important, because people are beset by all kinds of propaganda images, images that attempt to move people to some kind of action or set of assumptions, without their knowledge, and more often than not against their best interest. . . . Media literacy therefore also requires an attempt to clarify how the visual media have changed over time, both by the ever-growing sophistication of an ever more benumbed audience and also by the fact of media concentration. (Personal communication, August 2, 2002)

Beginning with the assumption that media education is a function of democratic society lends itself to an emphasis on media texts and the sophisticated consumption of those texts as they are given and received. The assumption that democratic society is largely a function of media education lends itself to examining the conditions under and through which texts and information are produced and received, for it assumes that the workings of media are now absolutely inseparable from the way democracy does or does not work. The first assumption takes democracy for granted; the second does not.

Taking democracy seriously, especially as the starting point of any examination of the value of American education, therefore requires not only that we refuse to take democracy for granted, but also that we not mystify the powers of literacy. Nothing in literacy, as such, lends itself to democracy. Literacy does not ensure democracy; it simply gives it a chance to function. Media literacy likewise ensures nothing if its base rationale and motive are simply to develop and to refine the competency of people who use media, to make them better consumers and, perhaps, technical producers of the media that everywhere shape their lives. In Giroux's words,

> I don't understand at all what it would mean to separate questions of meaning from questions of power. . . . I just don't understand why we would want to talk about Hollywood without talking about concentrations of power. It can't be done in any way that would do justice to questions of the circuit of movement and registers that would actually give a kind of breadth and depth to any definition of power.
>
> Meaning is always connected to power—the issue here is not to presuppose that meaning and power come together simply around questions of interpretation and text. That actually undermines a way to analyze literacy by suggesting that the opportunity for people to interpret what they see out there is simply a matter of individual choice and agency, and not something that's already in many respects been staged by apparatuses of power that have the ability to limit the range of choices that people actually have. (Personal communication, August 2, 2002)

We believe that media education can and must do more than what traditional notions of *literacy* can offer. Media education must give *context* to literacy. Being media literate may help us to read and to produce media texts with sophistication, but this alone means nothing in the context of democracy and the traditional value that we place on citizenship in a hypermediated political and social environment. For media literacy to mean something in the context of democracy, we need to take it a step further than competency and proficiency. At the same time that we place value on being media literate, we need to take seriously the importance of getting educated about the origin and nature of the mass media system that we have today, about where the system came from, the decisions that formed it, why these decisions prevailed, and how and why alternative visions failed. We need, in other words, not only to take seriously media content and technology, but also to take seriously the historical and institutional contexts in and through which media and technology have become what they have become. While media literacy can provide tools for functioning in and adapting to a mass-mediated world, media education can provide tools for understanding where that world came from and why.

We would argue, then, for media education strategies that begin with these working assumptions:

- A functioning democracy requires an informed citizenry.

- Americans rely on mass media, especially television, for the vast majority of their information.

- Mass media are the primary educational forces of our time.

- Media education is a democratic and educational imperative.

- A functioning democracy requires that diverse forms of information—including information about the business of media and media policy—are available to the public.

With these assumptions in mind, we would suggest that media education must therefore work simultaneously and with equal stress

- To empower citizens, students and nonstudents alike, to develop and refine their pragmatic and critical ability to access and to assess the range of information given them in a variety of media forms.

- To empower citizens, students and nonstudents alike, to develop and refine their critical understanding of why and to what end they have been given the media forms and content they have been given.

The Need for Media Education: Differing Premises

There can be little consensus about the definition and value of media education when there is so little consensus about why media education is necessary in the first place. Any discussion of the issues involved must therefore begin with a discussion of need. The determination of need will determine the very rationale and shape of media education: its purpose, its place, its focus, and its priorities.

- If you begin with the premise that *new technologies have created an explosion of information* that is too fluid and too complicated to be accessed, navigated, processed, and understood with the traditional skills of print-based literacy, then you are likely to make the pragmatic argument that media education is needed to help people understand and function in a mediated world. Media education is conceived as a means of helping us adapt to a new world.

- If you begin with the premise that *the transition from print to visual culture* demands more developed and refined aesthetic sensibilities, then you are likely to argue that media education is needed as a necessary complement to traditional forms of literary and artistic education. Media education is conceived as a means of adapting the traditional language arts curriculum to contemporary concerns to make it more relevant to the lives of young people.

- If you begin with the premise that there is *too much sex and violence in mainstream media*, then you are likely to argue that media education is needed to protect kids from media's potentially corrosive and harmful effects. Media education is conceived as a means of empowering young people and developing their values and self-esteem in ways that diminish the power of media's hold on them.

- If you begin with the premise that technology has provided *an ever-increasing array of media content of wildly varying quality*, then you are likely to argue that media education is needed to help people discern the good from the bad, to cultivate tastes and a more refined appreciation of quality content. Media education is conceived as a means of taste making and aesthetic refinement.

- If you begin with the premise that media institutions, for all their faults, are first and foremost *outlets for and of free expression*, then you are likely to argue that media education is needed as an alternative to government censorship. Media education is conceived as a means of developing free and critical choices, an essential antidote to the abridgement of free expression in media by those who speak through media.

- If you begin with the premise that *new forms of interactive technology* have *given media users unprecedented power and choice*, then you are likely to argue that media education is needed to help people recognize and realize this power. Media education is conceived as a means of developing competency in media use.

- If you begin with the premise that commercial media content, especially advertising, *operates via sophisticated forms of manipulation*, then you are likely to argue that media education is needed to understand and to defend against such techniques. Media education is conceived as a means of developing the critical capacity to read and to interpret individual media texts.

- If you begin with the premise that *critical thinking* in the most general sense is the aim of all good education, then you are likely to argue that media education is needed as another way to achieve this goal. Media education is conceived as a supplementary means of developing critical thinking as an end in itself.

- If you begin with the premise that we must always guard against *bashing the media*, then you are likely to argue that media education is needed to foster a more nuanced understanding of *the potential benefits offered by media*. Media education is conceived as a means of developing a critical capacity that can produce new appreciation for the potential of mass media.

- Finally, if you begin with the premise that mass media are overwhelmingly *purveyors of unthinking, lowbrow trivia*, then you are likely to argue that media education is not needed at all, that its presence in schools distracts from more traditional and substantial intellectual pursuits. Media education is conceived as synonymous with the dumbing down of our kids and schools.

Each of these premises, sometimes in combination with one another, has led to distinctly different conceptions about the necessity, shape, and future of media education. Sophisticated arguments for and against each of these conceptions have recurred throughout the relatively brief history of the media literacy movement, often in the name of positioning one form or another of media education as viable or unviable, as workable or unrealistic, as being uniquely in touch or out of touch with the subject or the times. But a larger issue has been and continues to be concealed in and by such debates. Despite the real divergences in opinion and philosophy that these positions and this ongoing debate would seem to reveal, two common assumptions ground all of them: That media literacy and education, no matter what form they take, should focus on *individual* responsiveness to media culture, and that media literacy and education must, by definition, be considered within the institutional frame of *schools*, with their attendant curricular and disciplinary pressures and demands.

Whether these assumptions translate into media literacy and education as a means of managing information flows or rejecting the specific content of these flows outright, as a means of appreciating quality programming or developing the ability to understand and critique its limitations, or as a means of using media content and technology to further traditional educational ends or to revise traditional forms of education, the common assumption is that media education should take media culture as it is given and as a given. In this way, media education functions either to help us cope better with media forms as they are or to defend ourselves against them. What goes largely, if not completely, unquestioned is why media education should take for granted the media we have been given at all, and why this should be the necessary starting point from which all else derives. Forgotten is McChesney's most crucial and persistent insight: that there is nothing natural about the media system and the content it generates and that democracy is threatened, by definition, when citizens lack information about the political and policy decisions that make the system what it is.

A different set of assumptions, based on a different set of realities, leads to a dramatically different set of questions. And these, in turn, lead to a fundamentally different approach to media education—one founded on the uncontroversial notion that education is fundamental to democracy and that democracy depends fundamentally on an informed and responsible citizenry with enough power and voice to participate and to deliberate meaningfully in the democratic process. Once again, there are two beginning assumptions here: that education is the lifeblood of democracy and that media education, despite all of its cool and seemingly alternative surface appeal, must be conceptualized from the outset along traditional, even traditionalist, democratic lines of thinking. Simply put, *if we take democracy seriously, and if we take education seriously as fundamental to democracy, then we need to understand clearly what media education can do to enhance democracy and democratic citizenship.*

Of course, even at this seemingly benign stage of the discussion, fault lines are likely to emerge. For example, if your view of education in a democracy is that it should first and foremost prepare the young for work, then you might well be willing to pay only lip service to the claims of those who believe that education should do more than give people professional or vocational training and skills, especially for kids at the primary and secondary level. If there is disagreement over whether education should be in the business of empowering young people to empower themselves to participate meaningfully in the decisions that will affect their lives as adults, then there will be fundamental disagreement about the purpose of media literacy and education. Likewise, if the democratic imperatives of education are acknowledged but placed in line with or behind a list of allegedly equal or greater concerns, then there will be fundamental disagreement with those who see the democratic mission of schools, and education generally, as fundamental to media education itself.

We believe that if media education is to be meaningful, it needs to engage an entirely different set of realities, specifically and explicitly the ways in which commercial media have come to dominate public space and discourse. Media education needs to take seriously and to draw from a wide and growing body of work that has examined the nature and consequences of corporate ownership of media. David Bollier's book *Silent Theft: The Private Plunder of Our Common Wealth* (2002b) is characteristic of a spate of political economic work (see Lessig, 2001; Frank, 1998; Baker, 1995, 2001; Stiglitz, 2000) concerned with just this threat to democracy: the corporate colonization of public discourse and previously public domains, a full-scale market takeover of "that vast range of resources that the American people collectively own, but which are rapidly being *enclosed:* privatized, traded in the market, and abused" (2002a). Bollier, consistent with the work of others concerned about the disappearance of public space and the commercialization of public discourse, examines the corporate takeover of media and the commercialization of the broadcast airwaves, the Internet, and childhood experience. The point is that *media education must of course help people to critically engage media texts, but that it must also help them to engage media institutions as institutions.*

That said, for media education to move beyond text-driven approaches, it needs to do so against *three key barriers:*

1. The perception that challenging media ownership is somehow too left wing or anticapitalist to take hold in essentially conservative institutional settings, such as public schools;

2. The perception that challenging ownership somehow represents a brand of a priori thinking that renders students passive to the radical anticorporate agendas of teachers;

3. The perception that challenging corporate ownership threatens to alienate the increasing availability of corporate funding for media education and literacy programs.

These three barriers themselves speak to the need for supporting the development of media education approaches outside the narrow frame of the public schools. Schools do not exist in a vacuum. They themselves exist within the very media culture that media literacy and education are ostensibly designed to understand and to challenge. The policies, curriculum design, and funding, among other things, of public institutions are never free of the commercial imperatives and corporate logic that increasingly drive mainstream American politics and, therefore, mainstream political and popular views of education. One of the key goals of media education, then, needs to be to change the politics of public education by changing the way that the public understands media. With so much of what we know of media delivered by commercial media outlets themselves, media education becomes a necessary means of doing what media, by definition, cannot: *taking a step back from its baseline commercial motives to account for the larger social and political impact of media on democracy.*

When we persist in thinking that this kind of education is something solely for kids in school, we perpetuate a long-standing, historical confusion about the point of media education. It becomes a subject in school, rather than a basic requirement for informed citizenship; in the process, it loses to institutional concerns and demands its most important justification: understanding who and what drive media policy and how it affects our lives. When the politicians who make educational policy are the same politicians who make media policy, and when those same politicians are financed by the very corporate interests that fund and profit from media, then media education needs to be more than a way to prepare kids for life in the digital age. As McChesney puts it,

> Every day the federal government generates communication policies, regulations, and subsidies that determine the nature of our media system, our journalism, and our culture. The politicians on the relevant congressional committees are swimming in contributions from these corporate lobbies. . . . That is why the airwaves were handed over to commercial interests, why copyright has been

transformed into protective legislation for powerful media firms, why advertising and commercial ballyhoo permeate our lives. (2002, p. 11)

The need for media education grows out of precisely this: the threat to media education posed by the way media themselves work to exclude real discussion of just these issues. In McChesney's words,

> these policies have not been the topic of much public debate. They get little press attention, except for the occasional 'business' story, of interest to investors and managers, not citizens in a democracy. And the overwhelming majority of Americans, not to mention most members of Congress, are largely oblivious to them. (2002, p. 13)

Media education, framed this way, needs to happen outside of school, in the wider public domain, to change the very political culture that shapes the way schools view media education. If media education is to take hold in the schools, it needs to make sense *outside* of schools first.

A Brief History of Media Literacy in the United States: From Cooperation to Opposition and Back Again

A review of the history of media education and literacy in the United States is a review of its life and death in American schools. The history of media education in the United States is cyclical, and, in many ways, we find ourselves today where we began. Initial calls in the 1930s and through the 1960s for media education to provide students with the ability to adapt better and to consume with more sophistication the media content targeted at them gave way to the critical viewing movements of the 1970s, which challenged the very essence of what it was kids were being asked to adapt to and to consume. Industry-friendly approaches were replaced by approaches that were hostile to what the industry was producing. This critical turn gave way to mid-century–style, industry-friendly approaches in the 1980s, when the momentum of the critical viewing movement was defunded and ridiculed outright for its belief that television was a worthy object of study and for its allegedly reductive take on media content and its presumed effects. The critical media literacy and education movement therefore withered under a combination of pressures. Conservative politicians and traditionalist educators questioned the very validity of media education. And a host of media literacy educators themselves argued that consumers of media were not simply passive recipients of unhealthy messages in need of protection from educators who knew less about the pleasures and complexities of mass media content than their students.

The circle is now complete. *In the 1990s, and up to the present, the most influential and pervasive media education initiatives in the country now fit well enough within the demands and logic of the commercial media industry to win its approval and funding.* How we got here is telling.

Calls for media literacy began with the rise of commercial radio in the early 1930s, when "a group of English teachers who were part of the local chapter of the American Association of University Women (AAUW) in Madison, Wisconsin, became concerned about the new medium and decided to form a study committee on radio evaluation" (http://www.nationaltelemediacouncil.org). The group's mission was to "develop awareness, critical evaluation, and appreciation of quality programming" and has remained so through several incarnations to the present. With the arrival of television, the original council renamed itself the American Council for Better Broadcasting (ACBB) in 1953, and in 1983 it changed its name again in response to "new technologies" that "further expanded" its "choices and horizons," becoming the National Telemedia Council (NTC). Since 1950, the organization's work has included polling audiences about radio and TV programs, creating a syllabus for TV content analysis, and developing media literacy curricula.

Despite name changes, changes in focus, changes in technology, and changes in the media industry, to this day the NTC remains committed to its original evaluative mission, a mission that it continues to frame in opposition to what it perceives as misguided criticism of the media industry. In its view, media literacy is a form of critical awareness that provides the means for greater appreciation of "excellent" media content. As the NTC homepage declares,

> While the scope has expanded over the years, our purpose, which was already well defined in those early years, has become further strengthened—to develop an aware, critical audience, and to take a positive attitude toward achievements in excellence rather than a negative attitude toward mass media.

Stressing its "more difficult" desire to "help our young people to turn the television experience into an active, constructive part of their lives," its overall mission remains grounded in a definition of media literacy and education as a means of adapting to the status quo—its primary aim is to inspire kids to "cooperate" with the media industry as it is: "From the beginning we have taken a positive, non-judgmental attitude and embraced a philosophy that values reflective education and cooperation rather than confrontation with the media industry."

The example of the NTC is important not because of any excessive influence it wields as an organization, but because its informing principles so clearly reflect one side of the ongoing debate between those who emphasize the need for media education to fit with or within the basic commercial and corporate logic of the media industry and those who see media education as a necessary way to protect young people from that logic, whether in the name of morals, values, or a basic concern for the health and well-being of young people. Our concern, here, is not with whether the former perspective—what we might call the *prag- matist group*—has sold its soul to the very corporate media industry it claims to be critically examining, nor is it with whether the latter perspective—representing what some might call the *protectionists*—suffers from moral panic that blinds it to the aesthetic complexities of media content and the complicated dynamics in which media texts are interpreted differently from person to person. These kinds of characterizations on both sides are so common in the media literacy literature that they warrant little attention here. Our argument, instead, is that these very arguments have tended to deflect attention away from a broader conception of media education as a democratic imperative.

The cooperative stance was countered at the end of the 1960s and through the 1970s with the rise of the critical viewing movement and the development of "critical viewing skills (CVS) curricula" (Tyner, 1998, p. 134). In 1969, respond- ing to concerns about television violence, the National Education Association (NEA) recommended the development and inclusion of critical viewing curri- cula. At the same time, independent researchers James Anderson and Milton Ploghoft joined with Ohio University to develop the Critical Receivership Skills Project, producing media literacy curricula for a number of U.S. school districts. These first attempts to organize a critical approach to media gained momentum at the start of the 1970s, when two widely publicized reports, one from the Sur- geon General's Advisory Committee on Television and Social Behavior in 1972, the other from the National Institute of Mental Health, trained a critical light on the potentially destructive effects of commercial television and mass media content on viewers. As Tyner notes, media literacy was coming into its own, driven by public concern, a political mandate, and significant financial backing from both public and private sources: "Buoyed by ample funding and a sense of optimism, media education in the 1970s was at its peak" (p. 134).

For all of this activity and promise, the momentum of the media literacy movement in the 1970s was reversed in the 1980s. The federal funding of CVS projects by President Jimmy Carter's Office of Education dried up almost as quickly as it materialized during the presidency of Ronald Reagan. In Tyner's view,

> The media literacy projects of the 1970s were amply funded, the materials were professional and creative, and the curricula received high evaluations from teachers who used them. In spite of this, as soon as funding ran out for these projects, around 1981, media education activities ground to a halt in the United States. (1998, p. 138)

The small amount of activity in the 1980s reflects both sides of this cyclical dynamic. From the so-called protectionist front, the U.S. Catholic Conference in 1982 released a new curriculum called *The Media Mirror: A Study Guide on*

Christian Values on Television. And, in the same year, from the don't-bash-media front, the NTC launched Project Look-Listen-Think-Respond.

In 1982, despite the relative regression and stagnation of the movement in the United States, an International Symposium on Media Education was held by the United Nations Educational, Scientific and Cultural Organization (UNESCO) in Grünwald, Germany. The result was a "Declaration on Media Education" that called for the international development of media education at all grade levels. The purpose: "To develop the knowledge, skills and attitudes which will encourage the growth of critical awareness and, consequently, of greater competence among the users of electronic and print media" (http://www.unesco.org).

In the late 1980s, back in the United States, Kathleen Tyner and Liz Thoman emerged as key figures in the movement. In 1987, Tyner founded Strategies for Media Literacy in San Francisco and set about developing media education materials and training workshops. And in 1989, Thoman founded the Los Angeles–based Center for Media and Values, which, in 1994, became the Center for Media Literacy.

The 1990s saw the publication of a number of new media education curricula and a number of conferences on media literacy and education, the most influential sponsored by the Aspen Institute in 1992. The goal of the conference was to define and to stabilize a field that, up to that point, was perceived as being what Patricia Aufderheide characterized as "a blizzard of idiosyncratic projects, typically driven by the passion of individual teachers and organizers" and lacking "a central mission or mandate" and basic "infrastructure" (Heins & Cho, 2003).

While the impetus behind and recommendations of the Aspen conference led to an increased focus on teacher training and development, it also pointed to a difficulty that persists today: *not only how to fit media education within the existing curricula of public schools, but also how to do so successfully within the structural dynamics, pressures, and limitations of public educational institutions that are themselves subject to the very political dynamics that shape media institutions.* The point, again, is that while it may be true that attempts to develop and to implement meaningful media education programs in the United States have been short circuited by cyclical debates, it may also be true that the very nature of the debate has reproduced itself by systematically excluding a key point of consensus.

The reason why this perennial debate—between the so-called protectionists and those who feel they offer a more sophisticated take on the nature of media and media experience—is worth considering is precisely because it underscores the need for an entirely new way of looking at media education.

Consider that, while Tyner lays blame for the shift in policy in the 1980s to new concerns with drugs and crime and conservative calls for a return to traditional basics in education, she also places blame on the CVS movement itself—specifically, what she sees as its limited and limiting focus on television, and, more specifically, the pernicious effects of its content. This dual emphasis, she argues, continues today to inform a misguided media literacy approach in the

United States that blames mass media and seeks to protect children from their negative effects. In her most recent work, speaking in the present, she is therefore led to the conclusion that "media literacy movements in the United States tend to be cyclical . . . never venturing far from top-down, protectionist rhetoric" (Tyner, 1998, p. 140). The question that needs to be posed and seriously considered is whether the very way this debate continues to get framed may itself be at least partly responsible for the tentativeness of the movement to date.

Tyner cites as one of the failures of the critical viewing movement in the 1970s its reductionist focus on television, arguing that "media education was narrowly confined to a television universe devoid of troublesome cultural context," mistakenly "isolated as a medium of study because . . . its 'power' was simply assumed" (1998, p. 136). In this way, she advances two lines of argument that continue to shape media literacy debates today: the belief that protectionist approaches to media literacy and education are culturally unsophisticated and out of tune with culture, and the belief that the power of television cannot be assumed, that "the public's response to television is one of ambivalence" (p. 137). Tyner's critique of these assumptions, while perhaps insightful about the limits of media approaches that aim only to protect kids from media content, itself reproduces an assumption that limits the potential scope of media education. While it is important that television be understood in the context of other cultural factors, as Tyner argues, it is also important to understand that culture can no longer be so easily bracketed off from something called television, a move she makes that, in a sense, reproduces the very technicist mentality that she critiques.

Television is culture, and media are culture. And, as such, to talk about the power of television or mass media is to talk about the power of culture to shape impressions of the world cumulatively, not only in terms of the isolated or isolable messages or content within it, but also in terms of what TV does to recycle and to repeat certain ideas, commercial motives, cultural forms, and phenomena. The point must be to examine and to understand the power of TV, given its sheer presence in American culture, to promote certain points of view and to crowd out others. The content issue therefore comes down to nothing more complicated than a question of the diversity of content, or the lack thereof; it is not a matter of believing that certain kinds of content should be censored but of believing that democracy requires that some space be cleared in the public airwaves—and in our public schools—for a greater diversity of content and ideas.

To her credit, Tyner herself sees a way out of this cyclical history via "critical democratic approaches to media education," which, she observes, "show promise in moving the field" away from protectionist approaches that seek to blame media, rather than to critically understand and more efficiently use and experience them (1998, p. 162). Hailing such a democratic-minded approach for its dedication to "strengthening democratic institutions," Tyner explains its rationale as follows:

> If an informed electorate is the cornerstone of a democratic society, and, if the polls that report that most North Americans get their news and information from electronic media are correct, then it is imperative that students must learn to read and write electronic media, as well as print, in order to fully participate in a democratic society. (p. 162)

Without providing anything further about what this kind of democratic media education might comprise or do, in the remaining ten paragraphs of her discussion she focuses on how teaching democratic principles in U.S. classrooms presents a "problem" because "most schools do not operate as democratic institutions," because of school safety concerns, because school architecture is out of synch, and because of class size (Tyner, 1998, p. 162). While her point seems to be that all of these issues present barriers to what she calls "democratic pedagogy" (p. 163), it is never quite clear why she makes this shift to structure and pedagogy at all—why, for example, the same concerns would not be relevant to a discussion about the traditional teaching of American history and democracy in general.

For our purposes, Tyner's comments are instructive because they are characteristic of some of the basic misunderstandings that have deflected serious consideration away from the democratic necessity and value of media education. What matters most here is that the argument that "critical democratic approaches to media education" need to focus on helping students "read and write electronic media, as well as print," fails to make explicit what such "reading" would entail (Tyner, 1998, p. 162). Given the democratic rationale for this kind of media education, would it mean reading the way media policy gets made? Would it mean reading those views and texts that technically cannot be read by virtue of the fact that they are systematically excluded from mainstream media? Regardless of the answers to such questions, the larger point is this: The stakes are simply too high to settle for such ambiguity in serious discussions about media, education, and democracy. The effect of such ambiguity is to complicate what otherwise might be a clear, straightforward, and potentially consensus-building picture of the need for media education at a time when, as Tyner herself notes, democratic participation and deliberation are so dependent on media.

The Debates: A Closer Look

These contested framings of the very meaning of media education lie at the heart of ongoing debates within the field. By looking at how these debates have been framed, we might begin to understand not only why there seems to be widespread consensus that media education has foundered in the United States, but also whether and to what extent the way in which the debate itself has been framed may be partly responsible for reproducing this lack of consensus. Once again, the point here is not simply to recycle debates that have already been extensively recycled. It is to determine how media education might (a) begin to achieve cohesion in focus and meaning as a movement in our schools and (b) begin to develop and to take hold outside of schools in order to change the way that we think about the social and political role of education in light of the social and political role played by media.

Arguably, the most influential and widely quoted account of these debates comes from media literacy expert Renee Hobbs (see also Brown, 1998; Kubey, 1998). In "The Seven Great Debates in the Media Literacy Movement," Hobbs argues that there are seven key debates that are "foundational, that is, that these seven questions define the field of inquiry for practitioners at the present time," that they are "essentially framing questions that explicitly or implicitly guide the classroom practice of those educators who teach with and about the media" (1998, p. 18). According to Hobbs, these debates involve questions about the following: (a) whether or not media literacy should "aim to protect children and young people from negative media influences" (p. 18), (b) whether production should be "an essential feature" of media education, (p. 20), (c) whether pop culture texts are a valid focus of media education, (d) whether media literacy should have "a more explicit political and ideological agenda" (p. 22), (e) whether media education belongs in the K–12 curricula, (f) whether media literacy is best taught as a discrete subject or integrated throughout the existing curriculum, and (g) whether media literacy efforts should be financed by media organizations.

Hobbs's account of the framing of these issues is essentially descriptive, but her description allows her to frame the issues herself, especially with regard to questions about the protectionist impulse and the "political and ideological agenda" that she sees at work in some approaches. Hobbs critiques approaches that seek to protect young people from the negative influence of media on the grounds that there is no clear evidence that such negative influence exists. She argues that to proceed as if it does risks reducing not only the complexity and potential of media to its most pathological content, but also the complexity of students' experience of media to mere passivity (1998, p. 19). A larger concern for Hobbs is that such a view places the teacher in a position of superiority over the student, short-circuiting both the sophistication of students' experience with media and student power in the classroom. As she puts it, "When media literacy skills are positioned in opposition to media culture, the quality of instruction is compromised," leading to a "rescue" fantasy with teachers who see students as "helpless victims" rather than engaging "the genuine pleasures" students may receive from media (1998, p. 19). The result of such reductions, Hobbs argues, may be "an instructor-focused classroom" that "may cause students to parrot the correct interpretations—the one the teacher has sanctioned"—in ways that may undermine the "authenticity" and "relevance" of media literacy education to students' lives (1998, p. 19).

This line of reasoning carries over into Hobbs's discussion and critique of what she sees as the explicitly political agenda of approaches that "serve as a means to achieve a range of progressive political ends" and "social change" (1998, p. 22). Citing Buckingham, she warns that the belief that media literacy education should call attention to the institutional and political-economic constitution of the media industry risks being "propagandistic" (1998, p. 22). In keeping with her critique of the "protectionist" (1998, p. 19) stance, she argues that this, in turn, may encourage students to "either play the game" of teachers and "learn to reproduce 'politically correct' responses without necessarily investigating their own position" or to "refuse to do so, in order to annoy the teacher and thereby amuse themselves" (p. 22). Hobbs makes clear the underlying assumptions that inform her characterization: that "knowledge, skills, and attitudes associated with media literacy education should be understood as independent goals, not simply as means to other ends" (p. 23).

What's important here is not so much Hobbs's contention that the kind of "explicit political" tenor of media literacy strategies that come out of a tradition of liberation struggles, like those advanced by educators such as Paulo Freire and Henry Giroux, "may be unlikely to be accepted in the de-centralized, and community-centered context of mainstream public education" (Hobbs, 1998, p. 23). More important is that she moves well beyond this understandably pragmatic consideration into the theoretical credibility of such transformative, democratic approaches. Media literacy education that focuses on ownership, political economy, media policy, and the institutional realities of commercial media is set in opposition to approaches "that maximize the students' potential for discovery and the realization of personal, social, or political action without pushing a specific agenda on students" (p. 23). Likewise, for Hobbs, "teaching students to question textual authority and to use reasoning to reach autonomous decisions" is a "radical enough" agenda, "without adding additional baggage associated with explicitly formulated political or social objectives" (p. 23).

Giroux takes issue with precisely this kind of common academic and political suspicion whenever media education attempts to focus explicitly on questions of democracy:

> It seems to me that any pedagogical intervention is precisely directive. I mean, as Paulo Freire said many times, when we talk about pedagogy, we're talking about an act not just of interpretation. We're talking about a direct intervention that recognizes that pedagogy is both a political and moral practice, and not simply a neutral practice, and not simply a technical practice. Now, knowing that, what does that mean? It seems to me we have to theorize what it might mean to make a distinction between molding students and providing the conditions for them to, in a sense, not only engage in a culture of questioning, but also to learn those knowledges and skills that would expand the possibility for them to be political and social agents.
>
> In that sense I'm guilty—yes. I believe that pedagogy is interventionist; I believe that at the same time it does suggest a project. Yes, I believe that it

is directive. But at the same time I do not believe in the notion that's being advanced everywhere, all of a sudden, in mass media, that any project associated with pedagogy is by default an act of indoctrination. I mean we need to make a distinction between what it means to set the conditions for students to become critical and, at the same time, empowered social agents, and what it means to not be able to engage in a pedagogy of terrorism. (Personal communication, August 2, 2002)

While we agree with Giroux, Hobbs's characterization and assessment of the kind of media education we recommend in this report are nevertheless instructive. The inherent institutional and political conservatism of many public school systems may, indeed, present a barrier to implementing media literacy education curricula that challenge the undemocratic structures of media control and production. But this is not at all the same thing as saying that such curricula are inherently propagandistic. The easy association of media education approaches that take seriously the nature and history of the media industry as necessary objects of study with political correctness and the degradation of students' individuality deflects attention, by way of caricature, from the essentially democratic value of such approaches. Ironically, in the name of complexity, ambiguity, and pluralism, Hobbs advances the argument that these approaches are reductive only by reducing their actual complexity and potential. McChesney puts it this way:

I don't think the idea of looking at the way the industry is structured, and the way government policies create a type of industry, presupposes the nature of the critique, any more than a critique of the content presupposes the nature of the critique. It's really a question of what's going to be part of the legitimate terrain, and what isn't, and it should be considered that way. It shouldn't be rhetorically dismissed as being propagandistic, because that's not relevant whatsoever. You know, if Renee Hobbs or others believe that media literacy should just deal with what exists and doesn't even ask why it exists, that's fair enough for her belief. I think that is a very short-sighted and one-dimensional view of media and culture, and one that sort of gets you into a sort of vicious circle of getting on a treadmill and never really understanding the system you're in, rather than of trying to defend yourself from it. (Personal communication, August 2, 2002)

Even if we are to grant Hobbs her argument that such approaches are unlikely to fit neatly within the highly contested and politically charged arena of our public schools, we would nevertheless draw a sharply different conclusion: that embracing media education as a form of democratic critique and social change does not mean that it is adding additional baggage to existing media education curricula as much as it means is seeing value in developing additional content to supplement what she herself feels should be included.

There are, then, two separate issues at stake here: The need to reconsider how media education debates have been framed within the limits of traditional educational spheres in ways that reproduce misrepresentations of what a truly democratic form of media education might actually look like and accomplish. And the need to think outside of these limitations about the nature and value of media education more generally conceived—not as a means to develop critical thinking skills as an end in themselves, *but as a means of assuring that we all, students and nonstudents alike, are truly educated about the nature of media and their relationship to democracy.*

This way of conceptualizing the issue focuses attention on places other than the public schools. In doing so, it helps us open up our definition of media literacy and education, so that we can focus on the needs of adults as well. Debates over differing definitions of media education that stay within the narrow limits of curriculum development, educational policy, and the pragmatic institutional pressures faced by educators in our public schools, reproduce the basic misconception that media education should somehow be something reserved for kids. This, in turn, lends itself to timidity with regard to larger questions of power and democracy, limiting how we might conceive of media education as a basic and necessary means of educating the general public about the political and public implications of media.

The more general focus we are proposing here points us in a number of new directions, all informed by the basic assumption that it is crucial to reinvigorate the public debate about the role of media as currently structured in relation to larger democratic ideals and concerns. It is essential that we focus our energies on opening up and enlivening the way that we understand and talk about media. And, given that the very objects of such an analysis—media institutions themselves—are the chief guardians of public discourse, *this means investing in alternative forms of public information.* Only by extending our notion of media education so that it takes into consideration the pedagogical power found in places such as community organizations, the full range of nonacademic institutions, books, and media content itself, can we begin to see the value of investing in the development and public distribution of information that is currently inaccessible to the general public.

The bottom line is that changing how media education might work to connect a critical examination of the commercial and corporate logic of media to the demands of a democratic society must happen outside, as well as inside, traditional educational spheres. Educational policy is always the product of educational politics, and politics derives always from those—institutions and individuals—who have the power to tell the stories that shape and justify policy. Until we challenge and change this larger cultural and political dynamic, until we demand space for the kinds of stories that have no place, motive, or stock in a commercial media system governed by other motives entirely, it is unlikely that the state of media education in our schools will overcome these crippling academic debates and achieve its truly democratic potential. Ironically, a media-educated public may be a prerequisite for media education to work in our schools.

Recommendations

Based on our previous discussion of what is at stake in the ongoing debates around media literacy and media education, and the necessity to reinvigorate a society-wide debate about the structures and organization of the commercial media, we offer the following recommendations.

1. Support media education approaches and organizations that frame media explicitly as a public space and that work explicitly to inspire a critical awareness of mass media's relationship to the public interest as a democratic imperative. The central goal of media education must be to enhance critical citizenship and social agency, and to foreground—rather than making it part of a list of potential approaches—the virtual impossibility of core democratic principles to flourish in a society so saturated by media that are themselves not democratized.

2. Support media education approaches and organizations that take into account how our schools are in direct competition with media, and therefore can no longer be taken for granted as the primary places where students learn. We must take into account how literacy itself—whether we want to recognize it or not—is increasingly shaped outside the traditional educational sphere.

3. Support the development and delivery of educational content that foregrounds issues of media ownership and political economy in relation to questions of democracy and democratic participation.

4. Support the development of innovative and interdisciplinary graduate programs in media literacy, bringing together scholars from disciplines such as education, communication, and film to provide teachers in training the skills that they need to wed aesthetic and formal concerns to issues of political economy and democracy.

5. Support efforts to do outreach to educators, school boards, and academics about the importance of media education in the public sphere—as well as to politicians and others involved with setting budgets and goals for education.

6. Support independent work that examines the relationship between media policy, technology, and democracy with the express purpose of educating the public about media.

Conclusion: Media Literacy Education and the Triumph of Conservatism

Media literacy, on the one hand, fights a battle for credibility, forever trying to justify itself as a worthy field of study as guardians of high culture attack what they perceive to be the dumbing down of curricula that have opened themselves to pop culture. Traditionalists, such as William Bennet, Diane Ravitch, and others who would purge pop culture from the curriculum for a return to the so-called great books, succeed in this regard: they fan the flames and define the terms of debate within the media literacy movement itself. Media literacy education becomes reactive to conservative political attacks rather than responsive to the incursion of commercial media into an ever-widening sphere of public life and discourse. It loses its potential to offer a sustained consideration of the corporate and commercial threat to traditional democratic values as it responds to criticism that is actually part of a larger liberal educational trend that has contributed to the erosion of traditional values. The end result in such an environment—an environment that itself points to the absence of and need for a countervailing public voice in the so-called culture wars—is that media literacy professionals spend a lot of time justifying themselves.

One effect is that the focus of media education on pop culture itself comes to demand justification. As discussed previously, this, in turn, leads to media literacy approaches that favor the inherent complexities of media's so-called higher forms and the ambiguities of content, feeding the constant need to justify the study of media content by forever pointing out that, at their best, media and their readers often engage traditional literary and aesthetic forms. At the same time, this line of thinking reproduces the very high-low cultural distinction that forces media literacy education to justify itself in the first place, even as it attempts to justify the place of pop culture in the curriculum.

One way this literary justification for media studies plays out involves the question of pleasure, a question that goes to the very nature and meaning of media content. The concept of kitsch has worked as a description of media content that is designed, at base, to appeal as widely as possible to mass sentiment and sensation, resulting in a shut-down of critical thought and deep experience. In contrast, pleasure models of media literacy attempt to disrupt the inherent bias they see in this formulation—a separation, again, between high and low that negates, they say, the actual lived experience of media by young people, the sophisticated pleasures that they take from media. This leads to the repeated suspicion or condemnation of protectionist media literacy approaches that seem to ignore the individual experience and potential pleasures that come from a deep engagement with media content. To bracket pleasure, the argument goes, is pedagogically dangerous, because it refuses to meet students on their own ground, refuses to take their experiences seriously, while reducing these experiences to the deluded products of a false consciousness waiting for treatment from an apparently pleasure-phobic teacher who knows better.

Of course, this repeated characterization derives much of its force from a highly restrictive notion of pleasure. An alternative conception of pleasure unaccounted for in such characterizations is what Henry Giroux calls "the learned pleasure of analysis" (personal communication, August 2, 2002)—the pleasure one derives from stepping back from immediate impressions to understand them more fully. Far from a radical proposition, this would seem to identify the very experience of education in its most traditional rendering.

The point here is that the essentially conservative framing of educational and cultural concerns generally has had the effect of deflecting serious consideration from media literacy education approaches that are committed to understanding the relationship between the corporate and commercial control of media and the demands of democracy. In such a context, literary justifications emerge to answer traditionalist charges that studying media is frivolous. Ambiguity then becomes the order of the day: ambiguity as an aesthetic, as opposed to a political, value, all in a way that feeds the tendency of liberal educators to prefer a plurality of media education approaches capable of matching the plurality of media experience. In this context, the goal of media education is to encourage critical thinking as an end in itself.

What ends up being pushed to the margins in such a political and theoretical environment is the crucial question of access. And how questions of access get framed are themselves intimately linked to these recurring debates about the place of pleasure and the agency of media consumers. For the question is whether the hypercommercial media system and content we have, at least to some extent, is simply a reflection, the end product, of what people want, and whether the ideas that dominate media—from the scripts of sitcoms, to the plots of big budget Hollywood thrillers, to the themes and flash of advertising, to the sensationalism in local news—have achieved this hegemony simply because of good market research and the responsiveness of media producers to the desires of the public. In this view, focusing on pleasure itself becomes a democratic act. If we fail to pay attention to people's desires, to the pleasurable aspects of consumption as they relate to media content, the thinking is that we risk missing how media institutions, while commercial, nevertheless must always account for the desires of the public in a democracy. We risk making the incredible claim that we can somehow stand outside the very system we believe is a key shaping force in our overall sense of reality, forever wagging our fingers, railing against the evils of pleasure, always looking behind the cool and often ironic surface of media content for some a priori meaning that reduces pleasure and the way people watch to economic determinants. The question, then, comes to this: Should we read the limited range and commercial mediation of ideas that we find in mass media as expressions of public sentiment for those ideas?

Coming to terms with this kind of argument requires coming to terms with questions about access. When Americans gave away the broadcast system to advertisers in 1934, the fact is that media content started to be shaped more by the demands of advertising revenues than the demands of the public interest (see McChesney, 1993). Content became a way to deliver audiences to advertisers. This logic alone, at the very least, raises basic questions about the ability of media to serve explicitly public and democratic interests. The blanket commercialization of the airwaves means that most of what goes on there places its highest premium on appealing to audiences as consumers, not as public citizens in a democratic society who require access to as great a diversity of information as possible—not least, access to extensive information about the very nature and source of those forms of public information that are readily and pervasively available.

Questions of access, then, lead back to questions of audience, and they raise larger questions about whether there actually exists an audience at all for the kind of alternative, public service–oriented, critical media content that we would argue needs to form the basis of any form of media education. One line of thinking seems to be that this kind of material is only likely to have an audience in schools, because, in schools, by definition, the audience is captive. The view that there are no real choices being made in such a situation seems to inform the beliefs of those, like Hobbs (1998), who see this kind of approach as contradicting its very democratic pretensions by forcing views on others rather than cultivating their ability to make their own choices. But what this view misses is the question of diversity and whether we believe that education, the ability to access information necessary to the public interest, and democracy itself require as great and wide a range of expression as possible. Such views may be unpopular, but the expression of minority views—if this is indeed what they are, when properly understood—is a fundamental pillar of democracy.

These competing perceptions about the kind of work our schools should be doing expose another persistent inconsistency at the heart of conservative claims about the value of so-called traditional literacy and the perhaps unwitting submission of liberal media educators to the essential logic of these claims. Conservative, so-called high-culture defenders, such as William Bennett, Diane Ravitch, Allan Bloom, and E. D. Hirsch, have argued precisely for a return to traditional education and curricula, for a return to what Harold Bloom calls the "more difficult pleasures" offered by something like "canonical" literature (1995). It is just this line of thinking that made its way into the Bush Administration's education plan, the No Child Left Behind Act, which includes a specific provision that federal funding be allocated to history departments that teach so-called traditional history (http://www.whitehouse.gov/news/reports/no-child-left-behind.html). Key here is that advocates of this position argue for a return to the so-called basics of education, to fundamentals and the great books, precisely and explicitly against what they perceive to be the popularization of education. Leaving no child behind means leaving what is worst in the child's culture behind.

It means resisting the misguided progressive agenda to dumb down curricula in order to meet the needs of overstimulated and numbed masses of kids who have consumed too much media, too much TV, and who now equate learning with the so-called easier pleasures of pop culture. At the same time, media education approaches that are motivated by a desire to understand media in relation to democracy and to help democratically transform media are viewed by many liberals in the field as essentially undemocratic, because they are averse to peoples' actual enjoyment of and emotional investment in media. This negative view of the kind of critical and democratic pedagogy advanced by Paulo Freire rests on the notion that media content reflects the desires and tastes of the people, on the free-market ideal that the best idea will sell better than the worst idea and that this itself is a reflection of popularity.

We would argue, simply, that one cannot make the case, on the one hand, that unpopular or minority views simply have no audience, and that to advance them is therefore necessarily to engage in propaganda, and then, on the other hand, claim that education should precisely be about slowing things down, slowing the media-saturated world of kids down long enough for them to catch their breath and do some critical thinking. This latter view depends precisely on what the former rejects: that there is value in countering the limitations of media culture with less popular alternatives. This is what schools do and have always done. In this way, the logic of traditionalists with regard to literacy might actually be more in line with media education approaches that stress democratic issues.

The question, then, is whether and to what extent we believe that media education should address the way power operates in the public sphere—whether we believe, and take seriously, the basic idea that some people have more power than others and that not everyone's voice gets heard. These are, of course, fundamental democratic questions, despite the advanced ambiguity of debates within academe about the nature of aesthetics and aesthetic experience. The nature of aesthetic experience is, of course, crucial to any kind of comprehensive understanding of how media content works, but it cannot be separated from the nature of the very media through which such experience is produced and delivered. If we agree that the free flow of information is the very ground of informed democratic consent, then, when we look at media, we are looking at an already fundamentally political arena. Media literacy education cannot, then, shrink under the pretentiously apolitical claims of those who style themselves as guardians of tradition without at least making the case for media education as a democratic imperative. Most every school in the country, as well as parents of all political stripes, would agree that the overriding mission of schools is to prepare kids to think and to participate as informed citizens in a democracy that demands informed participation. Media education at its best has the potential to advance this traditional mission.

The focus of media education needs to move away from an exclusive consideration of content and pleasure as separate or separable fields of inquiry to the very environment within which people make decisions. When we do that, we need to ask whether or not this environment—the very field of play from within which we come to know the world and understand the issues that matter most to us—is in any sense undemocratically dominated by one very narrow segment of the population.

Meaning-making—how people make meaning individually, collectively, as active agents acting on their world in distinctive ways—must, of course, be a central concern of any serious form of media education. But the conditions and context through which meaning gets made must also be central; both of these must be considered together, especially in their reciprocal relations with one another. Solely considering inherited institutional conditions or contexts leads to a consideration of power and manipulation only. Looking solely at how people make their own meanings (as in some versions of reception theory or reader-response theory) leads to undue emphasis on individual freedom and choice. To separate one from the other is itself a political act, even if it is done in the name of avoiding political reductions, undermining the potential of meaningful media education in a democracy.

Notes

1. This is the preferred and widely circulated definition of media literacy within academe. See, for example, the Alliance for a Media Literate America (AMLA) literature at http://www.amlainfo.org.

References

Action Coalition for Media Education Web site. (n.d.). Retrieved from http://www.acme-coalition.org

Alliance for a Media Literate America Web site. (n.d.). Retrieved from http://www.amlainfo.org

Bagdikian, B. (1983). *The media monopoly.* Boston: Beacon Press.

Baker, E. C. (1995). *Advertising and a democratic press.* Princeton, NJ: Princeton University Press.

Baker, E. C. (2001). *Media, markets, and democracy.* Cambridge, UK: Cambridge University Press.

Bloom, H. (1995). *The Western canon.* New York: Riverhead Books.

Bollier, D. (2002a, Summer). Reclaiming the commons. *Boston Review, 30.* Retrieved from http://www.bostonreview.net/BR27.3/bollier.html

Bollier, D. (2002b). *Silent theft: The private plunder of our common wealth.* New York: Routledge.

Brown, J. A. (1998). Media literacy perspectives. *Journal of Communication*, 48(1, Winter), 44–58.

Center for Media Literacy Web site. (n.d.). Retrieved from http://www.medialit.org

Center for Media Studies Web site. (n.d.). Retrieved from http://www.mediastudies. rutgers.edu

Citizens for Media Literacy Web site. (n.d.). Retrieved from http://www.main.nc.us/cml

Eco, Umberto (1979). "Can television teach." Screen education, 31, Summer, pp. 12-19

Frank, T. (1998). *The conquest of cool: Business culture, counter culture, and the rise of hip consumerism.* Chicago: University of Chicago Press.

Garnham, N. (1990). *Capitalism and communication.* London: Sage.

Heins, M., & Cho, C. (2003, Fall). *Media literacy: An alternative to censorship.* Retrieved from http://www.fepproject.org/policyreports/medialiteracy.html

Hobbs, R. (1998). The seven great debates in the media literacy movement. *Journal of Communication*, 48 (1, Winter), 9–29.

Just Think Web site. (n.d.). Retrieved from http://www.justthink.org

Kubey, R. (1998). Obstacles to the development of media education in the United States. *Journal of Communication*, 28(1, Winter), 58–69.

Lentricchia, F. (1983). *Criticism and social change.* Chicago: University of Chicago Press.

Lessig, L. (2001). *The future of ideas: The fate of the commons in a connected world.* New York: Random House.

McChesney, R. (1993). *Telecommunications, mass media and democracy: The battle for the control of U.S. broadcasting 1928–1935.* New York: Oxford University Press.

McChesney, R. (2002, Summer). The place of politics. *Boston Review, 27*, 34.

MediaChannel Web site. (n.d.). Retrieved from http://www.mediachannel.org

Media Education Foundation (1997). Representation and the media. [video]

Media Education Lab Web site. (n.d.). Retrieved from http://www.reneehobbs.org

Media Literacy Clearinghouse Web site. (n.d.). http://med.sc.edu

Media Literacy Review Web site. (n.d.). Retrieved from http://interact.uoregon.edu/ MediaLit/mlr/home

National Telemedia Council, Inc., Web site. (n.d.). Retrieved from http://www.nationaltele-mediacouncil.org

New Mexico Media Literacy Project Web site. (n.d.). Retrieved from http://www.nmmlp.org

No Child Left Behind Act. (n.d.). Retrieved from http://www.whitehouse.gov/news/reports/ no-child-left-behind.htm

Project Look Sharp Web site. (n.d.). Retrieved from http://www.ithaca.edu/looksharp

Schiller, H. (1996). *Information inequality: The deepening social crisis in America.* New York: Routledge.

Stiglitz, J. (2000). *Economics of the public sector.* New York: W.W. Norton.

Tyner, K. (1998). *Literacy in a digital world: Teaching and learning in the age of information.* Mahwah, NJ: Lawrence Erlbaum.

UNESCO (1982). *Declaration on Media Education.* Presented at the 1982 International Symposium on Media Education, Grünwald, Germany. Retrieved from http://www.unesco.org

The Media Education
Foundation, Politics,
and Public Pedagogy

Beyond the Ivory Tower: Cultural Studies, Politics, and Public Intellectuals

An Interview with Sut Jhally
Edited by Jeremy Earp

This interview, conducted by Lynn Comella and Jeremy Earp of the University of Massachusetts in January of 2005, explores the relationship between cultural studies, the educational work of the Media Education Foundation, and the relevance of both to contemporary American politics.

Cultural Studies, Determination, and Difference

Can you talk a little bit about how you use cultural studies in your own intellectual work?

I came across the value of contemporary culture studies when I was working as an undergraduate at the University of York in England. I went there to study history and sociology, and I quickly became interested in the intermingling of sociology, pop culture, and politics and what was necessary to understand a society that was essentially undergoing a seismic shift in its major institutions. Stuart Hall talks about how cultural studies was a response to this need for a new way of looking at a society that was transforming in front of our eyes. And I guess cultural studies also helped me make sense of my own life and what came to be called the postmodern experience, in that identity wasn't so fixed and stable any more.

Could you elaborate on that thought?

Well, in an important sense, I was always culturally—and in terms of identity—at the margins or in the margins. I was never at the center. I was the center of my own world, of course, like all of us, but that was always a kind of marginal world. I was born in Kenya, my parents are Indian, and, when I was six years old, we moved to England, where I grew up and was formed. So England is really home to me culturally, but throughout that whole process I was being pulled in a myriad of different directions. Was I Indian? Was I English? Was I a mixture of the two? These questions pointed to the very basic question of identity—my relationship to masculinity, race, nation, and so on.

So it was because I was thrust into this very particular, and peculiar, situation that I always experienced myself as somehow on the margins. On the one hand, I was always regarded as an immigrant in England, even though that's still what I regard as home. Then I moved to Canada. And now I've been in the United States for the last twenty years. But again, I have been kind of marginal to this kind of central dynamic of identity in all of those places. And what's significant, I think, is that you can see things differently from the margins. I don't necessarily think you can see things more clearly, but you do see them differently. It forces you to pose questions that are not so straightforward, that don't have such clear-cut answers. The questions you ask and the answers you get end up being kind of messy. And I think that's exactly what intellectual work is all about: you have to get the clarity, but you cannot avoid the mess.

When did you do your undergraduate studies, and was there something about that time period that affected how you initially came at this work?

I started at York University in the north of England in 1974, around the time Hall and his colleagues at the Center for Contemporary Cultural Studies at the University of Birmingham were coming out with all this incredible new stuff. It was the heyday of cultural studies. In fact, I remember I got Paul Willis's Ph.D. dissertation on language and the cultural differences between biker and hippie communities—he'd only just completed it, and I got it on interlibrary loan, so I was actually reading this stuff exactly as it was being produced. This was also the same time that the Working Papers in Cultural Studies series was being published. It wasn't like there was a tradition of cultural studies; it was developing at the same time it was emerging. The point is that there was no set way of doing these things, and, even as an undergraduate, I could see that you had to come up with new ways of understanding the shifts that were taking place. So right from the start, cultural studies was important to my intellectual development.

It sounds as though cultural studies allows you to marry your interests in history to your interest in sociological analysis in certain ways. There is so much of a tradition in cultural studies of doing exactly that.

Cultural studies allowed me to develop an interdisciplinary perspective, drawn not just from sociology, but also from literary studies, history, anthropology, and linguistics—from all of these different places. It was really kind of an exciting intermingling of traditions and fields that allowed you to see what was going on in the moment, or at least gave you the possibility of seeing what was going on in the present in exciting new ways. That was really very energizing for an undergraduate to be involved in that kind of work, and it continued with my initial master's thesis work at York as well.

What was that about?

It was about the birth of Thatcherism, although Hall had not quite yet coined that term. There was a key moment in 1977 when Thatcher did an interview on TV where, it seemed to me at least, she shifted the very terrain on which you could talk about race. For the first time, you had a major politician in a mainstream interview saying that the problem with immigration wasn't just about jobs—which had been the established and somewhat rational way of talking about immigration as a problem to that point—but that it was essentially a cultural issue. The specific term she used was *swamping*. She said that these people were swamping the English way of life and English culture—both of which had given so much to the world that they had to be protected from this siege of immigration.

Before this moment, that kind of talk was limited to what we would now call the radical and racialist right, to people like Enoch Powell and extremist parties like the National Front. I thought this was a key moment, because what she was doing was bringing this kind of fringe stuff into the mainstream. Here we had a mainstream politician saying really extremist things, and, rather than the extremism being transferred to her, what was happening was that her respectability was being transferred to extremism itself, making it more acceptable and normal. I thought this was a transformative moment, and I also thought it wasn't being recognized for what it was: the unleashing of a dangerous racial discourse into the mainstream of society. And as a result of the work that Stuart Hall has so tirelessly done, we now know that the racial appeal to an English identity was absolutely fundamental to why Thatcherism was able to take shape and then survive as a political, cultural, and economic project.

And I'm assuming that this appeal to English identity was an appeal to a white identity?

It was absolutely framed in racial terms. The English, who had given so much to the world, were white, they were carriers of the famous "white man's burden." And there were these hordes of brown and black people swarming in from the outside world who were threatening to change all of that. And, while there had always been a good deal of immigration from the West Indies, Thatcher was explicitly talking about Asian immigration.

There were two huge Asian migrations into England, both from East Africa, one from Kenya and one from Uganda. Those migrations really did, in many senses, transform at least parts of major cities. As Hall says, just as the British Empire was trying to cut the umbilical cord, everyone arrives on the doorstep and says, "You said you were the mother country, so here we are!" At the very moment the Empire is dissolving, in other words, the Empire quite literally comes home. It really is, in this sense, the chickens coming home to roost.

And that was part of the revolution that Hall talks about, where a very old and traditional industrial society was being transformed—first by commercialization and the expansion of the market, then by immigration. This produced a kind of cultural trauma that is still very much unresolved in the English imagination. And Thatcher was expressing something very important about how this was all being experienced. My thesis was an analysis of the Thatcher interview and the resulting media coverage and how, discursively, the English understanding of common sense itself was shifting. Obviously, the new translations of Althusser and Gramsci were vital to this analysis, providing a new way of thinking about the relation between ideology and conventional wisdom, all of which coincided with what was developing in cultural studies at virtually the same time.

The cultural studies tradition that you reference is very much connected to the Birmingham Center, where a struggle with and over Marxism is at the core of the project. But American cultural studies, even of the critical variety, seems to be less connected to that problematic. Is that an important difference for you?

I think it is. And it's around issues of difference and sameness where that dynamic can be seen most clearly. First of all, it's important to stress that Marxism is still relevant in the modern world, not just politically, but intellectually. In a very important sense, one of the central thrusts of the Western Marxist tradition has been to work out not just the economic side of capitalism, but also the less developed analysis of politics and culture. It's really been a working out of the very particular problem around agency and structure surrounding the many complexities of the base/superstructure model or metaphor—and I do think, by the way, that it is much more a metaphor than a model. Western Marxism offers a way of thinking about the key relationships to which any social scientist is drawn—the relationships between agency and structure, individual and society, and individual and collective. And the central question is the question of determination. The reason why Marxism is important, in my view at least, is that it gives the most nuanced and complex way of understanding determination. It's a way of talking about difference and sameness in a way that remains coherent.

For instance, when we talk about difference and sameness, we immediately need to ask which questions are most interesting and productive for us to focus on. It strikes me that *difference*, from an intellectual perspective, is not all that interesting to study. I know that, within the world of cultural studies and American cultural studies in particular, this may seem almost heretical to say, but the reason for posing it in this way is to recognize that difference and variation are built into the human species at a very fundamental level. They are built into our individual lives in the most basic sense, so that no one else has lived, or can live, by definition, precisely the life you've lived, I've lived, anyone has lived. We are all, in one sense, unique in human history, in terms of the experiences that we've had that have landed us in this place at this time. The combination of discourses that surge through us as we try to make sense of the world is absolutely unique. And that's built into us as a species. We're always active, always trying to understand the world, always interpreting, and, of course, always communicating. We're a storytelling species that always needs to communicate, always needs to understand, and that understanding is always mediated through culture and through our individual, lived experience. So no one has exactly the same understanding of reality, because we all bring our different experiences to that process.

Let's look at this more specifically from within the context of the tradition of audience studies. To me, the interesting question is not why people would make different meanings from the same text. That's simply what we should expect when we recognize our uniqueness. In fact, we should expect infinite meanings, because people bring so many different elements to their interaction with stories.

We now know from the work that's been done in cultural studies that there can be no meaning in the text itself, that meaning is always an interaction between the text and what readers bring to it. And it's precisely that interaction that should be the focus of study. When people bring all of these huge and varied experiences, the infinitely different lives that they have lived, to the reading of culture, you'd expect to find difference. In fact, if you didn't find difference, there'd be something weird going on. So for me difference is not the interesting question; the infinite meanings of the social world are simply part of us as an active, interpreting species.

So the question, then, is this: given the possibility of infinite meanings, why is it that in concrete and specific circumstances only a *few* meanings are given? That seems to be the more interesting question. Not why are people different, but why—given that there is so much difference built into us—are people so much the same? What are the structures that make us so much the same?

This is why I think the Marxist discussion of determination is so valuable. It gets to the heart of what actually brings people together, given that the possibilities of being torn apart are built into our nature, in a sense, as a species. In this way, Marxism gives us the most elaborate way of understanding sameness and difference, of understanding why people come to believe the same thing. While it's true that not everyone ever believes exactly the same thing, and while there are always important exceptions, nevertheless, a Marxist orientation helps us come to terms with why so many people do indeed come to embrace virtually identical and unquestioned sets of beliefs. And why they construct understandings and institutions around these beliefs that come to organize the fundamental belief structures of entire societies.

What you're talking about goes against a great deal of recent work in cultural studies that seems to shift emphasis away from power and to focus on the activity and agency of audiences in their interactions with media. How would you respond to criticism that says that, in the end, you may simply be reproducing the one-dimensional analysis of a crude Marxism that is no longer capable of explaining how media operate in a postmodern context?

I have no doubt that many people would read what I'm saying in that way. That is, they point to differences in interpretations as evidence that media power is very limited and that audiences are very savvy in how they interact with media forms. Diversity of interpretation is used as a way to show that power is not operating, when, in fact, what I think you have to look at is how power works through diversity. Popular forms can only be popular if they work in diverse ways, and no popular form works in only one particular way. For example, in the work I did with Justin Lewis on *The Cosby Show*, we identified the show's ambiguity as the key to how power and, more generally, popular culture operate to reproduce racial discourses that are deeply troubling. You have to have an analysis that is complex enough to actually look at that diversity. But you also have to frame it within a context that looks at how that diversity of interpretation can be used, how it can be put to use by particular institutions for their own ends.

There seems to be an inflection here on the reception side. What of the production side in all of this?

On the production side, there will always be ambiguity and complexity, because people can't control how messages are read. Producers might have all kinds of ideas about how the messages they create are going to work but, in the end, they can't control that. That's the difference, I think, between doing literary studies and doing cultural studies. Literary studies is really looking at the message and the complex ways in which the message is put together. I don't want to deny that. In fact, even with the focus on the audience, I don't want to get too far away from the focus on the message, because, in fact, people are always interacting with specific things. People can't just make any meaning they want. They're interacting with the messages that come to them, which have already been framed in a very particular way. So you've got to be able to look at that. You have to have the tools to be able to deconstruct the text in its full complexity. And, at the same time, you've got to be able to show not only how wide open a message is, but also how closed down it is. In other words, that there is a limit to how it can be interpreted. But the point that I want to make is that, if you only stand on the side of textual analysis, then you have no idea how the text is actually being used, how it is actually being interpreted, and how those texts are actually operating in the world of real meaning.

Hall says that cultural studies is about examining "the dirty semiotic world," where power meets meaning. And to understand this dirty semiotic world, you have got to be able to look at the messages, you have to be able to look at audiences, and you have to look at the broader context, the political, economic, and social context within which those things take place and circulate. And that's very difficult to do. I mean, you can't just sit in your office and look at an image or a video on MTV and figure that out. It requires a huge amount of work.

The issue of pleasure is hotly contested right now in communication studies. What would you say to those who might criticize Hall, or you for that matter, for not taking a full enough accounting of how power meets meaning meets pleasure? Isn't there a danger of reducing the ambiguity and potential power of experience here?

Meaning is always connected to pleasure. When I talk about meaning, I am not just talking about abstract meanings or structures of knowledge. I am talking about the way that people actually interact with and experience the world. And, again, that is the question of popularity. When I talk about popularity, I am talking about the question of pleasure. You have to be able to explain what it is that, in fact, drives people toward these kinds of messages, toward this kind of media and popular culture. But if you highlight pleasure exclusively, then everything comes down on the side of the audience and the side of agency, especially if you find that there's diversity in interpretation. Activity and diversity get the stress, and, suddenly, you've lost the centrality of power within this analysis.

The best example of someone who does this is John Fiske. He became quite well known about fifteen years ago because of his focus on pleasure. What he did within this body of work was that he essentially defined diversity as evidence that textual power was not operating in the way we previously thought about it . He essentially said, "Well, people are deriving different meanings from this, so that must mean that the text is not very powerful." On the one hand, he's right that you have to recognize that there is diversity in interpretation. But, if you stop there and only stay on that side of the equation, then you're going to be floating off into the world of pleasure and agency, looking solely at how people are making meaning and more or less exercising full control over their own lives. You can then say, as many do, "Look at how little effect the media has on people." And, when that happens, you enter the world of apology for the existing order of things. And that's right where some pop cultural critics have gone. The point is this: By saying that this issue of power has been overplayed, that *effect* has been overplayed, some people have gone to the other extreme and fixed their focus solely on the question of what drives people, what motivates people in their interactions with media. Everything then starts to resemble what used to be known as *uses and gratifications* research: What uses do people get out of this? How are individuals' needs gratified by and through their interaction with the media? And, to me, that's disastrous, both from an intellectual and a political perspective, because it completely loses touch with the context within which media messages matter and operate in the first place. It loses the context in which people interact with messages, with how messages are constructed, with the very things that condition how people think about and experience pleasure.

I'm all for pleasure; who isn't? But we also have to recognize that pleasure can be used against people. In fact, pleasure has always been used against people. That is the essential nature of how power operates. That is the essential nature of how ideology operates. Pleasure masks the work of ideology precisely when it seems as though you are making meanings that come from yourself. If I had to choose one way to make sure that a population was under my control, that's the way I would do it—make sure that the population actively controlled itself in pleasurable ways. And, from there, it's a short step to ensuring that people take actions that are against their own material interests.

With all of this in mind, if a young scholar were interested in popular culture, what advice would you give her about the types of questions she should be asking? What would mark a political question as worthy of asking, in your view?

In my view, there are two aspects, always, to the kinds of analysis cultural studies should be doing. On the one hand, we have to deal with the question of popularity. That is, why do some cultural forms take hold at particular times and become popular? Even in the case of moguls like Rupert Murdoch, powerful media producers cannot simply impose their views on the population. For something to be popular, it has to interact in meaningful ways with what is already going on in the lives of people. So that's the first question to ask: What, exactly, is the basis of a particular phenomenon of popularity? And this then provokes much more fundamental questions about what's actually happening in people's lives. So it's not simply "Why is this message popular or why is this song popular?" But instead, "How is a specific song tapping into what's going on in the concrete and material lives people are actually living?" So that's the first question, the question of popularity.

The second question then emerges from the uses of that popularity. That is, how is meaning—meaning made in the interaction between a popular culture and an audience—being used politically? And to get to the core of that question, we always need to bring in the question of power. In this sense, it really goes back to a very old debate between agency and structure. And the point is that the best cultural studies approaches never fail to take both of these things into account. So, yes, cultural studies has to look at agency—because people are not simply dopes or dupes, they are not dumb, and they actively engage with cultural forms to make sense of their lives. But—and this is crucial—we do so *not* under conditions of our own choosing, as Marx said. What's imperative, what this dynamic demands, is that we focus on both sides of this dynamic: the active side, yes, but also the side that people do not have under their control. Part of the problem with some recent trends in cultural studies is that they have lost touch with that second part.

Media Education Foundation: Building Institutions

A lot has been said about how the Media Education Foundation (MEF) evolved out of MTV's threat to sue you over your video Dreamworlds, *but I think less is known about how MEF has grown and evolved as an organization over the past decade and a half since then.*

I wish I could say I had this grand vision for MEF that predicted where we would be as an organization today. But the fact is that MEF, like virtually all institutions, developed within some very concrete conditions, in response to a number of very specific situations. First, as you note, was the *Dreamworlds* controversy. The major decision I made at that time was to distribute *Dreamworlds* myself, so that meant that MEF, from the start, was not simply going to be a production company, but also a place that would try to distribute things as well. But the truth is that this was less a decision than a reaction to circumstances. I went to a number of independent distribution organizations with *Dreamworlds* but none were all that interested in it. So MEF, more or less at its inception, was set up to distribute one video—with the passing thought that if we could generate any funds from it, we could then think about supporting another project.

And were you still an organization of one at that time?

More or less. But in the very beginning I did bring on somebody part time to help with sales. Actually, I've been thinking a lot recently about the history of this organization. MEF started in 1991, and from June of 1991 to June of 1992 I had one unpaid intern who dealt with the sales of *Dreamworlds*. We then moved into our first offices, consisting of four small rooms, in June of 1992. I'll never forget standing in this empty space with four rooms wondering what the hell I had done. But as money came in, we started to buy furniture and computers, and before long I was asking myself, "Okay. But what now?" The answer was a video on tobacco advertising.

Why tobacco advertising?

First, because I thought it was an important topic. Second, because I thought there would be a demand for it from educational institutions. In fact, that's precisely the rationale that informs, in very broad terms, how we function to this day. Two things always: social importance and market viability. And I think this is a combination that some progressive or alternative film producers sometimes forget or miss entirely. They have a topic they want to do, and market considerations are secondary. That's why there have been some fantastic films that very few people have seen—because, on the Left, distribution has not been thought through as much as production has. My reason for highlighting this was really pretty simple: it was the only way that we were going to survive, and to succeed you first have to survive. And I just didn't have the resources to start writing grants and raising money that way.

All of that said, we didn't choose topics just because we felt that they could make money. MEF has never done that. If we did that, there would be no reason for us to exist. So we've always operated with two questions in mind up front: Is this is a topic that needs to be studied? And if so—and only if it is so—can we sell it?

Playing devil's advocate for a moment: Isn't it hypocritical to operate this way—given that so much of your work critiques the excesses and injustices of the capitalist market? Aren't you just using the market yourself and producing something as a commodity and then selling it?

I couldn't disagree more. I don't see it as a contradiction at all. Because one positive aspect of the market is that it gets you in touch with different groups. That's what the market is good for. If you don't cater to the demands of certain groups, you don't survive, so in this sense the market links us to where we want to be. Politically and pedagogically, we wanted to be in classrooms, and the market was a way of linking us to that aim. That was where my work as a professor really paid off, in the sense that I had a pretty good feel for what would work in classrooms and what was necessary. This is just what MEF has always been balancing—the topics that need addressing, with the necessity to get the distribution and resources needed to continue doing the work we do.

I'm always thinking in these terms, and in this sense, yes, an awareness of the market is always there. In the early days it had to be there. It was necessary to our survival. And there's no doubt this produces some negatives. You always have to produce and sell, produce and sell, produce and sell. There's an incredible pressure for new products, and that pressure has been pretty unrelenting over the last fifteen years. In many ways, I haven't really had a chance to sit back and reflect a lot on these kinds of things.

So all of this demands a certain kind of growth. If you have to produce new things in order to have economic viability, and you need that viability to fuel your organization, then you have to grow. And even if that growth isn't always registered outwardly in terms of hiring more staff, for example, it would seem that you nevertheless do constantly have to be giving people new reasons to come back.

True. But it's also political. To produce more things means that you're getting more ideas out there and into classrooms. The market is the means of doing the critical work we do. As I said, the pressure has been more or less unrelenting, especially as we incurred debt from the start. The main reason, I think, was that I made a pretty crazy decision—which was to say that we were going to both produce and distribute. People generally don't do that because each of these takes huge amounts of resources.

For a lot of reasons, I don't think ours is a model that can be easily repli-cated. Sometimes, when people ask how we did it, they're looking to duplicate it. And I'd be lying if I didn't say that it's very tough. Still I do think it's possible, in the United States especially, because there is a large educational market here. The key is to think carefully about all of the dynamics involved with that market and to produce very specifically for it. It would be a lot more difficult, I think, to duplicate this in other countries, because there isn't the same kind of large edu-cational market capable of sustaining an organization like this in the way it needs to be sustained.

So on the one hand, the reliance on sales alone to sustain MEF has had some very negative side effects in terms of this constant pressure to produce more things. But the same time, there is a positive aspect to it: if you can get to a posi-tion where you can sustain yourself economically, it does actually give you the freedom to take on projects that you otherwise wouldn't be able to take on. And I'm talking specifically here about dealing with subjects that most philanthropic foundations would never fund because they're too sensitive and controversial. That's actually what we did with *Peace, Propaganda, and the Promised Land*. There's just no way that *Peace, Propaganda, and the Promised Land* could've been made by an organization that depended on foundation grants to survive, because the Israeli-Palestinian conflict, in the United States at least, is a topic that is more or less off-limits, even for most left-of-center foundations. But we were in a position that allowed us to fund the initial stages of this ourselves. I remember talking to one of our advisers about this, and he said: "Someone just needs to do this. This is one of those statements that needs to be made, even though we're not going to make huge amounts of money out of this." Our funding structure allowed us to take a risk on a project we believed in. We would not have been able to do it otherwise.

In that sense, I never want to be solely reliant upon foundation grants. If you come to rely too much on foundation grants, you're also going to have to rely on program officers who may change suddenly. That's exactly what hap-pens sometimes, and it can create big problems for nonprofits. The program offi-cer changes, the priorities change, and suddenly half your budget is gone, and you're laying off the people you'd been supporting with that money. So while I'd certainly like to get money from foundations to support some of our work, I never want to be dependent on it. The market is something we can control, for the most part anyway. We don't have to worry about one person making all the decisions. If we produce the right things, and they're important and useful to teachers, then we know we can get our stuff out there and, in turn, reinforce the stability we need.

So the bottom line in all of this, I guess, is that the structure of MEF poses chal-lenges, but it also presents huge opportunities to do things we wouldn't otherwise be able to do in the traditional nonprofit world. Even though MEF is nonprofit, in the sense that no one owns it, and in terms of the normal way nonprofits are described, the ways in which we support ourselves are not at all typical.

What other challenges have you faced in running MEF over the years?

There have been, and there continue to be, many challenges, some financial, but also others that have to do with organizational culture. It's an issue that a lot of progressive organizations struggle with—the tension between mission and daily operations. On the one hand, our mission is to produce materials that help people deconstruct the world in which they live, begin to understand the structures that shape their everyday environments, and also envision alternatives, possibilities, and different ways of seeing the future. All of this is guided by a progressive vision that is not at all political in the everyday, partisan, Democrat-Republican sense but that is very political in the sense of embracing values of citizenship that demand individual autonomy and awareness in the face of any kind of power that would undermine these democratic imperatives. On the other hand, there are always additional questions about which values should govern MEF's concrete operation as an organization. That is, how do you actually get films made under time pressure? How do you get them distributed under fiscal constraints? This has been the constant challenge, and not just for us, but for all progressive organizations. In fact, it's just this challenge that Stuart Hall said eventually drove him away from the Birmingham Center—the tensions created by this developmental dialectic. MEF is not unusual in having conversations around these things.

On the issue of how you select topics, can you talk about some of the considerations involved beyond financial concerns?

First of all, I think MEF is in something of a privileged position at this point, because the videos we do produce and distribute have the potential to raise the topics we choose to a certain level of importance. The videos will get out there, and people are likely to talk about them and use them in classrooms. But it's an important question, because we're constantly thinking about the topics we should be looking at. And there are political and commercial decisions that come into play, in the sense that we're required to think about what's important not only at a specific moment in time, but also into the months and years ahead. We have to think about issues in terms of transitory versus lasting social relevance. The challenge is to pick those topics that you know are going to be around for a while. You don't want videos that are outdated by the time you make them. We've sometimes come close to that, in that we've sometimes taken so long to do a specific title that it loses its initial relevance. You've got to be able to look into the future, and this is a good thing, because it challenges us always to address issues in a way that moves beyond cultural symptoms into the very structures and conditions that produce them.

As for the actual decision-making process, the challenge is to meld all of these factors and also to ask some other basic and fairly mundane questions.

Will a certain topic be too difficult for us to treat in a video? Can the topic be addressed adequately with one expert, given that single-interview videos are the easiest to produce? Do we know enough good people who are well enough versed on a topic to invest time in a multi-interview project? Are we looking at something that seems very important but lack the expertise, or access to expertise, to do a good job with it? What kind of research will be required to get a project even to the point where we know what we need for expertise? All of these practical factors, and many more, come into play.

Do you have a personal favorite or favorites?

There are videos that have been extremely important to MEF, so let me come at your question that way. I think we can identity five or six titles. *Dreamworlds* was the first vitally important video, of course, for the simple reason that it started everything. Then we have a period in which MEF made videos about health and media issues, the most important of which was a video called *Slim Hopes*, which was produced in 1995 with Jean Kilbourne. That took us to another level, because the response was so positive, and the sales were very high. It allowed us to expand from the first office, the four small rooms, into the rest of that space and a whole other part of the building. It allowed us to grow in terms of staff as well. The next pivotal videos, and they came out around the same time (2000), were *Killing Us Softly 3* and *Tough Guise*. Their success propelled us even further. Again, it's gender issues that were driving all of this to this point: *Dreamworlds* was about gender, *Slim Hopes* was about gender, *Tough Guise* was about gender, and *Killing Us Softly* was about gender. And the success of the last two allowed us to think about expanding again, and in 2003 we bought this great, old, broken-down fire station in Northampton and were able to fix it up so that we had the space to do what we do better.

That was huge for the organization, no?

It was. And, if not for those videos being made and embraced, it wouldn't have been possible. Then I would have to say that the next pivotal video was *Hijacking Catastrophe* in 2004. That video, which I believe is the best we've produced, expanded our reach—taking our material beyond institutions, professors, academics, and students to ordinary citizens and activists.

Was that film made with an eye toward that market?

Absolutely, in the sense that it was made with an eye toward serving as a useful resource for Americans as they approached what many people regarded as one of the important elections in history. Our mission is educational, and after 9/11 there wasn't a lot of information coming from mainstream media. The trauma, the sense of patriotism, the fear in the media of being labeled un-American, all of this created a media climate that shut down thinking and debate about the policies we were seeing emerge right after 9/11, then in the lead-up to the war and beyond. So the question became how MEF could use its resources to provide materials that would help citizens make more informed choices. The result is that MEF is now at a very interesting stage. *Hijacking Catastrophe* has given us a different kind of profile, one more explicitly connected to the requirements of democratic citizenship, the fundamental demand in a democracy for information. And our challenge now is to build on that while maintaining our baseline mission to provide material to universities and colleges that continues the crucial work of addressing the important cultural and social issues—issues that always seem to be caught up, at base, with issues of gender, race, sexuality, class, and the like.

And do you have one favorite from this list?

Those are the videos that have been important to MEF. In terms of my own favorite within those, it's difficult to say because I tend to like every video we make. But I do think the video that did the most to change the way people saw MEF was *Tough Guise*. In general, *gender* has tended to mean *women*, and I think we inadvertently kind of went along with that. I think *Tough Guise* really got masculinity onto the gender map in a very mainstream way. To be able to intervene, to be able to say something meaningful about the social construction of masculinity, and to do so in a nonthreatening way to that kid in the back of the lecture theater was very important. That's the core of what cultural studies should be about, and that's what cultural intervention is about. In terms of the classroom, it's not just about talking to the front row, but also being able to talk to that student in the back row who doesn't really want to be there, who's there because he has to be there. You've got to be able to reach into that back row and to have a presence there. I think that *Dreamworlds* did do that, and I think that *Tough Guise* did that as well.

What you're describing is pedagogically challenging, to say the least. Anyone who has taught will tell you that it's easier to reach people who are already committed.

I think it's the central challenge of pedagogy, and cultural pedagogy, to talk to people you otherwise wouldn't talk to, and may not have a lot in common with. The reason that *Dreamworlds* worked is that it dealt with images of pleasure; if they weren't images of pleasure, they wouldn't be in music videos. The function of these images is to draw people in. And with regard to *Dreamworlds*, men have told me that their initial reaction when they were told they would be watching the video was, "Wow, we're going to get a whole hour of watching beautiful women in our classes." There's no doubt that that's what hooks people in, and the reason for that is that these are images of desire. And I think we have to explicitly recognize that. Given that we don't have the same resources that record companies have or that Hollywood has, we've got to exploit the power of those images and turn them back on themselves, much like martial artists redirecting the power coming at them. We've got to turn the power that's coming at us directly back on its source. The challenge, then, for something like

Dreamworlds is to make sure that people do not get lost in the seductive power of the images and to make the images problematic, to take familiar images and make them strange, so that they can be seen at a critical distance in new ways. That is why there are so many images, one after the other, until the moment of pleasure turns into overload. The other thing that I did in *Dreamworlds* was to rip out the music from the music videos and to replace it with my own voice. So, to get the images, they also have to have my analysis at the same time. You can't take one without the other.

So you're interrupting their normal consumption of popular culture?

Yes. So that, the next time they're watching music videos, these ideas, these alternative ways of seeing things, are in their heads. That's what cultural intervention is about. It's not about control; it's about intervening and having a presence. With *Dreamworlds*, it's also very important that the voice over the images was a male voice. And, in fact, some of the early feminist response to *Dreamworlds* was pretty negative. Some people said, "Well this is just the same old patriarchal voice from above telling us how to think. Why wasn't there a woman's voice in there?" I recognize that I could have made that choice, but the fact is that I made a very deliberate decision to feature a male voice. If your ultimate target is that male student in the back row, a male student who's likely to be defensive or outright dismissive in the face of any serious talk about sexism and misogyny in something like MTV, the risk—as unfair as it assuredly is—is that he will be more likely to dismiss a woman on these issues. That's what he's been trained to do by the culture. Boys will be boys and all of that. And it just becomes, in his mind, another puritanical woman moaning about images and feminism and whatever, and he's tuned out. Already in his mind are all the stereotypes that go along with that female voice, and he's tuned out to the analysis already. But if it's a male voice, it's harder for him to do that. If nothing else, it presents a moment of confusion, productive confusion, I hope. If he's going to reject it, he has to reject the ideas; he's got to deal with the ideas. So it was very important for me, strategically and pedagogically, that it be a male voice saying these things. It's not until men take this on, it's not until men use their privilege to deal with these things, that you can intervene effectively in those places. Not exclusively, of course. I'm not saying only men can do it, obviously. What I am saying is that, unless men have a very important role within that, it's going to be impossible to deconstruct male culture.

I think *Tough Guise* works in very much the same way. The fact that it's a man talking about these things allows entry into a world that might otherwise be closed off. In some ways, it gives men permission to engage these issues. And it doesn't hurt when the man, as with Jackson Katz in *Tough Guise*, is someone who, in some stereotypical senses, embodies traditional masculinity in that he's an ex-football player. And the way he talks about these issues resonates with a lot of men who have never thought seriously about these things. He can't be rejected straight away as a soft or male-bashing guy who's been taken in by feminism. In that sense, his body is very important to him, and his voice is very important to him. And this means that, if you're going to reject his analysis, you've got to reject the ideas, not some stereotype that's already in your mind.

The Media Education Foundation and Politics

To what extent do you see the MEF as an explicitly political organization?

Well, it is and it isn't. It's a political organization in the sense that we want to be active in the world and that we want to inspire people to be more active in the world. But we're not political in the sense of being connected to the political process, particularly to a political party. A lot of our work takes aim at the concentration of power, and, in this way, it has been fairly relentless in exposing the antidemocratic bias in our supposedly liberal media, for example. If our work is political, then, it's political in a small *d*, democratic sense that transcends parties and establishment politics as it exists today. We see our work as simply advancing the demands of citizenship: helping people to critically examine the bombardment of images and information that constantly come at them, so that they have more control over their lives and those who act in their names—whether Republicans, Democrats, or media executives. In that sense, we're political in that we believe that knowledge matters. And our basic mission is to help get as much knowledge as we can into places where it matters most and can make a difference. We feel that the way to do that these days is not only to write books and articles. The way to do it is by making videos and films that are capable of intervening in the world in which people live. In that sense, it's highly political.

How has this political orientation been reflected in the actual subject matter of MEF's projects over the years? Has the nature of the kind of political intervention you're talking about changed or evolved over the years?

To some degree, yes—but, from the start, we've remained an intellectual and pedagogical organization, so the nature of the questions that we focus on pushes us in a very particular direction. In that sense, I actually don't think that MEF videos have changed very much. The core of our mission has always been to take the latest cutting-edge knowledge, from the academy or from wherever else people are dealing with media issues, and to translate this knowledge into forms that ordinary people can understand, so that you don't have to be a scholar or an expert to understand the analysis. In this sense, I see what we do as democratizing information. We simply try to make this stuff accessible, so that the ideas can actually intervene in the world. That impulse has been there from the start, and it hasn't changed.

Let's move a little deeper into this relationship between intellectual, scholarly work and what you're saying about accessibility. Do you see your work as a media scholar, as a cultural studies scholar, as in any way separate from this pedagogical emphasis at MEF?

To me, cultural studies scholarship has always been not only about understanding the world in the best ways in which it can be understood, but also about staying attuned to how knowledge can be made to matter in the world. It was that particular perspective that actually engaged me in the project of cultural studies to begin with. What engaged me was that cultural studies was looking at stuff that was going on right now, that you needed new knowledge to be able to understand that, and that this new knowledge was going to be able to intervene in the world at which you were looking.

Is it safe to say, then, that there's a sense of urgency that attaches to this kind of orientation and work?

I do think that we're living at a unique moment in human history. There are some things that we know we are hitting the limits of, the physical environment, for example, which we're consuming and destroying. There's no question that that's new and has never happened before in history—that we could actually be destroying the world. We also have the capacity now to destroy the world with nuclear weapons. So both of these things are radically new, unique. We have never had those possibilities before. And, obviously, they produce a sense of urgency, or at least they should.

But, more fundamentally, what we are talking about is the dialectic between democracy and power. I think that one of the fundamentals of human existence is the drive toward democracy and the drive toward freedom. I think that there's no doubt that we are, as a species, probably freer now than ever before, that more people are free now than at any point in human history, and that more people are able to control their lives in unprecedented ways. That's the result of the longing for democracy, about which a lot of people have talked. But the project is in no way complete. In fact, the democratic project, the impulse toward freedom, can never be satisfied. Freedom ceases to exist the moment it becomes complacent. And that's why there's always a necessity for vigilance in a democracy, a sense of urgency that keeps us on guard against the institutionalization of democratic power centers that undermine what they claim to be serving, advancing, or realizing.

Alex Carey, the Australian theorist, says that there are three great developments in the twentieth century. First is the growth of democracy. Second is the growth of corporate power. Third is the growth of corporate propaganda to protect corporate power against democracy. Although I think that, throughout history, elites have used culture to maintain control, what seems to be different right now is the specialization involved—the specialized institutions that have now grown up around this propaganda. The advertising industry and the public relations industry have now become specialists at tapping into the emotional core that drives people. So the open question right now is whether or not human beings are ever going to get to that stage where we will be able to save ourselves—and the planet—before our economic models destroy the environment or before our weapons and wars destroy everything. This, I think, is the great question of the twenty-first century: Can we save ourselves from unprecedented dangers in the face of unprecedented propaganda bombardments that keep us numb and uninformed?

What can cultural studies, as we have been talking about it, bring to political analysis that political science and other forms of communication studies have not already been doing for years?

What cultural studies brings to politics and political analysis is an explicit and deep focus on how political meanings are mediated—that is, how public opinion is structured, or controlled and manipulated outright, by means of techniques like advertising and public relations. Cultural studies allows an engagement with the myriad meanings that attach to the relationship between these techniques, our political structures, and the political meanings that result from and, in turn, affect this relationship. Again, I don't think that the use of public relations by elites is anything new. I just think that there's more awareness of the phenomenon now, and I think that cultural studies gives us good tools for understanding political movements and processes in new ways.

Very early on, I did some work with Justin Lewis and Michael Morgan, colleagues of mine at the University of Massachusetts, which we funded with proceeds from sales of *Dreamworlds*. (In that sense, I guess, there was a connection between gender and politics right from the start.) We did a survey during the first Gulf War in 1991. At that time, there were all kinds of opinion surveys circulating that measured how much the American people supported the invasion of Iraq and the drive to oust Saddam Hussein from Kuwait. Poll after poll showed that between 80 percent and 85 percent of people supported what the Bush Administration was doing.

We saw all of this, and we began to think of ways to enlarge our understanding of the political situation. And what we quickly realized was that nobody was asking about the *basis* of that support. Nobody was taking things a step further to determine *why* there was apparently so much support for the war. What we wanted to get at was the underlying discursive structure that was informing people's understanding of the world and allowing them to support this kind of action. So we conducted a survey that asked not what people believed, but what they actually *knew*. We thought, up front, that there was a relationship between what people believed and the actual knowledge that informed their understanding of the way in which the world worked.

We asked a number of questions about the Middle East and about world affairs. And what we found was that Americans had very little knowledge about what was going on around the world. In fact, the study showed that the more people supported the war, the less they knew. So there was an inverse relationship between support for the war and actual knowledge about the events that were connected to that region. We also wanted to link this to media coverage of the world, so we also asked people how much media they watched. And we found an extremely interesting relationship: The more people watched television, the less they actually knew, and the more they supported the war. So the media seemed to be centrally connected to Americans being systematically misinformed about a major part of the world and, therefore, about the actions being taken in their name in that part of the world. It was an interesting study that allowed us to move deeper into the nature of support for the war. And I think this is precisely what cultural studies can do. I think it allows us to pull apart some of these broader notions of public opinion and to get a sharper sense of the ways in which people are really thinking about things.

A 2004 study of public opinion by the University of Maryland's Program on International Policy Attitudes (PIPA) came to similar conclusions about the current war in Iraq.

Yes. That survey used a strategy similar to ours, which is to look at knowledge rather than simply opinion. And they found essentially the same thing we did a decade and a half ago. Here again, there was very, very strong support for the war, but that support was based on almost no knowledge. No real information. And when I talk about knowledge, I'm talking about very basic facts that are indisputable about that region. Not opinion about the region—just basic facts about the region and aspects of the war. And again, this study found that media was at the center of this. I think the most famous finding of the PIPA study is that the more people watched FOX News, the less they knew about the war, the less they knew about the region, the less they knew about the world, and the more they supported the war. So watching FOX News not only makes you more conservative, it also makes you more ignorant. What all of this suggests is that there may be a relationship between ignorance, political propaganda, and corporate media coverage of the world and where American politics is right now.

But I think we can also take things further than that. I don't think people are simply misinformed, because there's a lot of information out there now, even among mainstream sources. Take the twin issues of weapons of mass destruction and the connection between Saddam Hussein and Al Qaeda as framed in the run-up to the war in Iraq. Saddam Hussein did not have weapons of mass destruction. And even Congress has come out with official reports saying that there were no links between Al Qaeda and Osama Bin Laden. And yet the majority of people who voted for George Bush still believe that weapons of mass destruction were found and that there was a link between Saddam Hussein and Osama Bin Laden. They actually believe that the war in Iraq is somehow connected to the attacks of 9/11.

The question, again, is why people believe this. Are people just dumb? Or have the media really done their job in ways that prevent real knowledge from getting through? The interesting thing is that the fact that there were no weapons of mass destruction and the fact that the link with Al Qaeda is nonexistent are now mainstream ideas. They are not ideas that simply exist on the margins, and, if you watch regular news, you will come across these ideas. So I think that now we need to ask or to complete the question, which is this: Why, in the face of countervailing evidence, do people still believe that weapons of mass destruction were found? And I think that, at that point, you have to look at the relationship between knowledge and identity.

I think that one of the reasons why large numbers of Americans still believe these things is because if they didn't, if weapons of mass destruction and the connection to Osama Bin Laden didn't exist, then the war in Iraq is illegal and possibly about nothing more than a giant power or resource grab. And this just won't cut it given the kind of self-identity Americans have, given the belief that America is always on the side of good, always on the side of freedom and democracy. I think that this belief in America is so strong, and that the very ideal of America is so strong, that a lot of people simply will not allow facts to get in the way.

But it should also be said that, in one sense, if this analysis is valid, there is hope. Because it shows that people's support for the war is based on noble reasons. They do not support the war because they support empire or because they support genocide or because they support expending the blood of American troops to control oil reserves. Instead, it seems clear that a lot of Americans really did think that Saddam Hussein was a threat and, therefore, that America had to take just action against this threat. It's in this sense that we can see the positive dimension here, because the support is based upon a noble set of values. What's interesting is how these noble ideas and motives can be exploited by people with no real interest in democracy and no interest in upholding any America ideal of virtue. If we don't dig deep into the discursive structure of these stories, if we ignore the issue of American identity and focus only on arcane policy details, I think we end up with a very superficial, one-dimensional way of understanding how and why people actually come to support government policies.

But you're not suggesting that people are simply passive consumers of media coverage and propaganda, are you? That people are brainwashed?

Absolutely not. The one thing that cultural studies has always shown us is that you cannot think about media in a simple, one-dimensional way. There are always highly contradictory dynamics at work. We always have to remember that ideology can work through contradiction. Two contradictory ideas can exist simultaneously within the same kind of discursive structure, and a standard political analysis doesn't give you any real insight into that. A standard Marxist analysis doesn't give you enough insight into that. As I have said before, we have got to look at both identity and ideology at the same time, look at how they hold together and how power works within this relation. And this is exactly what cultural studies gives us—nothing if not insight into what Stuart Hall calls "the dirty semiotic world of power and knowledge." The job of cultural studies is to try to unpack that Gordian knot. And it's really difficult to do because it's so tightly wound and consists of so many different strands.

Hijacking Catastrophe *is about empire. And* Peace, Propaganda, and the Promised Land, *on one level, shows how the imperial drive of the United States to control the Middle East is often fundamentally at odds with claims that our presence there is all about spreading our values and supporting democracy. How do you think the notion of an American empire sits within the larger frame that you're describing of an American identity?*

That's the key question. What would happen if Americans actually understood themselves as an empire and actually regarded themselves as an empire? I think that Americans have a huge, almost built-in resistance to thinking about themselves as an empire. This notion that America only works for the good persists, and I think it does so directly against the notion of empire as global control of the world for its own sake. Empire then gets framed not as empire, but as the natural expression and expansion of exceptional American ideals.

Isn't that true of past empires? Empires have never really said that they exist to control and crush people simply for the sake of controlling and crushing people, have they?

I think there's a certain way in which democracy distinctively inflects the operation of the American empire. The Roman empire, for example, not being a democracy, didn't have to worry about controlling the population. The British didn't particularly have to worry about controlling the population either. At the start of the British Empire, Britain was not a democracy, so it didn't need to channel its imperial designs through democratic ideals. You could do two things together: You could serve British economic interests, and you could also bring civilization to the heathen hoards. And that was part of what the white man's burden was. I am not too sure how much that went beyond the elite circles.

I think what is really significant about American empire is that this notion that we are doing the right thing actually works in the opposite way. I don't think that elites now think that way at all. I think that when the architects of empire were sitting around trying to figure out how to control oil in the Middle East, they were talking about economic factors and what they needed to control. And then they were saying, "Well, how can we sell this?" So, right now, I think it actually works opposite, in some ways, to how the British Empire worked, in that elites don't believe any of this stuff. They know that none of this is about democracy and freedom, but that it has to be sold to the population within the context of these ideals. And it has to be sold to the population precisely because it is a democracy, because, in a democracy, you need to bring the people along—or at the very least assure that they don't rebel. Again, coming back to Alex Carey's notion about the growth of democracy and the growth of corporate power and the role that corporate propaganda plays to curb the potentially anticorporate excesses of democracy—what this means is that propaganda becomes a baseline necessity in democracies in a way that it is not in dictatorships. Saddam Hussein didn't have to worry about this kind of thing in Iraq, because he could simply control the people through blunt force and fear. The Soviet Union, likewise, for all of its propaganda efforts, could always control the population by military means and state policing powers. But when you have a democracy, propaganda and ideology become much, much more important. This is why you have to have your specialized institutions, like advertising and public relations—to be able to fulfill that function.

Beyond actual content, how much of the public relations mobilized in the buildup to the war do you think simply functioned as a form of distraction for an already distracted public?

Distraction seems to imply that they don't want you to really think about this. As long as you aren't really thinking about what's going on, then it's fine. Some analysts who I greatly admire think that this is actually what popular culture is—simply a distraction and deflection from the so-called real world of politics and policy. But I don't think that it's enough to say that it's merely about distraction, because they actually do need to bring the population along. They need to win active support. Again, this is not just acquiescence. They need to get part of the population to be active supports of their policies, so that the population comes to invest in government actions. There's no doubt that, right now, there is, in fact, a large section of the American population—perhaps not the majority, but a large enough section of the population—that is very motivated politically and very active in the Republican Party, that is also very invested in empire and this war effort. And we are not talking only about rich people. We are not talking about oil barons. We are talking about people of modest means, who actually have no economic interests in empire but who are now invested in it ideologically. That, I think, is new. I think that is something that is distinctive right now.

Simply talking about ideology and deflection doesn't get at that. At some point, if you really want to fight this fight within the United States and you want to be able to have this democratic debate around this, then you have to be able to deal with that. You have to be able to deal with the level of identity that people have invested in empire. You are not going to simply take it apart by pointing out the facts to them. And that's what I think is interesting about the issue of weapons of mass destruction and the issue of Saddam Hussein's link to Al Qaeda; it's the fact that, when people came to understand that these things were not true, it didn't make any difference.

You have got to intervene at another level. You have to intervene at a level that shows people exactly what is at stake for them personally: how they are invested in war policy and empire, how they are losing through these policies, and the way in which these things affect their concrete lives, their material lives—how much debt they have, whether or not their sons and daughters will come back maimed, either physically or psychologically from this war. Unless we engage people at that level, we are not going to have much hope in changing the discursive structures that inform how Americans understand the world.

Can you talk about how this analysis plays out in the context of Peace, Propaganda, and the Promised Land?

I think that if ordinary Americans knew exactly what was going on in the Middle East, if they understood exactly what was happening in the Israeli-Palestinian conflict and knew their own government's role within that, they would be horrified about the role that America has played in enabling one of the most horrendous events of the last thirty-eight years, Israel's occupation of the West Bank. I think that if people knew what was really happening in their name, policy would change. So we made *Peace, Propaganda, and the Promised Land* as a way to show how Americans are systematically misinformed about this subject. If it didn't particularly matter how you thought about the world, then there wouldn't be this incredible propaganda effort to make sure that Americans thought about the Israeli-Palestinian conflict in one very narrow way. And so the film was designed to show Americans how media coverage of the conflict affects their own understanding and, therefore, American foreign policy itself in that part of the world. Perhaps it is based on a kind of naive idea that, if Americans only knew what was really going on *and their complicity in it*, then something could change.

Is there a certain kind of racism at work here as well?

That's a different thing, I think. I don't think that you have to be racist to turn away from the information that exists out there about the Palestinian conflict. There is simply very little information available to mainstream audiences, so I don't think that you can make that equation. Perhaps if there were a lot of information available and people were still turning away from it, then you could make a different kind of argument. But, right now, I don't think you can do that. I don't think that the Israeli-Palestinian conflict is about race or even religion in terms of how it has played out here with American viewers. There is a racial element to it in the sense that Israel is framed as a white, European democracy set against Arabs who want to drive the Jews into the sea. That kind of broad framing definitely exists, but I don't think it is essentially sold through the racial aspect; I don't think race is the central aspect of how this conflict has been mediated. On the contrary, I think it is largely mediated through absence. One of the things that you find when you start looking closely at this is that Americans know almost nothing about the Israeli-Palestinian conflict. And, sometimes, it's not only that they know nothing; it's that what they do know is simply factually wrong. They think the opposite of what is true.

You said that this is more about absence than anything else. A lot of the groups that you document in Peace, Propaganda, and the Promised Land—*pro-Israel, Zionist organizations—they obviously do not view themselves as anti-Palestinian or racist organizations. They see themselves as guardians against a long tradition of anti-Semitic racism against Jews. That seems to be in the forefront of their work, and you seem to be putting it on the side. How would you respond to that?*

I think there are two issues about anti-Semitism that are crucial. One is the existence of anti-Semitism in the world, the existence of anti-Jewish sentiments and the impact that they have on the actions that people take. The Holocaust is the prime example of what happens when anti-Semitism is taken to its logical conclusion. Anti-Semitism exists in the world, has existed for a long time, and actually has existed in the Christian world much more than in the Arab world. In fact, in the Arab world, anti-Semitism was a very, very minor phenomenon until the start of the Zionist movement in the early part of the twentieth century. Anti-Semitism in the Arab world, in fact, doesn't exist until well into the twentieth century. It exists, in a huge way, of course, among Christian nations. So that is one crucial fact: the existence of anti-Semitism.

The second question, for me, at least from the perspective of what we are looking at here, is how the *accusation* of anti-Semitism can actually work to silence people. And I think that you have to separate out those two things—that is, you have to look at how anti-Semitism is used discursively. And I think that you have to look at how anti-Semitism is used discursively to make sure that, in fact, anti-Semitism in the real world does not increase. I think anti-Semitism, as an accusation, especially around the Israeli-Palestinian conflict, has been a great silencing mechanism. That is, any criticism of the policies of the government of Israel is automatically labeled as being anti-Jewish and, therefore, anti-Semitic. It has often kept people quiet, because no one wants to be accused of anti-Semitism. No one wants to be accused of being a racist. And, whenever you deal with this issue in a critical way, frequently, this is the first accusation that is made, and it is a very, very powerful silencing mechanism.

In fact, I can tell you that, for over ten years, it kept me silent about the conflict in the Middle East. I did not start dealing with this issue explicitly until about 1996, and yet, for years prior, I had been teaching courses at the University of Massachusetts on issues of ideology and identity. There's no question, as a simple matter of intellectual honesty, that I should have been looking at how the media was representing the Israeli-Palestinian conflict. The fact that I didn't amounted to personal cowardice, in my view. When you are dealing with questions of propaganda, how can you avoid so primary an example of propaganda with regard to American foreign policy? You can't. It's simply there, kicking you in the teeth, and you actually have to make an effort to avoid it. And, in fact, I think I did. And the fact is that I knew that, if I dealt with the issue, if I raised the issue of propaganda in my classes and was in any way critical of the policies of the

Israeli government, there were going to be rumors of anti-Semitism and rumors of racism. Here I was a tenured, full professor at a liberal university, and yet I was worried about what was going to happen, what some people were going to *say* if I brought this issue into the classroom. For ten years, these fears silenced me, and I didn't touch the issue. I talk about it as cowardice, because cowardice means not doing what you have a responsibility to do because of the possible consequences. I'm not talking about cowardice as failing to act in the face of grave dangers, like the threat of violence or death. I'm talking about cowardice as failing to speak—in a democratic society, no less—for fear that people are going to say nasty things about you. And that was enough to keep me silent. Imagine how that works for other people who don't have the protection of tenure that I have.

All of this was actually brought home to me in the most powerful way at a talk by Edward Said that I attended in 1996 at Hampshire College here in western Massachusetts. It was an event celebrating the work of the great third-world activist and intellectual Eqbal Ahmed. Noam Chomsky was there. Howard Zinn was there. Dan Ellsberg was there. Anyone who was anyone connected to the Left was there celebrating his work. And the last person who spoke was Edward Said. When he got up to speak, he actually had tears running down his face, tears of happiness. He said, "The reason I am here is that when the rest of the Left forgot about the Palestinians, Eqbal did not, and for that he paid a great price in terms of his intellectual career and his own academic career." I remember thinking when he said that—in a moment of shame—"Why haven't I dealt with this?" And I made my mind up at that moment that I was going to deal with it. I was no longer going to hide from this issue in the way that I think most intellectuals have hidden from it, out of fear of the repercussions.

This is, in fact, exactly how propaganda works. It can actually stop people from raising questions that make things uncomfortable. When I talk about absences, that's what I mean by absences. You can control people in that way. So one of the first things that I started to do at that point was to think about making a film on how the media has covered these issues. We are media critics at MEF, and this film was really about the media coverage of that conflict and how it shaped what people knew about the issue.

At the same time, I started doing surveys in my classes to find out what my students knew about the conflict, and they yielded some very interesting answers. One of the questions that I asked was about the occupation of Palestine. I asked what country has been continually condemned in the United Nations for illegally occupying someone else's land in the Middle East. And I provided four possible answers: Kuwait, Lebanon, Israel, and, because I couldn't say Palestine, Palestinians. Those were the four possible choices. That is an objective, factual question. The answer, of course, is Israel, which, since 1967, has been involved in the illegal occupation of the West Bank and Gaza, and has been condemned continually in U.N. resolutions around those issues. These are students at a good, liberal university, but, a lot of times, they would say, "Well, actually, I don't know." And I'd tell them that they had to at least guess, because I felt that, guessing, rather than simply being random, might actually reveal something interesting about what was going on in their heads. And over the years, between 58 percent and 65 percent of my students have answered that they think Palestinians are illegally occupying someone else's land in the Middle East.

What does that tell you?

What that told me was that the propaganda system was working really, really effectively. It wasn't just the propaganda system working through the news. It was also the propaganda system as extended in TV programs and movies and video games, where Arabs are always presented in this very narrow way as terrorists and as murderers. It was clear that, when my students thought about the Middle East, they thought, "Okay, I think I know where it is," and when they then needed to make a decision between good guys and bad guys, in their minds, they had this idea that Palestinians are, by nature, terrorists and therefore must be doing something bad. If someone is occupying something illegally, then it has to be those people who, in my imagination, are connected to those kinds of negative, barbaric things.

It would seem that some of this sort of thing extends to the political environment after 9/11—in which offering any kind of explanation of the root causes of terrorism got framed as either a rationalization of horrible crimes or downright treason.

Absolutely. But I think you have to distinguish 9/11 the event and then the way that 9/11 has been used—the discursive construction of 9/11. And again, there is no doubt that it has been constructed in such a way that it is designed to shut off debate, to shut off any kind of thinking. The moment that you start to talk about why 9/11 might have happened or how it has been used politically, the moment you start to talk about any of that, you are shut down. You're told that you don't care about the troops, or that you don't care about the victims that died that day, or that you're on the side of Osama Bin Laden and the terrorists who carried this out. I think this has worked very effectively not only to shut down debate, but also to push all discussion about 9/11 in a very particular direction that requires unquestioning—and therefore fundamentally antidemocratic—support for American foreign policy.

What's really interesting is how soldiers, the people who are actually in Iraq, think about these things and how they interpret why they're there. People who come back after visiting occupied Iraq say that one of the things you notice when you talk to soldiers is that they say they are there to avenge 9/11. In fact, we know that, when they staged the demolition of the statue of Saddam Hussein, the American flag that they initially draped on it actually came from Ground Zero. In a lot of soldiers' minds, there is a very direct connection between the towers coming down and what is happening in Iraq right now. And in one sense, there *has* to be. If you're a soldier on the ground, why are you there? Why are you engaged in an occupation of a foreign country? Why are you treating ordinary civilians in this horrible way? Once the idea of weapons of mass destruction is gone, you are not there because Saddam Hussein is really dangerous. Once the idea that this is somehow connected to terrorism is gone, why are you there? You are simply there as a mercenary. So, for the soldiers in particular, what do you push? You cannot push the rationale of weapons of mass destruction, because it's objectively false. But what they have been able to put forward is this other idea that, in fact, Saddam Hussein is connected to Al Qaeda and that what they are engaged in is a response to 9/11. On that basis, you can do all kinds of horrible things.

Again, there's a kernel of nobility in this. You are no longer just a mercenary acting on behalf of wealthy interests driven by sheer power politics or hunger for other people's resources. You are not there for the oil. You're there because you are protecting America by making sure that another 9/11 doesn't happen. When I talk about discursive structures, that's exactly what I'm getting at: the rationalizations that people have in their minds that allow them to do what they need to do. Again, I don't think that we can generalize about what goes on in the hearts and minds of American troops—they are not all bad, and they are not all good. But a lot of them are, by definition, very ordinary people who have been driven to the military because of economic reasons. And you have got to somehow get that population to go along with the imperial adventure. And the way that you do it is not by selling empire. You don't do it by selling empire. You do it by saying that this is about terrorism. This is about protecting the people back home. You hear it from soldiers all the time. If you look at some of the letters they've written, they're heartbreaking. They say again and again that they're fighting terror there, so that we don't have to fight it in New Jersey. That's the kind of image that they have in their mind. That they are on the front lines, and, if they don't do what they're doing, then these heathen, Islamic hoards are going to be at your door in New Jersey. Again, it is an incredibly effective propaganda tool.

All of this—advertising, public relations, and political advertising—seems to be drawing from this reservoir of values, morals, nobility, the stuff of deep human longings. A lot of commentators have talked about just this in the context of Bush's 2004 reelection victory, the whole moral values dynamic. How do you read this?

I don't think that the last election was won or lost on values. I think that the last election was decided on the basis of fear. And again, this comes back to how 9/11 was used. Those of us who live in states that actually didn't matter in the election, who don't live in swing states, lived in a very different world from those in places like Ohio and Pennsylvania. They were inundated with messages and bombarded with campaign rhetoric from the start of the campaign to the end of the campaign. And what the Republicans pushed time and time again was a message of fear. They pushed the idea that electing John Kerry was going to make you less safe, was going to invite more 9/11s. But let's remember that the vote was

51 percent to 49 percent. This was not a landslide victory. Even within some of those states that absorbed the brunt of this barrage of fear, Bush won a very, very narrow victory. So I think that we have to be careful about separating America into blue and red states and suggesting that there are differences between regions of people based on something like inherent values. On the other hand, there is unquestionably a difference in the ways people were appealed to, and I think fear was decisive in this regard.

How much do you think that media reform can change the political environment that we've been discussing?

Media reform could make real political analysis and real information more accessible. Right now, the vast majority of money that campaigns collect goes straight to the media to buy advertising time. So the media don't actually have an incentive to engage in real critical analysis. And the result is that we end up getting only what comes from the political parties themselves. If you had true reform of the system, if you made advertising less important, if we insisted that media have a responsibility in a democracy to provide information and programming that is useful to citizens, there's no question that would change things. You'd get a different kind of discourse emerging out of that.

Short of that, is there a way to accomplish some of these things within the existing system?

I think that the way into it is by talking to people. I mean, people aren't just all about values. People are also interested, I think, in material issues. My colleague Justin Lewis wrote a book on this. In fact, when you look at the American population, they are very progressive around a whole host of issues: taxation, for example; the environment; health care. But what's happened is that the political parties have simply not dealt with those issues. That, I think, is the great trick that corporate America has played. They bought out the Democratic Party by providing money both to the Democrats and to the Republicans. For Democrats, corporate money outranks labor money about seven to one, so that corporate money is very important to both Republicans and Democrats. And what that means is that Democrats will simply not raise the fundamental and structural economic issues, the very issues that have the potential to rally the majority of the American people to their side.

They do raise economic issues, but in a limited way?

Yes, it's within a very limited frame, within the strict contours of corporate values. The Democrats simply don't tap into popular progressive values. So the only real separation between Republicans and Democrats emerges on social and cultural issues—abortion and religion and homosexuality—rather than health care, taxes, jobs, student loans, the things that really affect people's lives. I think that the only way to get it back to progressive issues is either to reform the Democratic Party, so that it once again becomes the party of economic populism, or through a third party that explicitly raises and addresses these kinds of issues. Short of these two things, there is no way that you are going to change the structure, because, otherwise, you are simply in the domain of values. What corporations have done, in one warped sense, is brilliant. How do you take the major issues off the agenda? You fund both political parties. You fund both political parties, and those issues are then taken off the agenda, and politics then becomes about what? Politics then becomes about social and cultural issues.

Not only issues such as guns or abortions, but also issues of identity, like you said.

Absolutely. It becomes about these broader ways in which we think about the world, and that's why masculinity was so important in the last election. There is also the incompetence of Democrats. Kerry's campaign was literally incompetent. And it was incompetent because it didn't answer the attacks on his ability to lead, on his manhood, as it were. The Swift boat ads had an effect because the Kerry campaign didn't respond aggressively, which meant that the Republicans could then dominate those issues as well. But the key here is that, if this is what politics is all about, then Democrats, and certainly progressives, will never win. Let's say that the Democrats won on that basis, by playing this game better. And let's say that Kerry had carried Ohio. Would it make a difference in terms of fundamental economic policy? No. It would make a difference in terms of protecting a woman's right to abortion and some other important cultural issues around gay rights. But would it have made any difference to the major things that actually structure people's lives around jobs and around trade and taxation and those things? Absolutely not.

I think that what you have to look at is how to move economic issues back into the agenda. I mean, it really is very strange. In America, economic issues, in any meaningful sense, have been all but taken off the political table. In the rest of the world, meanwhile, economic issues are what politics is always about. And that gets back to the responsibility of progressive intellectuals and progressive organizations like MEF. The role of progressive intellectuals is to try to understand that you cannot think about the future without understanding where you are right now. You have to understand the present in all its complexity, in all its many dimensions, and, once you've done that, you have got to be able to take that knowledge out into the world—so that knowledge actually starts to matter, actually starts to have an impact on the everyday, concrete lives of people.

And that's all we're trying to do at MEF. We're trying to take knowledge and get it into an accessible form, so that it's available to more than just elites, specialists, and experts. So, while at the heart of this, the starting point is always about education, we can think about education in a more broad and democratic way. We can think beyond the classroom about the demand for a public pedagogy as well, and that's the greatest challenge of all.

Okay. But given the size of mass media, its expansion, its concentration, the new forms of technology that are making it more and more personal and accessible to people, what kind of hope do you have that the kind of work that MEF is doing can stand up to the incredible resources and concentration of power on the other side working against it?

It is tough to look at the situation and to be optimistic in any kind of way, because you don't have access to the main means of communication that exist in society today. And there's no question that it's hard to know how you can actually be influential when you don't have that. The only thing that you can do is to keep working in the cracks of the mainstream institutions that are in control, because people actually do want to talk about these things. People are desperate for this kind of information, and you have to go where they actually are. You have to go where they're talking and gathering to address these kinds of issues: unions, churches, and the places where people actually live. But at the same time, I don't want to downplay the classroom. Given how widespread secondary education is in the United States—about 50 percent of the population actually goes to schools—I never want to diminish what can happen in the classroom; it's a great form of public outreach in and of itself. That is what gives me hope.

Fundamental change isn't going to happen in the short term. But if you can raise these issues, especially with young people, and if they take critical conscious-ness on as part of how they think about the world, then there's hope. Gramsci said it best: "Pessimism of the intellect, optimism of the will." If you don't have both of these things together, if you don't have the intellectual analysis, along with the reason why you need to do intellectual analysis in the first place, and faith that change can always happen—if those two things are divorced from each other, then people will actually devolve into paralysis. I worry about that some-times. I worry that people sometimes look at MEF videos and say, "I never real-ized the situation was so bad." But I also know that we're doing everything we can to inspire people to believe that the world can be changed.